ESSAYS ON
SEX EQUALITY

ESSAYS ON SEX EQUALITY

John Stuart Mill

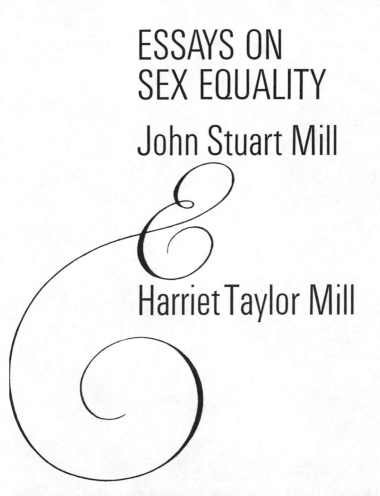

Harriet Taylor Mill

Edited and with an Introductory Essay by
Alice S. Rossi

The University of Chicago Press
Chicago and London

Alice Rossi's introductory essay, "Sentiment and Intellect,"
appeared in abridged form in *Midway,* Spring 1970, © 1970 by
The University of Chicago

The University of Chicago Press, Chicago 60637
The University of Chicago Press, Ltd., London

ISBN: 0-226-52545-7 (clothbound); 0-226-52546-5 (paperbound)
Library of Congress Catalog Card Number: 78-133381

Contents

Preface

When the University of Chicago Press approached me in the fall of 1969 with the invitation to write an introduction to the republication of John Stuart Mill's classic essay, *The Subjection of Women,* I accepted with pride and delight at the prospect of this essay's becoming more generally available once again. I had no idea at the time what an adventure in social-historical scholarship lay ahead for me.

The *Subjection of Women* had absorbed me at two previous points in my life. The first time I encountered the volume was as a college undergraduate interested in Mill's general ideas on liberty. A number of years then passed until I "rediscovered" the *Subjection* essay early in the 1960s when I was deeply involved in the analysis of sex roles and the status of women in American society. A quote from Mill's famous essay graced the beginning of my "Equality of the Sexes: An Immodest Proposal," which appeared in *Daedalus.*

That was the extent of my general knowledge of the essay or the larger work of John Stuart Mill until the fall of 1969, when it seemed desirable that I familiarize myself with Mill's life and work as preparation for writing the introductory essay. It was with a delicious sense of intellectual indulgence that I gathered up the autobiography, his major works, and commentators' studies in anticipation of a scholarly feast during the winter holiday from college teaching. I had not proceeded far in that reading before the figure of Harriet Taylor loomed as significant to an appreciation of Mill's concern with the issue of equality between the sexes. The very marked contrasts in scholars' views of Harriet Taylor and of her role in Mill's life and work soon provided sufficient mystery for me to determine on a search for an explanatory interpretation. That search took me far from the life and work of John Mill himself, to the literature on the Unitarian Radicals and the Utilitarian Radicals of early- and mid-nineteenth century England.

The more I read, the more the plan for the book changed, until it took the form of the present volume: bringing together all the known writings of both Harriet Taylor and John Stuart Mill on the topic of sex equality, coupled with a rather different and certainly longer interpretive essay on their relationship and writings on sex equality. In December therefore I plunged into an exciting month of intensive reading and writing to meet a January deadline for a manuscript.

Many people shared in that month-long intellectual marathon. A dedicated and scholarly librarian at Goucher College, Dr. Sarah D. Jones, and my student assistant, Carol Misialek, were particularly helpful in locating reference materials and assisting in manuscript preparation. Above all, my husband and children shared and indulged my almost total absorption in "John and Harriet," as they became familiarly known to the family, throughout the holiday season. They took gleeful pleasure in the numerous occasions on which I misnamed other, contemporary people "John" or "Harriet" during the hours away from my study.

Finally, I would like to express my appreciation to David Riesman, for his careful reading of the introductory essay, and to Professor Friedrich A. Hayek, who kindly checked the early essays and correspondence against his original manuscripts of the Mill-Taylor correspondence which he published in 1951. Grateful acknowledgement is also made to Routledge & Kegan Paul for permission to republish these same materials from the English edition of the Hayek volume.

ALICE S. ROSSI

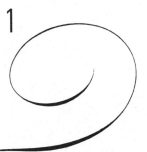

1

Sentiment and Intellect
The Story of
John Stuart Mill and
Harriet Taylor Mill

ALICE S. ROSSI

Sentiment and Intellect
The Story of
John Stuart Mill
and Harriet Taylor Mill

f we could go back to the town of Avignon in the year 1860, we might take a two-mile stroll along the banks of the Rhone, through meadows and groves of mulberries, to the house in which John Stuart Mill wrote the first draft of *The Subjection of Women.* As we approached the house, we would see an oblong garden with an avenue of sycamores and mulberry trees, and at the end the small square house in which Mill lived and worked. A white stone building with a tile roof and green blinds, Mill's home commanded a view of green fields, backed by ranges of mountains. Here Mill wrote during the morning hours, passed the afternoons roaming the surrounding countryside, and spent the evenings with reading and correspondence. Close to this secluded house is the cemetery in which Mill's wife Harriet was buried two years before (1858), a quiet place John Mill visited daily.[1]

1. The description of Mill's home and the mode of his life there during his last years come from a letter by W. T. Thornton to his friend, Henry Fawcett. See Hugh S. R. Elliot, *The Letters of John Stuart Mill* (London: Longmans, Green & Co., 1910), 1: 261–62.

This then is the setting in which Mill wrote his major volume on women. When he finished the draft of the essay in 1861, Mill intended to keep it among his other unpublished papers, "improving it from time to time if I was able, and to publish it at the time when it should seem likely to be most useful."[2] By "useful" Mill meant politically expedient, and that time did not come for another eight years. The intervening years were very full and active ones: a prodigious amount of writing that brought to fruition a lifetime of intellectual effort, and a culmination of Mill's active political commitments in the three years (1865–68) he served as a member of the House of Commons. In 1868 Mill retired again to his home near Avignon, where he revised the manuscript of the essay on women for publication in 1869.

One hundred years have passed since *The Subjection of Women* was published, yet it stands almost alone as an intellectual analysis of the position of women and an appeal for political action to secure equality of the sexes. Nothing quite like it had been published before 1869, and nothing like it was to appear again until the publication in 1898 of Charlotte Perkins Gilman's *Women and Economics,* and another fifty years until the publication in 1951 of Simone de Beauvoir's *The Second Sex*. These three volumes are landmarks in both the long history of the women's movement for political and economic rights and the shorter history of intellectual analyses of sex roles and the relations between the sexes. All three share that rare quality of rigorous intellectual analysis combined with passionate commitment to the goal of sex equality. *The Subjection of Women* is of very special interest as the first and as the only one of the three written by a man.

Many men in the history of western intellectual thought have been deeply committed to the fight against tyranny over the minds and bodies of the powerless in nation after nation. Generations of young people have been stirred by intellectual and

2. John Jacob Coss, ed., *Autobiography of John Stuart Mill* (New York: Columbia University Press, 1924), p. 186.

political battles against a host of "establishments": the church, the aristocracy, the bourgeoisie, the military-industrial complex. The subjection of peasants, slaves, religious dissenters, and workers to a variety of ruling elites has stirred liberal and radical thinkers and activists for the past two centuries. John Stuart Mill stands as the solitary male intellectual figure who devoted his efforts to tracing the analogous subjection of women. It is a measure of the snail's pace at which the movement toward sex equality has progressed that *The Subjection of Women* is typically merely cited by title by scholars of Mill, but hardly ever analyzed, summarized, or included in collections of his essays on liberty and egalitarianism.[3]

John Stuart Mill was a man of sixty-three when the essay on women was published. A man of towering intellectual importance to his contemporaries, he stands as a significant figure in the history of ideas, one who straddled the eighteenth and nineteenth centuries and anticipated the twentieth. How did this man come to write a book on women? Why had this Victorian Englishman withdrawn to a secluded village in France to live and write? When during his lifetime did he develop an interest in the position of women? To answer such questions requires an examination of the development of Mill's thought and the course of his personal life, for a long period of gestation and a complex personal history preceded the publication of *The Subjection of Women*.

A scholar need proceed no further than a reading of Mill's autobiography and the prefaces he wrote for most of his work following the 1848 publication of the *Principles of Political*

---

3. An example of this tendency is the collection edited by Max Lerner, *Essential Works of John Stuart Mill* (New York: Bantam Books, 1961). This collection includes the *Autobiography, On Liberty, On Utilitarianism* and *The Utility of Religion*. Although Lerner makes the point that Mill's writings and ideas have a continuing relevance to the issues with which men and women in the 1960s are struggling, he makes no mention of the essay on women as sharing this continued relevance to modern issues. It seems clear from its omission from the collection, that Lerner did not consider *The Subjection of Women* to be among the "essential" works of John Stuart Mill.

Economy to encounter Harriet Taylor as a central figure in Mill's intellectual and personal life. It is doubtful that *The Subjection of Women* would ever have been written if it were not for Mill's twenty-eight-year relationship with Harriet. Hence it is not only Mill's own development, but the history of his relationship with Harriet Taylor, that must be examined if we are to understand why Mill wrote a book on women and why the book has such remarkable survival power and impact.

John Mill and Harriet Taylor were in their early twenties when they first met. Harriet was at that time a young married woman with two young children, but within a year the relationship between Mill and Mrs. Taylor was one of intellectual and spiritual intimacy. For the next twenty years, Mill continued to live at home with his mother and younger siblings, while Mrs. Taylor remained in her husband's household, yet it is clear that the unconventional relationship they enjoyed with each other was the very core of their lives. It was not until 1851, two years after her husband's death, when they were in their forties and suffering very poor health, that they married. Just seven years later, Harriet died at Avignon, and Mill bought a home near the cemetery in which she was buried. The nature of their relationship, and the exact contribution of Harriet Taylor to Mill's thought and writing, has been the subject of controversy for over a hundred years.

In an era in which sociology has confined itself to the here-and-now, and to a methodology that focuses on the quantitative analysis of survey and experimental data, it may seem strange that a sociologist like me should attempt an essentially biographic investigation into nineteenth-century historical materials. There is, however, a sociological tradition with which this is fully consistent. C. Wright Mills argued, to that minority of sociology graduate students who listened to him, that social science was basically the study of human variety, which consists of "all the social worlds in which men have lived, are living and might live."[4] Mills argued that a proper sociological

4. C. Wright Mills, *The Sociological Imagination* (New York: Oxford University Press, 1959), p. 132.

perspective involves the study of biography and of history, and the intersection of the two in particular social structures. It is in keeping with this sociological tradition that I attempt a selective review of the personal lives and the work of John and Harriet Mill, with particular attention to the two distinct, though overlapping social and intellectual circles—the Philosophic Radicals and the Unitarian Radicals—in which they moved during the critical early years of their relationship.

This analysis has a further relevance to contemporary concerns about sex equality. In 1970 there are two quite distinct levels to the new renascence of concern for the position of women. One concentrates on the reformist, liberal pursuit of widening and consolidating the legal rights of women in the political and economic spheres. This activity builds on the long tradition of the women's rights movement throughout American history of the past 120 years, symbolically initiated by the Declaration of Sentiments at the Seneca Falls convention in 1848. The second, more radical approach focuses attention on the private as well as the public sector and pushes both for an analysis of human sexuality in general and for a critical examination of marriage and the family as social institutions. This approach has involved a search, romantic as well as radical, for a new vision of relations between the sexes, based on the hope that it is possible to blend physical sex, sentiment, and intellect in the husband-wife relationship. As yet few notable examples of such marriages have appeared, and so a contemporary sociologist is strongly inclined to widen the sample of such relationships by turning backward in time to earlier, prominent examples in history. A cross-sex relationship, inside or outside marriage, in which sex and intellect, family and work, are blended, is a dream in the heart of many young women searching for liberation in 1970.

Any scholar who attempts to examine Mill's personal history faces two special difficulties, and it will be well if we confront these at the outset. One difficulty is rooted in the image Mill both wittingly and unwittingly projected of himself. For his contemporaries, as for those who read his famous autobiography, the major features of this image are Mill's high moral tone, deep commitment to intellectual effort, and rigorous rational analysis. The image is aptly caught in Gladstone's characterization of Mill as the "Saint of Rationalism." This is nowhere more apparent than in the autobiography itself, which is remarkable for its impersonality. It is so nearly a pure intellectual recital of Mill's development that John Jacob Coss could say: "In many ways it is primarily an account of the social history of England in the first three quarters of the Nineteenth Century."[5] It was because of this quality of the autobiography that Coss used the book in his philosophy courses at Columbia University, along with Plato's *Republic,* Aristotle's *Ethics,* and Bacon's *Advancement of Learning.* In a more recent commentary, Hayek made a similar observation: "Of what in the ordinary sense of the word we should call his life, of his human interests and personal relations, we learn practically nothing."[6]

Hayek's contribution to our understanding of the personal side of Mill's life was the publication of the John Mill–Harriet Taylor correspondence in 1951. Even this volume of correspondence is far from complete, for many of Mill's personal letters were destroyed during World War II while Hayek was attempting to gather them in London; others appear to have been destroyed by Helen Taylor after her stepfather's death, and a good number remain unpublished in private collections in England and America. When the first full collection of Mill's work began to issue from the University of Toronto Press in the 1950s, Hayek wrote that no other major figure of the nineteenth century has had to wait almost one hundred years before his collected works were published. In 1970 several volumes remain to be published by the Toronto press.

It is interesting that an earlier draft of the *Autobiography* has come to light only in recent years. This document has had

5. Coss, *Autobiography of John Stuart Mill,* p. v.

6. Friedrich A. Hayek, *John Stuart Mill and Harriet Taylor: Their Friendship and Subsequent Marriage* (Chicago: University of Chicago Press, 1951), p. 17.

a curious history. It was bought in London in 1922 by Jacob Harry Hollander, a professor of political economy at Johns Hopkins University, and at the time of his death in 1940 the manuscript had apparently been read by only one other person —A. W. Levi, who subsequently wrote two essays based on a psychoanalytic study of it.[7] With the rest of Hollander's library the draft was stored in a Baltimore warehouse after his death and remained there until 1958, when the University of Illinois purchased the collection. Finally, in 1961, the early draft, edited by Jack Stillinger, was published by the University of Illinois Press.[8] This earlier version is less exclusively an intellectual document than the later one. The basic draft was written by John Mill, and Harriet penciled in suggested revisions and comments. When Mill accepted her suggestions, he penned over her penciled emendations, thus permitting Stillinger to examine the written evidence of Harriet's contributions to the "life," as they referred to it in their correspondence. Stillinger's examination of the manuscript led him to comment that Mill and his wife (and to an even greater degree, Mill alone, in his subsequent rewriting in the early 1860s) had made it progressively more "public" and less "human" than it had been at the start. As a result of the long unavailability of both the early draft of the autobiography and so much of the correspondence, it is clear that a great deal of the scholarship on Mill's personal life is still to be done.

Where Harriet Taylor is concerned, the scholar's task is even more difficult. Mill himself rejected the idea that an adequate memoir could be written on her life. When the American suffragist Paulina Wright Davies asked Mill about such a possibility in 1870, he responded:

Were it possible in a memoir to have the formation and growth

7. A. W. Levi, "The Mental Crisis of John Stuart Mill," *Psychoanalytic Review,* 32, (1945): 86–101; and "The Writing of Mill's Autobiography," *Ethics,* 61, (1951): 284–96.

8. Jack Stillinger, ed., *The Early Draft of John Stuart Mill's Autobiography* (Urbana: University of Illinois Press, 1961).

of a mind like hers portrayed, to do so would be as valuable a benefit to mankind as was ever conferred by a biography. But such a psychological history is seldom possible, and in her case the materials for it do not exist. All that could be furnished is her birth-place, parentage and a few dates.[9]

A good deal more than a "few dates" remain to the scholar interested in forming a profile of Harriet Taylor Mill. It is clear that paucity of historical evidence has not prevented, and may even have stimulated, the long series of very opinionated views about her. I shall review some of these contradictory assessments and suggest my own at a later point in this essay.

A second problem for a late twentieth-century scholar is the difficulty of emphatically penetrating the mystique of Victorian morality where "passionate" relations between the sexes are concerned. Unwittingly, the reader falls in line with the Victorian writers and early twentieth-century commentators in drawing up a balance sheet of evidence of the "did they or didn't they sleep together" variety, until one impatiently calls oneself back to the perspective of our own time and place. We are dealing neither with a casual sex encounter nor with a conventional marital relationship, but with a complex and subtle mutuality of intellect and sentiment beween a man and a woman. It may be that in nineteenth-century Victorian England avoidance of the physical act of adultery and adherence to the formal obligations of the marital relationship were more significant than the existence of intellectual and personal intimacy between an unmarried man and a married woman. In the mid-twentieth century the ordering of these priorities would be reversed: intimacy of sentiment and intellect in a cross-sex relationship outside the marriage is a greater threat to the marriage than adultery per se. In any event one surmises that "passion" in the lives of both John Mill and Harriet Taylor was a sublimated and highly intellectualized emotion, and that Harriet made an apt characterization when she told Gumperz that from 1831 on, her relationship both to her

9. Elizabeth Cady Stanton, Susan B. Anthony, and J. A. Gage, *History of Woman Suffrage* (New York, 1889), vol. I, pp. 219–20.

husband John Taylor and to John Mill was that of "Seelen-freundin."[10] What remains of central significance to us today is the subtle and pervasive transformation that their love for each other brought about in the personal lives and in the ideas and intellectual efforts of John Mill and Harriet Taylor.

What follows is an account of Mill's life and development with special attention to the ideas on marriage, divorce, and the position of women that were current in the social and intellectual circles in which Mill and Harriet Taylor moved. At appropriate points in the unfolding chronology, I shall summarize and highlight the essays they wrote on women in 1832, 1851, and 1869.

Early Family Life and Education of John S. Mill (1806–21)

John Stuart Mill has described so fully the remarkable education he received under his father's tutelage, that there is no need to reproduce it here. From the evidence of the autobiography, his education began with Greek at the age of three, Latin in his eighth year, supplemented with mathematics, philosophy, and the experimental sciences as he approached his teens. His first attempt at serious writing began at the age of eleven when he wrote a history of the Roman government. Even in this first piece the imprint of Utilitarian thinking is apparent, for Mill's focus in this Roman history was on the struggle between the patricians and the plebeians. Within a decade of this early effort, Mill would join the Utilitarians' political battle to undermine the power of the English aristocracy through parliamentary reform.

Mill is cited in Terman's genetic studies of genius as probably having had the highest intelligence quotient of all recorded instances of precocious children. A reading of his father's entry on Education in the *Encyclopaedia Britannica*, however, gives a clue to the central idea in James Mill's education of his son: all mankind is born alike, with little or no significant variation

10. Hayek, *John Stuart Mill and Harriet Taylor,* pp. 56, 291.

in genetic potential for learning. Hence the child's mind was truly a tabula rasa on which a teacher could imprint anything he wished. With such a view, it is little wonder that James Mill, in collaboration with his intellectual mentor, Jeremy Bentham, could initiate a course of study for his three year old son with little concern for the boy's innate ability. By what is perhaps the most intensive study regimen any child has ever been subjected to, young Mill completed a course of education by his fourteenth year that would normally stretch into young adulthood. The objective of the two older men was to produce a "worthy successor" to carry on their work in utilitarian economics and politics.

It is scarcely surprising, in light of the rigorous long days of study Mill was subjected to as a child, that neither his emotional self nor his social skills were given much chance for cultivation. In addition to his own demanding study, he was gradually charged with the responsibility of tutoring his numerous younger siblings. In later years he described himself at eighteen as a "dry, hard logical machine," and this is how he impressed his young contemporaries as well. John Roebuck wrote that on early acquaintance with Mill he was struck by his obvious learning and knowledge of political life, but that he was

utterly ignorant of what is called society; that of the world, as it worked around him, he knew nothing; and above all, of woman he was as a child. He had never played with boys; in his life he had never known any, and we, in fact, who were now his associates, were the first companions he had ever mixed with.[11]

The highly rational, intensive education Mill received from his father need not have impoverished his emotional life. That it did so is partly a reflection of the suppression of feelings in his father's own personality. Mill characterized the personal qualities of his father as similar to those of the Stoic, a man who had

11. R. E. Reader, *Life and Letters of John Arthur Roebuck: With Chapters of Autobiography* (London, 1897), p. 28; cited in Hayek, *John Stuart Mill and Harriet Taylor*, pp. 31, 285.

scarcely any belief in pleasure. . . . He never varied in rating intellectual enjoyments above all others. . . . For passionate emotions of all sorts, and for everything which has been said or written in exaltation of them, he professed the greatest contempt. He regarded them as a form of madness.[12]

This is as far as the final draft of autobiography went. In an excised section of the early draft, Mill commented that he thought his father had greater capacities of feeling than were ever developed in him and that in this he resembled "almost all Englishmen in being ashamed of the signs of feeling and by the absence of demonstration, starving the feelings themselves." Then, in one of the few references to his mother, he explained further:

In an atmosphere of tenderness and affection he [his father] would have been tender and affectionate; but his ill assorted marriage and his asperities of temper disabled him from making such an atmosphere . . . my father's children neither loved him, nor, with any warmth of affection, any one else. . . . That rarity in England, a really warm hearted mother, would in the first place have made my father a totally different being, and in the second would have made the children grow up loving and being loved. . . . But my mother with the very best intentions, only knew how to pass her life in drudging for them. Whatever she could do for them she did, and they liked her, because she was kind to them, but to make herself loved, looked up to, or even obeyed, required qualities which she unfortunately did not possess. . . . I thus grew up in the absence of love and in the presence of fear.[13]

It was to this emotional impoverishment of his early life that Mill attributed his own quality of aloof reserve, a quality he frequently referred to in later years as an impediment to intimate relations with others. A good example can be seen in his correspondence with Thomas Carlyle, whom he befriended in early adulthood. When Carlyle chided him for reporting only his "thoughts" and not his "feelings" in his letters, Mill answered:

12. Coss, *Autobiography of John Stuart Mill,* p. 34.
13. Stillinger, *The Early Draft,* pp. 183–84.

Truly I do not wonder that you should desirate more "heartiness" in my letters, and should complain of being told my thoughts only, not my feelings. . . . But alas! when I give my thoughts, I give the best I have. . . . My case must be left to Nature, I fear: there is no mind physician who can prescribe for me. . . . I can do nothing for myself, and others can do nothing for me; all the advice which can be given (and that is not easily taken) is, not to bear against the bars of my iron cage.[14]

We shall see that this self-characterization is only a partial truth, for within a month of writing the above passage to Carlyle, Mill was in close and intimate contact with Harriet Taylor and the highly expressive, unconventional members of her social circle. Mill may have found it useful to invoke his tendencies toward reserve and rationality in order to hold at a distance people like Carlyle whose desire for intimacy he did not reciprocate. In light of his upbringing, it was no doubt a difficult task, running against the grain of his own tendencies, for Mill to be open and expressive in his relations with others. That he tried and often succeeded in doing so is clear from his correspondence with his wife and their mutual intimate friend William Fox.

Philosophic Radicals and Mill's Emotional Crisis (1822–29)

The formal phase of Mill's unconventional education ended in his fourteenth year when he went abroad for a year of study in France. There he lived with Jeremy Bentham's brother, Sir Samuel Bentham, and concentrated his studies on the sciences, French, and music. On his return, he began his life-long association with the East India Company, starting as a clerk directly under his father in 1822, and retiring from the company in 1858 as chief of the office of the examiner of India correspondence. Almost simultaneously with the beginning of his employment, John Mill and a group of young radicals formed

14. Letter to Thomas Carlyle, from India House, 9 March 1833, in Francis E. Mineka, ed., *The Earlier Letters of John Stuart Mill 1812–1848,* vol. 12 of *Collected Works of John Stuart Mill* (Toronto: University of Toronto Press, 1963), pp. 143–44.

the Utilitarian Society. James Mill was the intellectual and political mentor to this talented circle of politically ambitious young men, bent upon modelling themselves after the French *philosophes* of the eighteenth century. James Mill encouraged them to work toward parliamentary reform, either through active political careers or through vigorous political writing in the journals of the day. The *Westminster Review* was established in 1824 by Jeremy Bentham and his immediate followers, and within a few years this journal became the medium for the expression of the political ideas of John Mill and his Philosophic Radical associates.

This first relatively extensive social milieu of which John Mill became a part was a diverse group of radical thinkers that included both women and men, some of whom were self-educated and others Cambridge-educated. This circle included many people who were to become prominent in British politics and scholarship: George and Harriet Grote, John Roebuck, Charles Buller, Joseph Hume, William Molesworth, Sydney Smith, Charles and Sarah Austin, Francis Place, and Mill's first close friend, Eyton Tooke.[15] It is reasonable to assume that apart from his mother, the women in this social circle were among the first adult women Mill got to know well. Although George Grote served as the group's spokesman in Parliament, his wife Harriet, according to many other members of the group, served as its "tactician." From contacts with Harriet Grote during a trip to England, Charles Sumner characterized her as a "high-minded . . . masculine" woman, "one of the most remarkable women in England." Sydney Smith said she was the "queen of the radicals," and Francis Place that she "*was* the Philosophic Radicals." Her salon was the political center for deliberations about tactics during the peak of the radicals' activism in Parliament in the early- to mid-1830s.

15. An excellent analysis of the political ideology and parliamentary activities of this group, from its rise in the early 1820's to its break-up in disillusionment by 1839, is Joseph Hamburger, *Intellectuals in Politics: John Stuart Mill and the Philosophic Radicals* (New Haven: Yale University Press, 1965).

Harriet Grote was perhaps the first woman intellectual Mill had met, a living model of what women were capable of doing even in the restricted world of English politics early in the nineteenth century. Sarah Austin seems also to have been an early example to Mill of the capabilities of women. Though he later wrote of her with some asperity in the early draft of the autobiography, during these early years she was an important figure in his life whom he addressed in his letters as "liebes Mütterlein." There is no record of what Mill thought of these women when he was a very young man in the 1820s, though they may have provided content for his much later discussion, in *The Subjection of Women*, of women's administrative capacity and shrewd practical judgment of people and events.

Involvement with the Philosophic Radicals lay at the center of Mill's political life and writings for the major part of the period from 1822 to 1840. His employment at the East India Company precluded direct political participation, but he became the thinker and writer in the background of the radicals' attempt to achieve parliamentary reform in England. Some assessment of his own role and of the standard he imposed on the quality of his political writing may be read into his observation that "Journalism is to modern Europe, what political oratory was to Athens and Rome; to become what it ought, it should be wielded by the same sort of men."

Beneath the surface of Mill's busy life during the 1820s, however, a storm was brewing: Mill was attempting to define his own identity and to differentiate it from that of his father. His severe mental depression in 1826 was but the beginning of a transformation in Mill's intellectual and personal orientation. Had this crisis not developed, Mill might have been but a minor figure in English intellectual history, a mere exponent of the ideas developed by Bentham and James Mill.

Intellectual and emotional weaning from paternal influence would almost have to be severe following a childhood of such extreme domination of thought and morality as that young John Mill experienced under the tutelage of his strong-willed father. In the fall of 1826, Mill reports:

I was in a dull state of nerves. . . . It occurred to me to put the question directly to myself: "Suppose that all your objects in life were realized; that all the changes in institutions and opinions which you are looking forward to, could be completely effected at this very instant: would this be a great joy and happiness to you?" And an irrepressible self-consciousness distinctly answered, "No!" At this my heart sank within me: the whole foundation on which my life was constructed fell down. . . . I seemed to have nothing left to live for.[16]

Characteristically, Mill attempted to cope with his depression by turning to books, hoping to find "relief from . . . those memorials of past nobleness and greatness from which I had always hitherto drawn strength and animation." This did not help, and Mill felt there was no one he could turn to for sympathy or advice: "If I had loved any one sufficiently to make confiding my beliefs a necessity, I should not have been in the condition I was." His father, of course, was "the last person" to whom he could look for help. Mill made no mention of his turmoil to his friends among the Philosophic Radicals, but his reasons for not approaching them with his difficulty seem clear: he was struggling with an experience which he thought denied crucial premises of Utilitarian theory. If he, the outstanding product of the intense education of cognitive abilities, could experience a demise of pleasurable associations and feelings toward the goals of increasing happiness for the "whole," then perhaps "the habit of analysis has a tendency to wear away the feelings." Though his life went along its usual course, Mill characterized his efforts at writing and debate as spiritless and mechanical.

The worst of his depression lifted suddenly while he was reading Marmontel's *Mémoires*, the content of which, and Mill's response, provided the major elements for Levi's psychoanalytic imputation to Mill of "death wishes" toward his father.[17] The passage describes Marmontel's father's death, the distressed position of the family, and "the sudden inspiration

16. Coss, *Autobiography of John Stuart Mill*, p. 94.
17. Levi, "The Mental Crisis of John Stuart Mill," p. 98.

by which he, then a mere boy, felt and made them feel that he would be everything to them—would supply the place of all that they had lost." Mill's tension was resolved into tears with this reading. "From this moment," he relates, "my burthen grew lighter. The oppression of the thought that all feeling was dead within me, was gone. I was no longer hopeless: I was not a stock or a stone."[18]

One may or may not subscribe to the psychological thesis that Mill's crisis centered on a repressed death wish against his father and the guilt it engendered along with the dread that he would never be free of his father's domination. What matters most to the course of our present analysis is the consequence of this depression and of its lifting. In Mill's own words:

The cultivation of the feelings became one of the cardinal points in my ethical and philosophical creed. And my thoughts and inclinations turned in an increasing degree towards whatever seemed capable of being instrumental to that object. I now began to find meaning in the things which I had read or heard about the importance of poetry and art as instruments of human culture.[19]

This implied a direct criticism of the "pure" world of rationalism at the heart of his father's ideas on education and politics. This criticism was made even more pointedly in the early draft of his autobiography, where he commented that he and his friends in the Philosophic Radicals group "had no idea of real culture. In our schemes for improving human affairs we overlooked human beings."[20] In 1827, however, these thoughts left Mill essentially alienated, at a deep personal and intellectual level, from his political associates. Restlessly he began to read from a far wider range, turning with a new responsiveness to the work of Coleridge, Carlyle, the French Saint Simonians, Comte, and Macaulay. His personal loneliness and deep alienation from the Utilitarianism of the Philosophic

18. The brief Mill quotations in the preceding two paragraphs are from Coss, *Autobiography of John Stuart Mill*, chapter 5.

19. Ibid., p. 101.

20. Stillinger, *The Early Draft*, pp. 17, 103.

Radicals are reflected in a letter to John Sterling dated 15 April 1829:

> There is now no human being (with whom I can associate on terms of equality) who acknowledges a common object with me, or with whom I can co-operate even in any practical undertaking, without the feeling that I am using a man, whose purposes are different, as an instrument for the furtherance of my own.[21]

This is the personal mood that Mill was in just a year before he met the woman who was to share a wide range of "common objects" with him for the following twenty-eight years.

Unitarian Radicals and the Love in Mill's Life (1830–51)

Historical evidence is vague about the exact circumstances which first brought John Mill and Harriet Taylor together. Mill's new-found responsiveness to poetry and literature, and the long-standing interest in radical politics among Unitarians were clearly in the background of the encounter.[22] The connecting link is thought to have been William J. Fox, Unitarian minister of the South Place Chapel, whose parish included not only Harriet and her husband John, but Jeremy Bentham's leading disciples, John Bowring and Southwood Smith. Fox had himself contributed in 1826 to the Philosophic Radicals' journal, *Westminster Review*. As a voracious reader of contemporary journals, we may assume that Mill was a regular subscriber to the *Monthly Repository*, edited by William Fox since 1827, and that he was sufficiently attracted by William Fox's politics to overcome his anticlerical resistance to Fox's ministerial capacity.

21. Mineka, *The Earlier Letters*, 12:30.

22. There were close connections between the Unitarians and Utilitarians well back into the preceding century. Joseph Priestley, scientist and prominent spirit in Unitarianism, had written an essay on government in 1768 which gave Jeremy Bentham his idea of the "greatest happiness" principle, the lead idea of Utilitarianism. An excellent analysis of the political and personal ties between these two groups can be found in Francis E. Mineka, *The Dissidence of Dissent* (Chapel Hill: University of North Carolina Press, 1944).

Tradition has it that Mill and Harriet Taylor met at a dinner party at William Fox's home in the summer or fall of 1830, a social occasion that included two of Mill's Philosophic Radical friends, John Roebuck and George John Graham. Harriet Martineau, known personally by Fox since the early 1820s, was also a member of the party, and it was she who was very fond of telling and embroidering upon the occasion of John and Harriet's first meeting. Hayek concludes from an examination of a letter written by Eliza Flower, a close friend of Harriet's, that the relationship between John and Harriet was already intimate by the summer of 1831, a year or so after they met.[23] At the time of their meeting, Harriet was twenty-three, already married for more than four years, and the mother of two sons. Her last child, Helen, was born the following year, in July 1831.

Concern for the status of women and the relations between the sexes was no new idea in the social circle of the Unitarian Radicals in the early 1830s. Mary Wollstonecraft had herself been a Unitarian intellectual, and down through the years of the Unitarian journal, the *Monthly Repository*, there are numerous articles both friendly to and persistent in their demands for the education of women. Harriet Martineau had written one such article, "On Female Education," in 1823, in which she argued that women must be educated to be "companions to men, instead of playthings or servants." The Utilitarian *Westminster Review* had similarly been a champion for the cause of women almost from the first issue. This background makes somewhat curious Mill's later explicit denial that his views on the relations between the sexes had been adopted or learnt from Harriet. In a footnote to his autobiography he explained:

This was so far from being the fact, that those convictions were among the earliest results of the application of my mind to political

23. Hayek, *John Stuart Mill and Harriet Taylor*, pp. 36–37. Eliza asked Harriet whether a recent article (June 1831) she had read was by Mill or Harriet, suggesting Eliza was fully aware of the similarity of views between her friend Harriet and John Mill.

subjects, and the strength with which I held them was, as I believe, more than anything else, the originating cause of the interest she felt in me.[24]

It would be more accurate to say that the ideas on sex equality were not unique to either John Mill or Harriet Taylor. They had both absorbed much of the thinking on this issue of the two main social circles within which they moved, the Philosophic Radicals and the Unitarian Radicals.

We can probably assume that if an article appeared in a journal in 1832, the topic of that article was much discussed in the preceding year in the intellectually vigorous circles within which John and Harriet moved. It is of interest, from this point of view, to examine the content of one of William Fox's essays on women, "A Political and Social Anomaly," which appeared in the *Monthly Repository* in September 1832, for he may have aired and discussed the issues it touched upon in the group that included John Stuart Mill, Eliza Flower, Harriet and John Taylor, and William and Sarah Adams. (Sarah was Eliza's sister). Fox went some distance beyond the usual stress on merely improved education for women, to suggest quite radical ideas concerning women's potential for intellectual achievement and their right to the franchise. In an anticipation of the argument that genuine education for women might "raise them above their station," Fox, in his usual peppery fashion, replied: "All the better. They might thus shame men into something like intellectual progress." He summed up his argument thus:

We understand not why one half of the community should have no other destiny than irremediable dependence upon the other half; as long as women have nothing in the world to look to but marriage, they cannot become qualified, in the best manner, for a married life; so long as the modes in which property is inherited, acquired and distributed, leave them in utter dependence, they can never, in that institution, treat or be treated as independent parties, making a fair and equal contract for mutual benefit. Under the present order of things, a large proportion of them must remain as

24. Coss, *Autobiography of John Stuart Mill*, p. 173.

they are, fools to be cajoled, toys to be sported with, slaves to be commanded, and in ignorant pride that they are so.[25]

Sometime during 1831 or early 1832, John Mill and Harriet Taylor wrote essays for each other on women and their position in marriage. Written some thirty-seven years before Mill was to express himself in print on the subject of women, these two essays are of special interest. They show an understandable emphasis on the problem of divorce and provision for the children of divorce, in light of the fact of Harriet's marriage. The manuscripts, now part of the Mill-Taylor Collection in the British Library of Political and Economic Science (London School of Economics), were first published by Hayek in 1951. They form a natural first entry in this volume which brings together the written evidence of the ideas of John Stuart Mill and Harriet Taylor on the subject of women.

There are several points of contrast between the arguments developed by John and Harriet in these two early essays. Harriet Taylor was by far the more radical in her views. Impulsive and far less intellectually disciplined than Mill, she argued that there should not be any laws on marriage, and that a woman should take responsibility for her own children, thus eliminating from the divorce question the problem of providing for the children. She also argued that since a woman would be responsible for her children's maintenance, she would think carefully about how many children she should have, instead of considering the addition of children a means for increasing "her ties to the man who feeds her." John Mill was more cautious in his reasoning. He called for a revision of marriage law and urged that since people tend to marry young, there was always a risk of an error in choice which would require divorce. To avoid what Mill considered possible demoralization through repeated mistakes, he urged a postponement of child-bearing for a long period after marriage, during which the couple could test their compatibility. Writing at a time when the control of birth was largely by continence and

25. Mineka, *The Dissidence of Dissent*, pp. 286–87.

coitus interruptus rather than contraception, he was aware that many people would be unable to avoid pregnancies before the marital relationship was sufficiently secure, and hence that provision for children in case of divorce remained a problem. At this point Mill, perhaps thinking of the Owenite planned community experiments, almost anticipated the search among many young people in the 1960s for communal living with shared responsibility for the care of children:

It will therefore most commonly happen that when circumstances arise which induce the parents to separate, there will be children to suffer by the separation: nor do I see how this difficulty can be entirely got over, until the habits of society allow of a regulated community of living, among persons intimately acquainted, which would prevent the necessity of a total separation between the parents even when they had ceased to be connected by any nearer tie than mutual good will, and a common interest in their children.

A second point of contrast between John and Harriet concerns the use to which women should put their improved education in the future. Again Harriet took the more radical position: if women are not to barter their persons for bread, they not only must be well educated but must be permitted to enter any occupational field they wish. Mill took the more cautious position, that a woman's goal would continue to be marriage to a man she loved; her occupation after marriage would be to "adorn and beautify life" by sharing fully and intelligently her husband's occupations and interests. This view was not moderated with the passage of time; thirty-seven years later Mill was still arguing that he saw no benefit to a wife's contributing to the income of the family, on the grounds that her work in the household and the rearing of children were her contribution to the family unit.

Despite her radical views, Harriet ended her impassioned call for great change in the status of women with a plea that John Mill become the "apostle of all the highest virtues" and teach the world the way to true equality. An awareness of counterparts in the 1960s combining fiery verbal feminism and personal dependence on a man, helps to curb critical assessment of this contrast in Harriet Taylor. Liberation of the intellect is far easier to achieve than liberation of the deeper emotions. It should also be noted than in 1832 Harriet Taylor was a largely self-educated woman, with years of intellectual growth ahead of her. By 1851 she would show no such passive submission to John Mill's leadership.

The year 1833 was a critical year in the relationship between John Mill and Harriet Taylor, and there are sufficient historical data to describe part of the turmoil they passed through. For Harriet the dilemma centered on whether and how a pattern could be established that would permit her to continue her close contact with John Mill yet fulfill her obligations to her husband. For Mill the dilemma was more complex, for he was continuing to explore the new intellectual world opened to him following his earlier mental crisis as well as trying to cope with his new personal relationship with Harriet.

It is probable that within the privacy of the social circle of the Unitarian Radicals, even more extreme views were expressed on marriage and divorce and women's education than any William Fox, William Adams, John Mill, or Harriet Taylor would and did express in public print. The degree to which the public and private views of this group of radical thinkers departed from the customary patterns of the mid-nineteenth century can be appreciated by noting the response of their contemporaries to the clearly visible attraction and close association between John Mill and Harriet Taylor. This can be illustrated by the comments of Thomas and Jane Carlyle before and after they met Harriet Taylor and the circle of Unitarian Radicals. Thomas Carlyle strikes a contemporary reader as a nineteenth-century Podhoretz, busily trying to "make it" in the world of London letters and politics by cultivating contacts with the influential people of his day. But he is by the same token a good transmitter of the gossip of the time. Before they met Harriet, Jane Carlyle wrote her husband's brother of the local gossip that Mrs. Taylor had "ogled Mill successfully so that he was desperately in love." Yet when they met Harriet, Thomas Carlyle's sketch of her was greatly muted: he wrote his brother that "she is a living romance heroine, of the clearest insight, of the royalist volition, very interesting, of questionable destiny, not above 25." After the Carlyles were introduced to the social circle of the Unitarian Radicals, they showed both attraction to and repulsion from its members. On one occasion, Carlyle wrote:

[The] party we had at the Taylors' was the most brisk, the cleverest (best gifted) I have been at for years: Mill, Charles Buller (one of the gayest, lightly sparkling, lovable souls in the world), Repository Fox (who hotches and laughs at least), Fonblanque, the Examiner editor, were the main men.[26]

There is clearly a conflict in Carlyle's response between the cultural values of his time and his private individual response to Harriet and her social circle. The cultural values eventually win out. In another letter Carlyle drew a more pointed contrast between the Philosophic Radicals set and that of the Unitarian Radicals, commenting on the latter as follows:

Mill . . . is greatly occupied of late times with a set of quite opposite character, which the Austins and other friends mourn much and fear much over. It is the fairest Mrs. Taylor you have heard of, with whom, under her husband's very eyes, he is (Platonically) over head and ears in love. Round her come Fox the Socinian and a flight of really wretched looking "friends of the species," who (in writing and deed) struggle not in favour of Duty being done, but against Duty of any sort almost being required. A singular creed this. . . . Most of these people are very indignant at marriage and the like; and frequently indeed are obliged to divorce their own wives or be divorced: for though the world is already blooming (or is one day to do it) in everlasting "happiness of the greatest number" these people's own houses (I always find) are little Hells of improvidence, discord, unreason. Mill is far above all that and I think will not sink in it; however, I do wish him fairly far from it.[27]

The Carlyles did not know that 1833 was a year of personal

26. Hayek, *John Stuart Mill and Harriet Taylor*, pp. 82–83.
27. Ibid., p. 82.

crisis for two pairs in the set of Unitarian Radicals. William Fox, older by some twenty years than the other members of the group, had lived through an unhappy marriage for many years and had been strongly attracted to the young Eliza Flower, for whom, together with her sister Sarah, he was guardian after the death of their father. Unconventional, highly artistic, and endowed with unusual musical talent, Eliza became increasingly devoted to William, helping him in church, journal, and correspondence duties. Eliza was an intimate friend of Harriet Taylor's, and the similar complexity of their heterosexual relations probably served to bring the two men into a closer relationship. Certainly Mill confided to a greater degree in Fox than in any other man with whom he corresponded, judging from the Mill letters that have been published thus far. The fact that Fox combined so successfully the two poles of politics and art may also have encouraged Mill to unburden himself of the effects of his intellectual turmoil during these years. Early in the spring of 1833, he wrote to Fox:

If there are any rumors that I was writing anything for the *Monthly Repository* of this month, I am sorry I cannot confirm them. I have abundance of vague intentions of writing for you, but I have been very idle of late, and in fact never have been in a state more unfit for work: from various causes, the chief of which is, I think, a growing want of interest in all the subjects which I understand, a growing sense of incapacity ever to have real knowledge of, or insight into the subject in which alone I shall ever again feel a strong interest . . . I feel so unequal to any of the higher moral and aesthetic subjects.[28]

This was rather strong language from a man who was yet to write a *System of Logic* and the *Principles of Political Economy*. Mill was probably still on a honeymoon with the world of literature, art, and poetry, unsure exactly how his own philosophic and economic views would shape up or how far they would depart from his intellectual origins in Benthamism.

28. Richard Garnett, *The Life of W. J. Fox* (London: John Lane Co., 1910), p. 103.

The *Monthly Repository* became an important outlet for Mill, in which, Mineka suggests, he tried out ideas he did not publicly espouse for more than a decade.[29] Either under pseudonyms or in unsigned articles, Mill departed considerably from orthodox Benthamite economics in the essays he wrote in the mid-1830s. In a discussion of his advocacy of a property tax instead of taxes upon consumption and industry (a position the Philosophic Radicals would share), Mill went on to show his scorn of any assumed link between the accumulation of a personal fortune and intelligence or ingenuity—a view that would have very much displeased his Benthamite associates at the time. In an article in 1833 he made a point that would have shocked any laissez faire economist and that foreshadowed the turn toward socialist thinking that Mill would take only years later:

We hope the time is coming for more rational modes of distributing the productions of nature and of art, than this expensive and demoralizing plan of individual competition, the evils of which have risen to such enormous height.[30]

On a more personal level, Harriet and John Taylor agreed to a trial separation for approximately six months, apparently with the hope on her husband's part that she would decide to cut her tie to John Mill and return fully to him as his wife. Mill joined Harriet in Paris in the fall of 1833 for several weeks. They wrote joint letters from Paris to Eliza Flower and William Fox that give ample evidence of the quality of their relationship and the indecision that hung over them. This was also the first time the two had any long period of time for talk and mutual exploration. John Mill wrote his friend Fox:

I am astonished when I think how much has been restrained, how much untold, unshewn and uncommunicated til now; how much which by the mere fact of its being spoken, has disappeared. . . . There will never again I believe be any obstacle to our being together entirely from the slightest doubt that the experiment would

29. Mineka, *The Dissidence of Dissent,* p. 275.
30. Ibid., p. 277.

succeed with respect to ourselves. . . . And yet—all the other obstacles or rather the one obstacle being as great as ever—our futurity is still perfectly uncertain. She has decided nothing except what has always been decided—not to renounce the liberty of sight—and it does not seem likely that anything will be decided until the end of the six months. . . . I know it is the common notion of passionate love that it sweeps away all other affections—but surely the justification of passion, and one of its greatest beauties and glories, is that in an otherwise fine character it weakens no feeling which deserves to subsist, but would naturally strengthen them all.[31]

In the same letter, Harriet enclosed one of her own to her friend Eliza:

O this being seeming as though God had willed to show the type of possible elevation of humanity. To be with him wholly is my ideal of the noblest fate for all states of mind and feeling which are lofty and large and fine; he is the companion spirit and heart desire—we are not alike in trifles only because I have so much more frivolity than he.[32]

As might be anticipated from the mood of these letters, Harriet did not renounce the liberty of seeing John Mill, and her husband agreed to such an arrangement in exchange for retaining the external formality of residing as his wife in his household. From 1834 until their marriage in 1851 (two years after the death of her husband), John Mill and Harriet Taylor continued this pattern, seeing each other for dinner at Harriet's home when John Taylor was absent, and spending frequent weekends at summer places along the English coast, as Harriet moved restlessly about from place to place with her daughter Helen. Mill continued to live at home with his mother, working at India House, tutoring his younger siblings, and writing widely on numerous political topics of the day.

Like so many Europeans of their time, both John and Harriet had numerous bouts of ill health. Much of their correspondence reported on one or another aspect of their health,

31. Mineka, *The Earlier Letters,* 12:186–88.
32. Hayek, *John Stuart Mill and Harriet Taylor,* p. 54.

but avoided the realization that both were suffering from tuberculosis. During the 1830s and 1840s Harriet took numerous trips to southern France and Italy in the search of improved health through exposure to a sunny, warm climate. Mill's employment with the East India Company limited the occasions on which he could join Harriet in the south, but he did manage many short visits during these years.

Numerous scholars of John Stuart Mill have suggested that it was a growing awareness of the gossip about his irregular relationship with Harriet Taylor that led to his radical withdrawal from social life by the mid-1840s. A closer reading suggests a rather different interpretation. If it were merely social disapproval of the John-Harriet relationship, one would expect the social set of the Philosophic Radicals to have continued intact after Mill's withdrawal from it. This was not the case, however. What seems to have occurred was a total breakup of the Philosophic Radical group as the members became politically disillusioned by parliamentary defeat and empirical refutation of their theories.

Since this larger demise of radicalism was important to the development of Mill's thinking and later intellectual effort as well as to a correction of the interpretation placed on the social withdrawal of John and Harriet during the 1840s, we might examine what happened to the radical cause during these years. The Philosophic Radicals were dedicated to the central idea that the basic cleavage in English society was between the aristocracy and the "people." Bentham's idea of "sinister interests" was narrowed by James Mill to the sinister interests of just the aristocracy or ruling elite. They saw the church and the legal profession as mere props to the aristocracy, and the universities as only subdivisions of the church. When Karl Marx was a mere boy in 1819, James Mill was writing about and teaching this rulers versus ruled thesis, arguing for example that it was aristocratic control of government which fomented war, since only in times of international hostilities could the government increase the proportion of the national wealth at its command and the proportion of the population subject to its control. Where the Philosophic Radicals differed from radical working class organizations was in their view that the cleavage between the middle class and the working classes was based merely on ignorance and fear. Political education, they thought, would cement the two classes together in opposition to the aristocracy.

The political efforts of the Philosophic Radicals centered on the attempt to effect a realignment of the Whig and Tory parties. They counted on this realignment as a necessary stage to conform with the underlying struggle between the people and the aristocracy. Counter to their expectations, however, the Tories increased in strength during the mid-1830s, the radical factions within the Tories and the Whigs showed increasing enmity rather than a consolidation of mutual interests, and the Chartists, which two members of the Philosophic Radicals (Roebuck and Place) had in fact helped to establish, showed increasing hostility toward the middle class and increasing threats of violence. By 1837 the Philosophic Radicals were in despair at their failure to achieve party realignment and were angry with the moderate reformers for not identifying themselves as Radicals. Between 1838 and 1840 they saw an increase in class consciousness and conflict and mounting evidence that the party system they thought obsolete had a good deal of life and energy left in it.

By 1840 their political hopes were dashed, and during the next few years the group gradually fell apart. If we note the shift of interest and activity among other members of the Philosophic Radicals, it becomes apparent that Mill was far from the exception. As John Mill shifted from political articles in the radical journals to work on philosophic and historical topics in the early 1840s, so the other members also turned to scholarship. George and Harriet Grote tacitly agreed not even to discuss politics; George Grote returned to his studies of Greek history and soon started a new classical journal with G. C. Lewis. Harriet Grote wrote that their interests had shifted from politics to letters, philosophy, and "projects for the rational enjoyment of our lives." By 1841 this fiery anti-aristocrat was writing her sister that she had "made a number of new acquaintances among fine folks, which I think to follow up now that Radicalism is extinct and politics no longer absorb my energies." Molesworth turned to work on his edition of Hobbes, Sarah Austin to translating German books, and her brother-in-law Charles confessed to a disappointment so bitter that he would never take an interest in politics again.

Having already wrestled (during his mental crisis of 1826–29) with the painful task of piecing together a new credo from the shambles of an older one no longer acceptable to him, John Mill may have been better prepared to cope with political disillusionment than were his Philosophical Radical friends. In any event, by 1842 he wrote that he was out of heart about public affairs and "had almost given up thinking of the subject." Hamburger suggests that "having failed as politician, he now downgraded that role and looked for improvement through philosophy." Ever the optimist, Mill tried to "fashion a role for himself as a philosopher whose task was to synthesize the various themes current in a transitional era in order to prepare for the future."[33]

These then, were the political events which preceded Mill's return to scholarship and the eventual publication of the *System of Logic* in 1843 and his *Principles of Political Economy* in 1848.

Intellectual Collaboration between John Mill and Harriet Taylor

Controversy has raged for more than a century on what Harriet Taylor was like in personality and intellectual capability, as it has on the nature of her relationship to Mill and her contribution to his published writings. We have already seen that in his early contacts with her, Thomas Carlyle conceded that Harriet was an interesting and romantic figure with a high degree of insight and firm purpose. Mill himself was

33. This section on the disillusionment of the Philosophic Radicals relies heavily on Hamburger, *Intellectuals in Politics*, pp. 242–72.

lavish in his praise of her as a woman and as an intellectual. In the *Autobiography*, in several prefaces to his published work, and in the inscription he had carved on her tombstone in Avignon.[34] Mill was extravagant in his comparisons of Harriet with prominent intellectual and artistic figures in English history. He portrayed her as more of a poet than Carlyle, more of a thinker than himself, like Shelley in temperament and organization but his superior in thought and intellect.[35] Mill's friend and first biographer, Alexander Bain,[36] tried to prevent the publication of such excessive praise when he read the proof for the first publication of the *Autobiography* in 1873. He wrote to Mill's stepdaughter, Helen Taylor: "I venture to express the opinion that no such combination has ever been realized in the history of the human race."[37] Bain felt that Mill outraged all credibility in his descriptions of Harriet's "matchless genius." Mill's praise was retained in the published work, despite Bain's urging that it be deleted or toned down. Nine years later Bain's assessment of Harriet was that she stimulated Mill's intellectual faculties by "intelligently controverting" his ideas.[38]

34. The inscription, which is reproduced in Hayek, *John Stuart Mill and Harriet Taylor,* p. 267, is as follows: To the beloved memory of Harriet Mill, the dearly beloved and deeply regretted wife of John Stuart Mill. Her great and loving heart, her noble soul, her clear, powerful, original, and comprehensive intellect made her the guide and support, the instructor in wisdom, and the example in goodness— as she was the sole earthly delight—of those who had the happiness to belong to her. As earnest for the public good as she was generous and devoted to all who surrounded her, her influence has been felt in many of the greatest improvements of the age and will be in those still to come. Were there but a few hearts and intellects like hers, this earth would already become the hoped-for heaven. She died, to the irreparable loss of those who survive her, at Avignon, Nov. 3, 1858.

35. See Mill's introductory comments to the "Enfranchisement of Women" in this volume for an example of this extravagant assessment.

36. Alexander Bain, *John Stuart Mill: A Criticism* (London, 1882).

37. Letter from Bain to Helen Taylor, 6 September 1873, in Stillinger, *The Early Draft,* p. 23.

38. Bain, *John Stuart Mill,* pp. 171, 173.

William Fox was one contemporary who was warm in his feeling toward Harriet Taylor and high in his assessment of her ability, moral commitment, and devotion to Mill. When Harriet died at Avignon, Fox wrote to his daughter:

Mrs. Mill died on the 3rd at Avignon. She would not have objected to being buried there, in the ground in which Petrarch has given a wide-world fame; and of which it might . . . be said, "A greater than Laura is here."[39]

Fox's biographer, Garnett, commented that if Petrarch's Laura was, as is usually believed, a married woman, the correspondence between the relations of the two pairs was amazing, even to their connection with Avignon, although the "field of mutual interests common to the English lovers was infinitely wider and comparison might afford no fallacious measure of Woman's progress between the 14th and 19th century."[40] A more recent scholar, Francis Mineka, shares the sympathetic view of Harriet's influence on Mill:

However over colored by emotion his estimate of her powers may have been, there can be no doubt that she was the saving grace of his inner life. Without her, John Mill might well have been a different person, but one can doubt that he would have been as fine, as understanding or as great a man.[41]

Positive assessments of Harriet Taylor such as this have been few, and they are far outweighed by often harshly negative assessments. Many Mill scholars quote a reply Harold Laski gave Justice Holmes when the latter asked him about Harriet Taylor. Laski wrote:

I believe that he was literally the only person who was in the least impressed by her. Mrs. Grote said briefly that she was a stupid woman. Bain said she had a knack of repeating prettily what J. S. M. said and that he told her it was wonderful; Morley told me that Louis Blanc told him he once sat for an hour with her

39. Garnett, *The Life of W. J. Fox*, p. 99.

40. Ibid., p. 155.

41. Mineka, *The Dissidence of Dissent*, pp. 274–75.

and that she repeated to him what afterwards turned out to be an article Mill had just finished for the Edinburgh. . . . If she was what he thought, someone else at least should have given us indications.[42]

Closer to our own time, Keith Rinehart has portrayed Mill as a submissive man whose autobiography shows a movement from the "aegis of one demi-god, his father, to another, his wife."[43] Stillinger leaned heavily on the earlier negative assessments of Harriet, with no mention of the more favorable ones. He summed up his impression of her in the following way:

Harriet of the incomparable intellect . . . was largely a product of his imagination, an idealization, according to his peculiar needs, of a clever, domineering, in some ways perverse and selfish, invalid woman.[44]

Disregarding the state of their health, the typically English search for its improvement through winters on the Mediterranean, and the fact that when they were separated they wrote almost daily to each other, Stillinger suggests that Mill "enjoyed her more as a correspondent than as a companion." Max Lerner took a curious attitude toward the relationship between the two, pointing out that Mill himself was a proper Victorian in his attitudes toward sex and that Harriet Taylor was "in all probability a frigid woman." He softens the psychological imputation of the latter by suggesting that Harriet's frigidity was a matter of principle rather than of neurosis.[45] It is not clear what the difference is between "a proper Victorian attitude" and "principled frigidity." Why not merely suggest that both John and Harriet Mill had Victorian attitudes toward sex?

No one has exceeded Diana Trilling in the harshness of

42. Stillinger, *The Early Draft,* pp. 24–25.

43. Keith Rinehart, "John Mill's Autobiography: Its Art and Appeal," *University of Kansas City Review* 19 (1953): 265–73.

44. Stillinger, *The Early Draft,* p. 27.

45. Lerner, ed., *Essential Works of John Stuart Mill,* p. xiv.

her account of Harriet Taylor.[46] John Mill had characterized Harriet as his "intellectual beacon," but Mrs. Trilling suggests she had in fact "nothing more than a vestpocket flashlight of a mind . . . one of the meanest and dullest ladies in literary history, a monument of nasty self-regard, as lacking in charm as in grandeur," whose correspondence shows a "fleshless, bloodless quality" full of "injured vanity, petty egoism and ambition." Mrs. Trilling then exhibits the standard of femininity by which she assesses Harriet Taylor much more clearly than the male scholars who preceded her had done: Harriet Taylor had "no touch of true femininity, no taint of the decent female concerns which support our confidence in the intelligence of someone like Jane Carlyle."

It is difficult to see why Mrs. Trilling's confidence in the "intelligence" of a woman depends on her possession of "decent female concerns." One suspects that she means "normality" rather than "intelligence." If by a "normal" woman one means a clinging, uneducated, submissive woman of the nineteenth century, or a well-educated, supportive wife-companion of the twentieth century, then by either standard Harriet Taylor was indeed very far from "normal." For that matter, neither was John Stuart Mill a "normal" man of his age, in either personal qualities, intellectual style, or manner of relating to the woman of his life.

One must be cautious in assessing the views held of Harriet by either her male contemporaries or the scholars who read the scattered fragments of evidence from those contemporaries. Assertive women were undoubtedly an even greater irritation to Victorian men than they are to men today. In a man single-mindedness of purpose has always been considered admirable; in a woman, whether in Victorian England or contemporary America, it has usually been thought a sign of selfishness, a distasteful departure from conventional ideals of femininity. Harriet Taylor was no shrinking violet, no soft and

46. Diana Trilling, "Mill's Intellectual Beacon," *Partisan Review* 19 (1952): 116–20.

compliant woman. She had, after all, lived against the grain of Victorian London in an unconventional liaison with John Mill for twenty years before their marriage. Under his tutelage she had a most unusual opportunity to grow intellectually, and we may assume that over the years of their collaboration, Harriet's self-confidence also grew as she tested her mettle against the strength of Mill's intellect and fund of knowledge.

One element contributing to the negative views held of Harriet was no doubt rooted in general cultural expectations of the role of women. Then as now, women who are intellectually or politically brilliant are more readily accepted by men if they are also properly feminine in their style and deportment with men. This helps to assure that there will be few women of achievement for men to "exempt" from the general category of women, since the traits associated with traditional femininity —softness, compliance, sweetness—are rarely found together with the contradictory qualities of a vigorous and questioning intellect, and a willingness to persist on a problem against conventional assumptions. The hypothesis that a mere woman was the collaborator of so logical and intellectual a thinker as Mill, much less that she influenced the development of his thought, can be expected to meet resistance in the minds of men right up to the 1970s.

There is a second approach to interpreting the contradictory assessments of Harriet Taylor that is of special sociological interest. If one links the assessment to the social circle to which the writer, friend, or scholar belonged or was intellectually and politically attuned, one begins to see the influence of social structure upon attitude and belief. The negative assessments of Harriet turn out to be held mainly by members of the Philosophic Radicals or scholars interested in that circle, whereas the positive assessments are held by those associated with the Unitarian Radicals. Significant differences existed between these two circles in theory, politics, and morality. The Philosophic Radicals represented a pole of moral righteousness, theoretical commitment to Utilitarianism, and political concern for parliamentary reform. The Unitarian Radicals, by contrast, were individually more unconventional, more artistic, and passionately committed to a wide range of political and social reforms in the area of domestic affairs and the institution of the family. One member of the Unitarian Radical set, William Bridges Adams, went so far as to criticize conventional domestic arrangements for their waste of time and energy, advocating, in 1834, the building of what we would call apartment houses, with provisions for communal kitchens and laundries.[47] This was the social set with which Harriet Taylor was personally affiliated. Mill's association with the Unitarian Radicals was seen by his political associates as a threat to his allegiance to the Utilitarian cause, and Harriet was the symbol of that association.

In keeping with this thesis, the people whom Laski cited in his letter to Holmes, all of them very critical of Harriet, belonged to the Philosophic Radical circle: Harriet Grote, Morley, Bain, Sarah Austin, John Roebuck. These were all persons who disapproved of Mill's involvement with Harriet and with the Unitarian Radicals. Carlyle, in a letter quoted earlier, specifically referred to the Austins as disapproving of Mill's attraction to the Fox social set. At the time, the early 1830s, the Philosophic Radicals knew nothing of the intellectual distance Mill had traveled from Utilitarian theory, quite on his own, following his mental crisis in 1826. They may well have attributed the subsequent changes in Mill's thinking to the influence of Harriet and her social circle rather than to the intellectual ferment within Mill himself which had begun several years before he met Harriet and the Unitarian Radicals.

Scholars are more apt to do research on people whose thinking they find attractive than on people whose thinking they dislike or disapprove. Accordingly, one observes a division among modern scholars in their opinions of Harriet which reflects the division of the Philosophic Radicals and the Unitarian Radicals themselves. Bain, Elliot, Laski, and Stillinger

47. William Bridges Adams, "Housebuilding and Housekeeping," *Monthly Repository* Vol. 8 (1834); cited in Mineka, *The Dissidence of Dissent*, p. 350.

were primarily concerned with the development of Mill's philosophic and political thought, and they tended to view Harriet in negative terms. The more positive views were held by the scholars of the Unitarian Radicals: William Fox's biographer, Garnett, and Francis Mineka, who studied the Unitarian journal, *Monthly Repository*, through the years of Fox's editorship. Cutting across this division is the political perspective of the scholars themselves. Hayek, himself opposed to socialism (the new road to serfdom), was more likely to concede considerable influence to Harriet, since he could then interpret Mill's socialist phase as a temporary aberration due to Harriet's influence over him. Though careful to indicate that more detailed study is required, Hayek suggested that such a study would show that Mill withdrew from the more advanced (i.e., socialist) positions he took under her influence and returned in later years to views closer to those he had held in his youth.[48] The Victorian scholar Basil Willey tended to a similar interpretation of Mill's views on religion.[49] In contrast, Harold Laski, a socialist, did not wish to view Mill's socialist thinking as a product of a woman's influence and hence followed the earlier trend toward a negative view of Harriet and of her contribution to Mill's thinking.[50] The Fabian Socialists who followed Mill did not share Laski's hestitation; on the contrary, the ideal of a working intellectual partnership between the sexes became a traditional Fabian idea.

Throughout all this debate and controversy about the personal qualities of Harriet Taylor and her contribution to Mill's thought and work, there has been surprisingly little attention paid to direct historical evidence. We may forgive earlier writers who did not have access to the Mill-Taylor correspondence, but not for their neglect of the ideals John and Harriet ex-

48. Hayek, *John Stuart Mill and Harriet Taylor,* p. 266.

49. Basil Willey, *Nineteenth Century Studies* (London: Chatto & Windus, 1950), pp. 141–86.

50. Max Lerner draws this distinction between Hayek and Laski in his introduction to Mill's *Autobiography, Essential Works of John Stuart Mill,* p. 6.

pressed in their published work on the relations between the sexes and the status of women. None of the Mill scholars have examined the essays collected in this volume for clues to the kind of relationship John and Harriet tried to maintain in their years together. Nor has due allowance been made, in my judgment, for Mill's own intellectual toughness. Mill was not a man to be easily influenced and won over by any idea or person. He rarely lost his critical, sifting, integrative orientation to the weighing of an idea. As Mill described his own process of growth: "When I had taken in any new idea, I could not rest til I had adjusted its relation to all my old opinions."[51]

The scholars attuned to the Unitarian Radicals seem to have come closest to an appreciation of the role Harriet Taylor played in Mill's work. Garnett stands almost alone in going behind the effusive praise Mill extended to Harriet to a comparison of Mill's work before he met Harriet with that which followed. He points out, for example, that Mill's essay on Tennyson, written shortly after he first became attracted to poetry, is probably a clear reflection of the influence of Harriet Taylor. Garnett suggests that this essay's "appreciation of other poets and discussion of the principles of poetry in general, would have been impossible to Mill" without a large contribution from Harriet Taylor.[52]

Mill refers to many of his publications from 1840 onward as "joint productions" of Harriet and himself. Again it is Garnett who points out that this claim is far more believable than it would be if Mill had included his *System of Logic* among the joint productions. This Mill did not do but expressly exempted the *Logic* from Harriet's collaboration. It is the *Principles of Political Economy* which Mill cited as their first joint effort. An examination of the Taylor-Mill correspondence and of Harriet's letters to her husband, in which she explained the postponement of her plans to go to Brighton because of intensive work on this book, supports Mill's claim that it was

51. Stillinger, *The Early Draft*, p. 133.
52. Garnett, *The Life of W. J. Fox*, p. 98.

a joint effort.[53] Mill himself described the contribution of each to the writing of the *Political Economy*: what was abstract and purely scientific was generally his, while the more human elements and lively practical illustrations were from her. He acknowledged that his first draft of the book had no chapter on the future condition of the working class, and that the one which was finally included was "wholly an exposition of her thoughts, often in words taken from her own lips."[54] *On Liberty* Mill claimed was even more fully a joint effort:

[It was] more directly and literally our joint production than anything else which bears my name, for there was not a sentence of it that was not several times gone through by us together, turned over in many ways, and carefully weeded of any faults, either in thought or expression, that we detected in it.[55]

It remains a puzzle why, if her contribution was so great, everything appeared under Mill's name alone. Social expediency probably ruled out such joint authorship during the long years of their unconventional relationship, and by the time they married, they may have felt that his "established" name would draw larger readership and sales than her lesser-known name. There is some evidence that Harriet was not completely satisfied with such a state of affairs. When it came time to publish the *Principles of Political Economy*, Mill wrote a footnote comment that "her dislike of publicity alone" prevented the insertion of dedications in all but the gift copies of the first edition. In actual fact, Harriet had approached her husband, John Taylor, about such a dedication, indicating pleasure at the prospect, and suggesting precedents for it in other re-

---

53. Late in 1847 Harriet wrote to her husband: "I do certainly look more like a ghost than a living person. . . . I think I shall not be able to go [to Brighton] before the end of next week being just now much occupied with the book." By February 1848 she is still absorbed in the manuscript: "I am so taken up with the Book which is near the last . . . that I could not leave town before the beginning of April if even then." Hayek, *John Stuart Mill and Harriet Taylor,* pp. 119, 120.

54. Coss, *Autobiography of John Stuart Mill,* p. 174.

55. Ibid., p. 176.

cently published work. Taylor, however, was profoundly opposed to the idea. In a letter to Harriet he said that

all dedications are in bad taste, that under our circumstances the
proposed one would evince on both author's part as well as the lady
to whom the book is to be dedicated, a want of taste and tact
which I could not have believed possible. . . . The dedication will
revive recollections now forgotten and will create observations and
talk that cannot but be extremely unpleasant to me.[56]

Two months later, Harriet explained to William Fox that the
dedication was limited to copies given to friends "at my special request . . . my reason being that opinions carry more
weight with the authority of his name alone." Hayek concluded that Harriet contributed a considerable amount to the
Political Economy volumes and to their subsequent revision
for later editions. One can imagine Harriet chafing at the social
conventions that required her to remain unknown and unacknowledged by the reading public.

There is also dispute concerning the authorship of the essay
entitled *Enfranchisement of Women*. In writing to the editor
of the *Westminster Review*, Mill referred to this essay as one
he had almost ready. Yet two years before, in February 1849,
Mill wrote to Harriet criticizing an article on women he had
read:

I do not think that anything that could be written would do nearly
so much good on that subject, the most important of all, as the
finishing of your pamphlet or little book rather, for it should be
that. I do hope you are going on with it. Gone on with and finished
and published it must be and next season too.[57]

From an internal analysis of this essay, a comparison with
the earlier 1832 essays and Mill's later famous one in 1869,
I have concluded that Harriet was the primary author of the
Enfranchisement of Women. The essay has a central core of
analysis that is practically unconnected to its prelude and ending. It begins and ends with a discussion of the convention in

56. Hayek, *John Stuart Mill and Harriet Taylor*, p. 121.
57. Ibid., p. 138.

Worcester, Massachusetts, which took place in the spring of 1850. The letter quoted above which refers to Harriet's "pamphlet" on women was written in 1849, before the Worcester convention. I believe the first several pages and the ending were added to Harriet's pamphlet to lend the essay some topical appeal.

What makes the case stronger for Harriet as the primary author of the essay is the content of the argument. Several positions taken in this essay are identical to those Harriet took in her earlier 1832 paper but do not agree with anything Mill himself subscribed to either in his 1832 essay or in 1869 in the *Subjection of Women*. In neither of Mill's essays did he subscribe to the view that married women should seek employment. In one essay he argued that such employment would flood the labor market and hence lower the wages paid. In the *Enfranchisement* essay, Harriet took this point by the horn and demolished it in the following manner:

Even if every woman, as matters now stand, had a claim on some man for support, how infinitely preferable is it that part of the income should be the woman's earning, even if the aggregate sum were but little increased by it, rather than that she should be compelled to stand aside in order that men may be the sole earners, and the sole dispensers of what is earned. . . . A woman who contributes materially to the support of the family, cannot be treated in the same contemptuously tyrannical manner as one who, however she may toil as a domestic drudge, is a dependent on the man for subsistence.

In both of John Mill's essays he claimed that married women already had an occupation, the care of their homes and children, and that they should therefore devote themselves to being educated companions to their husbands rather than holding outside jobs. But in the 1851 essay Harriet argued strongly against the idea of training women to become mere "companions of men":

The modern . . . modes of education of women abjure an education of mere show and profess to aim at solid instruction, but mean by that expression, superficial information on solid subjects.

. . . High mental powers in women will be but an exceptional accident, until every career is open to them and until they as well as men, are educated for themselves and for the world, not one sex for the other.

Her conclusion was that "what is wanted for women is equal rights, equal admission to all social privileges, not a position apart, a sort of sentimental priesthood."

This was strong language for 1851, and I submit that it was written by a strong-willed and intelligent woman, Harriet Taylor. It was a far more radical position than John Mill ever espoused on the subject of women, either twenty years earlier or twenty years later.

The image of John Stuart Mill as primarily a logical rationalist can be supported if one takes into account only his autobiography and major books. As more of his correspondence becomes available, the dominant image of Mill as the Saint of Rationalism may undergo a subtle correction. A few scholars in the past twenty years have begun to balance this one-sided image of Mill as the "logic machine." The English scholar Basil Willey has paved the way for this more rounded assessment. With access to the British library collection of correspondence, Willey in his tart, brisk way made the following comment on Mill:

What a piece of work is Mill. The steam engine radical, frightened at his own progress, whistling for the flowery meadows, his power loom prose booming out the sentiments of Rousseau or D. H. Lawrence.[58]

58. Willey, *Nineteenth Century Studies*, p. 161. What preceded this exclamatory assessment of Mill by Willey was a long passage from the *Political Economy* in which Mill argued for a reduction in population growth, urging that men have need for space and solitude. Mill ended the passage with a comment we in 1970 have good cause to rephrase in our own terms: "If the earth must lose that part of its pleasantness which it owes to things that the unlimited increase of wealth and population would extirpate from it, for the mere purpose of enabling it to support a larger, but not a better or a happier population, I sincerely hope, for the sake of posterity, that they will be content to be stationary, long before necessity compels them to it."

So too Max Lerner has struck a new note in his comments about Mill, pointing out that for all his apparatus of rationalism, Mill was a committed and incurable romantic who saw everything in more than life-size proportions, whether it was Harriet Taylor or the idea of liberty or the blind malevolence of nature. Lerner wrote:

Here was no . . . sawdust-stuffed Victorian moralist, no prim and unctuous spokesman for a carefully ordered world. Here was rather a man of strong passions, large vision, tenacious will, powerful intellect, who used and fused all his qualities in the service of a vision of a better world for all his fellow men.[59]

Part of that vision included a new relationship between men and women, and I suspect both John and Harriet Mill would have been very responsive to the image caught in Elizabeth Barrett Browning's poem, *Aurora Leigh*, in which Aurora says:

The world waits
For help. Beloved, let us work so well,
Our work shall still be better for our love
And still our love be sweeter for our work.[60]

The mutuality suggested in these lines makes insignificant any shrewd calculus of the "how much was hers, how much his" variety in assessing the collaboration between John Mill and Harriet Taylor. Though it is couched in terms of detached scholarship, one senses in Mill scholars an unwitting desire to reject Harriet Taylor as capable of contributing in any

59. Lerner, *Essential Works of John Stuart Mill*, p. xxix.

60. Curious ties often link together many figures in nineteenth-century letters. Robert Browning was befriended as a young boy by Sarah Flower, and she brought some of his poetry to William Fox for his assessment. Fox was among the earliest critics to acknowledge Browning's poetic talents. In later years, Browning remained in close correspondence with Fox, viewing him as his "literary father." The slim volume, *Aurora Leigh*, by his wife Elizabeth Barrett Browning, also figured in the life of one of the leading nineteenth-century American suffragists: Susan B. Anthony carried it with her everywhere, as one of her main sources of inspiration, a model of what a future woman's life might be. See Alma Lutz, *Susan B. Anthony, Rebel, Crusader, Humanitarian* (Boston: Beacon Press, 1959), pp. 74–76.

significant way to the vigor of Mill's analysis of political and social issues unless it included some tinge of sentiment or political thought the scholar disapproved of, in which case this disliked element was seen as Harriet's influence. The upcoming generation of students and scholars, it is to be hoped, will work on less sex-biased assumptions.

Brief Years of Marriage (1851–58)

Harriet Taylor and John Mill had known each other for twenty-one years when they were finally married in the London Register's Office in April 1851. There is no better example of the manner in which they attempted to put in practice the principles they were so firmly committed to on the proper relations between the sexes, than the remarkable statement Mill wrote two months before his marriage. There is no record of what Mill did with this statement, nor of any discussion between them prior to his drafting the document, but it is so fine an example of principles put to practice that it is worth inclusion here. The necessity for drafting a personal declaration in the form of an individuated marriage "pledge" applies to our own time as it did in 1851, for legal and ecclesiastical strictures continue to be alien to the spirit in which many men and women committed to sex equality wish to join their lives:

Being about, if I am so happy as to obtain her consent, to enter into the marriage relation with the only woman I have ever known, with whom I would have entered into that state; and the whole character of the marriage relation as constituted by law being such as both she and I entirely and conscientiously disapprove, for this among other reasons, that it confers upon one of the parties to the contract, legal power and control over the person, property, and freedom of action of the other party, independent of her own wishes and will; I, having no means of legally divesting myself of these odious powers (as I most assuredly would do if an engagement to that effect could be made legally binding on me) feel it my duty to put on record a formal protest against the existing law of marriage, in so far as conferring such powers; and a solemn promise never in any case or under any circumstances to use them. And in the event of marriage between Mrs. Taylor and me I declare it to be my will and intention, and the condition of the engagement between us, that she retains in all respects whatever the same absolute freedom of action and freedom of disposal of herself and of all that does or may at any time belong to her, as if no such marriage had taken place; and I absolutely disclaim and repudiate all pretension to have acquired any rights whatever by virtue of such marriage.

6 March 1851 J. S. Mill[61]

A resounding ring of liberty for individual men and women sounds in this statement of Mill's as it was again to echo from the pages of their "joint production" in the famous essay *On Liberty*, and in Harriet's essay on the *Enfranchisement of Women:*

We deny the right of any portion of the species to decide for another portion . . . what is and what is not their 'proper sphere.' The proper sphere for all human beings is the largest and highest which they are able to attain to. What this is, cannot be ascertained, without complete liberty of choice.

Little is known about the first two years of their marriage, partly because they were together and it is through their correspondence that we get a view of their personal and intellectual affairs. The Mills spent the summer following their marriage in France and Belgium, returning in September to settle in Blackheath Park, at that time a rural district on the outskirts of London, from which Mill commuted by train to India House. The rural quality of the setting is caught by a contemporary description that the house faced "a wide open space of rolling meadows bounded far off by a blue outline of distant hills." Here the Mills lived a quiet and solitary life for two years, with only occasional week-end visitors such as William Fox and his daughter or foreign scholars.

Harriet's two youngest children, then in their early twenties, were members of the Blackheath Park household, and it is from their pens that Hayek provides us with the only scraps of evidence that suggest something of the personal routine of their home life. A few years later when Helen Taylor was off on a brief fling at a stage career, she wrote her mother:

61. Elliot, *The Letters of John Stuart Mill,* 1:58.

I like to think about nine o'clock that you are talking with him. I am unhappy at three because you are at dinner and I am not there to help you. I grow impatient at five because he has not come in but at six it is pleasant to think that he is making tea and you have got my letter (which he has brought home).[62]

Harriet's son Algernon provided another, little known side of their home life and of Mill's musical talent:

Mr. Mill used, now and then, to perform on the piano, but only when asked to do so by my mother; and then he would at once sit down to the instrument, and play music entirely of his own composition, on the spur of the moment: .music of a singular character . . . rich in feeling, vigour and suggestiveness. . . . When he had finished, my mother would, perhaps, enquire what had been the idea running in his mind, and which had formed the theme of the improvisation—for such it was, and a strikingly characteristic one too.[63]

There is more evidence on the period from 1853 until Harriet's death in 1858, though for the unhappy reason that their declining health led to numerous separations as one or the other sought the relief of southern or coastal climates. Their first separation was in 1853. Far from enjoying her "more as a correspondent than as a companion," as Stillinger suggests, Mill wrote his wife:

This is the first time since we were married my darling wife that we have been separated and I do not like it at all—but your letters are the greatest delight and as soon as I have done reading one I begin thinking how soon I shall have another.[64]

It must be noted that the Mills had had twenty-one years before their marriage in which to establish the style of their relationship. It was an intellectual and sentimental communion through discussion and written correspondence. From their own views of the place of physical sex in individual lives and the larger society, there is no reason to assume that sheer

---

62. Hayek, *John Stuart Mill and Harriet Taylor,* p. 183.

63. Ibid.

64. Hayek, *John Stuart Mill and Harriet Taylor,* p. 184.

physical togetherness was as necessary to their relationhip as it would be to us in our day.

Even during their most prolonged separation, when Mill was ordered out of England by his doctor (December 1854 to the summer of 1855), they were in constant contact by letter. Mill's correspondence during these months in Italy, Sicily, and Greece are not yet available in print, although Hayek has tempted us with some sample letters. They make fascinating reading, as one follows Mill on mule trips into remote parts of Sicily, or mountain climbing in Greece, all the while writing fully in a style that shows an expansion of his spirits and improvement in his health, as he visits the places of historic significance familiar to him from Greek and Latin reading in childhood. This "symbol of rationalism" often trembled with emotion in these encounters with the classical past. One sample must suffice here, from a letter Mill wrote to his wife from Naples in February 1855:

Nothing can be more beautiful than this place . . . now in this bedroom by candlelight I am in a complete nervous state from the sensation of the beauty I am living among—while I look at it I seem to be gathering honey which I savor the whole time afterwards.[65]

Throughout the correspondence between 1853 and 1858 there was an undercurrent of urgency, a feeling that they must quickly complete their work before death claimed them. Already in 1853 Mill wrote to his wife at Sidmouth:

We must finish the best we have got to say, and not only that, but publish it while we are alive. I do not see what living depository there is likely to be of our thoughts, or who in this weak generation that is growing up will even be capable of thoroughly mastering and assimilating your ideas, much less of re-originating them—so we must write them and print them, and then they can wait until there are again thinkers.[66]

In 1854 Mill worked on his autobiography, and there is an

65. Ibid., p. 221.
66. Ibid., p. 185.

interesting exchange of letters with his wife about what should be said in it concerning their personal life. Mill wrote Harriet in February that on "what particularly concerns our life there is nothing yet written, except the descriptions of you and of your effect on me," prophetically ending:

But we have to consider, which we can only do together, how much of our story it is advisable to tell, in order to make head against the representations of enemies when we shall not be alive to add anything to it. If it was not to be published for 100 years, I should say tell all, simply and without reserve. As it is there must be care taken not to put arms into the hands of the enemy.[67]

Within five days Harriet responded to this letter, in part as follows:

This ought to be done in its genuine truth and simplicity—strong affection, intimacy of friendship, and no impro.priety. It seems to me an edifying picture for those poor wretches who cannot conceive friendship but in sex—nor believe that expediency and the consideration for feelings of others can conquer sensuality. But of course this is not my reason for wishing it done. It is that every ground should be occupied by ourselves on our own subject.[68]

This Victorian concept of "reason" controlling the "lower," "base," or "animal" instincts is often present in their writings and is the one area bearing on the lives of the two sexes in which the twentieth-century reader experiences a discordant note. Radical though they may be in political and logical argument on the social and legal barriers which kept women in involuntary or voluntary captivity, these Victorians had a view of the body as an unfortunate trap of the human spirit and intellect, to be controlled, clothed, forgotten—save when its frequent illness forced attention. The liberation of women was not thought of in terms of sexual liberation of women in the modern sense at all. Helen Taylor, whose ideas one may presume were moulded by her mother and stepfather, expressed

67. Ibid., p. 194.
68. Ibid., p. 196.

the Victorian view very pointedly in a letter written in 1870, in which she said:

I think it probable that this particular passion will become with men, as it is already with a large number of women, completely under the control of the reason. It has become so with women because its becoming so has been the condition upon which women hoped to obtain the strongest love and admiration of men. The gratification of this passion in its highest form, therefore, has been with women conditional upon their restraining it in its lowest. It has not yet been tried what the same conditions will do for men. I believe that they will do all that we wish, nor am I alone in thinking that men are by nature capable of as thorough a control over these passions as women are. . . .[69]

The Mills espoused very advanced and radical ideas about the status of women, marriage and divorce laws, the right of women to education and the franchise, and the injustice of denying basic human rights to the female half of humanity; but in the area of human sexuality they were very much the products of their Victorian era. One might raise the question, however, whether this is not equally true in the 1970s. We have witnessed, over the decade of the 1960s, a legal revolution in the rights of women in the employment sphere, yet our literature continues to be dominated by infantile acts of physical rape in the pages of a Norman Mailer and of female-male encounters confined to genital contact in the pages of a John Updike. Young women by the score still limp away bruised in spirit from sexual encounters they initiate under the banner of sexual freedom, but with an archaic stance of "take me" that acknowledges the male as actor and themselves as objects. Women still face a long struggle to secure the right to control their own bodies through repeal of man-made laws on contraception and abortion.

So too we have not even begun to digest the implications of recent laboratory studies of human sexuality.[70] This research

69. Elliot, *The Letters of John Stuart Mill*, vol. 1, p. 241.

70. William Masters and Virginia Johnson, *Human Sexual Response* (New York: Little Brown, 1966).

has now dispelled the twin Freudian ideas of lesser female sexuality and the view that vaginal orgasm is distinct from and superior to clitoral orgasm. It is doubtful, however, that these findings will be quickly reflected in the literary work of our male writers. Even further in the future is a serious coming to grips with the Masters-Johnson finding that there is greater intensity to female sexuality than male sexuality, or that the human female is often still aroused and sexually interested when her partner is sexually satisfied. It is rare for anyone to conclude from these findings, as Mary Shurfey recently did, that we can at last reject the myth of relative asexuality among women as a biological absurdity and realize that women's sexuality has been suppressed in the name of monogamy at the service of a man-centered civilization. No one has traced the implications of these research results for the structure of marriage and the family.

Fifty years of acceptance of Freudian concepts of female sexuality will not be quickly undone by one set of empirical researches on the human sexual response. Psychoanalytic theories have penetrated deep into the modern scientific and artistic consciousness. This is nowhere more apparent than in the sociological and psychological literature on sex roles and sex differences. Hence it is perhaps not surprising that it is not a social scientist but a twentieth-century playwright, Genet, who has written the most perceptive analysis of sex as a caste and its effects upon the larger society. Kate Millett has analyzed Genet's plays—*The Blacks, The Balcony,* and *The Screens*—as rationalist blasts against the most fundamental of society's follies, its view of sex as a caste structure ratified by nature. In Millett's analysis of these plays,[71] Genet considers human sexuality not only hopelessly tainted in its own sphere, but the prototype of institutionalized inequality of all other sorts—racial, political, and economic. Genet is convinced that by dividing humanity into two groups and appointing one to rule

71. Kate Millett, "Sexual Politics: Miller, Mailer and Genet," *New American Review,* no. 7 (1969), pp. 7–32; also Kate Millett, *Sexual Politics* (New York: Doubleday, 1970).

over the other by virtue of birthright, the social order has already established and ratified a system of oppression which underlies and corrupts all other human relationships. Genet's plea is that unless we go to the very center of the sexual politic and root out the power and violence there, all our efforts at liberation will only land us again in the same primordial stews.

In her *Enfranchisement* essay, Harriet Mill commented that it was fitting that abolitionists, committed to the extirpation of the aristocracy of color, should join forces in the first collective protest against the "aristocracy of sex" at the 1850 convention in Worcester, Massachusetts. But if anyone had carried the idea of sex as a caste system into the intimate area of human sexuality along the lines Genet has now done, one can imagine what a feverish struggle John and Harriet would have had to fit this new set of ideas into the fabric of their thought! It is fitting in 1970 that many men who were active in the civil rights movement of the 1960s have now joined in the "second" collective protest against the same aristocracy of sex, the contemporary women's liberation movement. At the same time it is also clear that beneath the fine words of liberation, many of us are far from liberated in the deeper roots of our attitudes toward male and female sexuality.

There are so many points in the writings of the Mills that show an uncanny anticipation of things to come, so fine an ability to project beyond their own time and place, that one hesitates to assert that even the new radical perspective on human sexuality might not have been woven into their philosophy, if not their personal behavior. More than one hundred years ago, Mill and his wife must have discussed many of their ideas about solutions to social problems confronting the world. The ideas come fresh across ten decades, in such observations as the following:

The social problem of the future we considered to be, how to unite the greatest individual liberty of action with a common ownership in the raw material of the globe, and an equal participation of all in the benefits of combined labour.[72]

This is from the draft of the *Autobiography* written in the early 1850s when Marx was working away, unknown to Mill, in the British Museum. It is a judgment that Americans, who now consume over half the raw materials of the globe although they comprise less than ten percent of the world's population, have yet to confront. Mill was looking far ahead, extrapolating from the hopes engendered in him by the revolutions of 1848, seeing beyond nationalism to a world that shared the natural wealth of the globe, a socialist world with a more equitable distribution of the world's bounty.

Or the following, from a letter to Professor Carl Heinrich Rau of Heidelberg written in 1852:

it is to be decided whether Europe shall enter peacefully and prosperously into a better order of things, or whether the new ideas will be inaugurated by a century of war and violence like that which followed the Reformation of Luther.[73]

Again, Mill was referring to the uprising of the working class in nation after nation, anticipating increased class warfare unless men had freedom to determine their own economic and political destiny. By the 1850s Mill saw that the aristocracy had been replaced by what he called the "shopocracy," middle-class mercantile interests with no more concern for the welfare and rights of the working class than the aristocracy before them. Even before the French workers' uprising in 1848, Mill had confided to a friend in 1847:

In England I often think that a violent revolution is very much needed, in order to give that general shake up to the torpid mind of the nation which the French Revolution gave to Continental Europe. England has never had any general break-up of old associations and hence the extreme difficulty of getting any ideas into its stupid head.[74]

72. Coss, *Autobiography of John Stuart Mill*, p. 162.

73. Elliot, *The Letters of John Stuart Mill*, vol. 1, p. 170.

74. Mineka, *The Earlier Letters*, vol. 13, p. 713.

It is little wonder that Hugh Elliot reported the experience of turning over numerous pages devoted to Mill's work in the Catalogue of Printed Books in the British Museum to find one headed by the entry: "Mill (John Stuart): see AntiChrist."

Men and women in the nineteenth century may not have had our sense of the expanse of physical space, but they often show a grasp of man's place in the long sweep of history that our existentialist times lack. It is refreshing to encounter Mill in Palermo in 1855 reading Goethe, speculating about the vast accretion of knowledge since Greek times, thinking about Goethe's responsiveness to the Greek sense of symmetry, and then commenting in a letter to his wife:

the moderns have vastly more material to reduce to order than the ancients dreamt of and the secret of harmonizing it all has not yet been discovered. It is too soon by a century or two to attempt either symmetrical reproductions in art or symmetrical characters. We all need to be blacksmiths or ballet dancers with good stout arms or legs, useful to do what we have got to do and useful to fight with at times. . . . We cannot be Apollos and Venuses just yet.[75]

A nineteenth-century man reading an eighteenth-century poet in a setting steeped in pre-Christian history, speculating about man in the twenty-first century!

A last illustration of Mill's anticipation of the future can be shown by his alertness to the connection between the status of women and the problem of population growth, a connection made only in a few isolated quarters in the social sciences of our time. In the chapter he attributed to Harriet on the future condition of the working classes in his *Political Economy,* Mill stated this connection in the following manner:

The ideas and institutions by which the accident of sex is made the groundwork of an inequality of legal rights, and a forced dissimilarity of social functions, must ere long be recognized as the greatest hindrance to moral, social and even intellectual improvement. On the present occasion I shall only indicate, among the probable consequences of the industrial and social indepen-

75. Hayek, *John Stuart Mill and Harriet Taylor,* pp. 225–26.

dence of women, a great diminution of the evil of over population. It is by devoting one half of the human species to that exclusive function, by making it fill the entire life of one sex and interweave itself with almost all the objects of the other, that the "animal" instinct in question is nursed into the disproportionate preponderance which it has hitherto exercised in human life.[76]

When in 1848 an American reviewer of the *Political Economy* objected to Mill's ideas on population growth, Mill responded in biting fashion, linking the objections to the reviewer's nationality:

On the population question, my difference with the reviewer is fundamental, and in the incidental reference which he makes to my assertion of equality of political rights and of social position in behalf of women, the tone assumed by him is really below contempt. But I fear that a country where institutions profess to be founded on equality, and which yet maintains the slavery of black men and of all women will be one of the last to relinquish that other servitude.[77]

In 1970 the United States exports millions of contraceptive pills and devices to Asian and Latin American countries, but it exports little education on what John Mill and Harriet Taylor understood so long ago, that freedom of choice and a wider range of life goals would undercut women's desires for a bountiful maternity. A few years after the above letter was penned, Harriet put the issue very pointedly in the *Enfranchisement* essay:

Numbers of women are wives and mothers only because there is no other career open to them, no other occupation for their feelings or other activities. . . . To say women must be excluded from active life because maternity disqualifies them for it, is in fact to say that every other career should be forbidden them in order that maternity may be their only resource.

One closes a book of Mill's writings or correspondence with

76. John Stuart Mill, *Principles of Political Economy*, ed. J. M. Robson (University of Toronto Press, 1965) 3:765-66.

77. Mineka, *The Earlier Letters*, vol. 13, p. 741.

a nagging question: who among us in 1970 are now thinking and writing with a foresight that will speak meaningfully to our descendants in the mid-twenty-first century, as Mill so often did to us? On issue after issue our language is different from Mill's, but the problems are the same, and often we have yet to rediscover the solutions Mill proposed a century ago.

Harriet's Death and "The Subjection of Women"

John Mill retired from the East India Company in the autumn of 1858, and the Mills took off for the south of France in October, planning to stay during the winter at Hyères, where Harriet's health had improved during a previous stay, and then to spend the spring in Italy. They never reached their destination, for a cold that Harriet had caught developed into severe lung congestion, and she died in Avignon on 3 November. Mill's own words are the best description of the aftermath of her death:

Since then I have sought for such alleviation as my state admitted of, by the mode of life which most enables me to feel her still near me. I bought a cottage as close as possible to the place where she is buried, and there her daughter (my fellow-sufferer and now my chief comfort) and I, live constantly during a great portion of the year. My objects in life are solely those which were hers; my pursuits and occupations those in which she shared, or sympathized, and which are indissolubly associated with her.[78]

In keeping with this mood, the first things that Mill published after his wife's death were the first two volumes of his collected essays, *Dissertations and Discussions,* including the *Enfranchisement* essay of his wife's and the volume *On Liberty* that had occupied them the previous few years. During 1860–61 Mill drafted *The Subjection of Women.* In his autobiography he explained that the essay was written at his daughter's suggestion that there might be a "written exposition of my opinions on that great question, as full and conclusive as I could make it." Concerning its content, he said:

78. Coss, *Autobiography of John Stuart Mill,* p. 170.

As ultimately published it was enriched with some important ideas of my daughter's, and passages of her writing. But in what was of my own composition, all that is most striking and profound belongs to my wife; coming from the fund of thought which had been made common to us both, by our innumerable conversations and discussions on a topic which filled so large a place in our minds.[79]

An important idea in Mill's view of the equality of the sexes is tapped in this passage: the "fund of thought made common" to Harriet and himself. Mill shied away from any direct personal account of his marital relationship, but the reader feels he was speaking from a personal basis when he described a marriage between equals toward the end of the *Subjection* essay. Although he first rejected the desirability of giving such a description (on the ground that those who can conceive such a marriage need no description, and to those who cannot conceive such a marriage, it would appear but the dream of an enthusiast), he proceeded to describe just such a relationship —a marriage between

two persons of cultivated faculties, identical in opinions and purposes, between whom there exists that best of equality, similarity of powers and capacities with reciprocal superiority in them so that each can enjoy the luxury of looking up to the other, and can have alternately the pleasure of leading and of being led in the path of development. . . . This and this only is the ideal of marriage; . . . all opinions, customs and institutions which favor any other notion of it . . . are relics of primitive barbarism.

The idea of complementary skills and knowledge, such that each spouse can be both leader and follower, teacher and student, on a firm base of shared values and goals, reads like a description of the Mills' own marriage. There is an echo here of Mill's description of what he and his wife contributed to the analysis of the position of women. Mill acknowledged that before he became an intimate friend of Harriet's, his views on the position of women were nothing more than an abstract principle: he saw no more reason why women should be held

79. Ibid., p. 186.

in legal subjection to other people than why men should. Harriet's contribution he described as follows:

that perception of the vast practical bearings of women's disabilities which found expression in the book on the "Subjection of Women" was acquired mainly through her teaching. . . . But for her rare knowledge of human nature and comprehension of moral and social influences, I should have had a very insufficient perception of the mode in which the consequences of the inferior position of women intertwine themselves with all the evils of existing society and with all the difficulties of human improvement.[80]

Mill had a poor view of the capacity of men in his time to live out a marriage on a basis of equality. In fact he argued that the reason barriers are maintained against the liberation of women from their caste status is that "the generality of the male sex cannot yet tolerate the idea of living with an equal." John Stuart Mill clearly could and did.

There are several reasons why *The Subjection of Women* continues to be a powerfully effective essay, which people in the 1970s can find as stimulating as those who read it for the first time in the 1870s. It is grounded in basic libertarian values that ring as true today as then:

We have had the morality of submission and the morality of chivalry and generosity: the time is ripe for morality of justice. . . . The principle of the modern movement in morals and politics is that conduct and conduct alone entitles to respect: that not what men are but what they do constitutes their claim to deference. . . . It is totally out of keeping with modern values to have ascribed statuses; . . . human beings are no longer born to their place in life; . . . individual choice is our model now.

To the generations of the twentieth century who have seen tyranny and the suppression of human liberty in all forms of government—Fascist, Communist, and democratic—John Stuart Mill's invocation of the rights of men and women to liberty and justice have a strong, continuing appeal. And to the women of the twentieth century, who have seen very little

80. Ibid., p. 173.

difference in the actual condition, if not the formal rights, of women under any existing form of government, *The Subjection of Women* continues to serve as a resounding affirmation of their human right to full equality and a sophisticated analysis of the obstacles that bar their way to it.

A second basic reason for the continuing relevance of the Mill essay on women is that it is not burdened with the dead weight of any of the social and psychological theories that have emerged during the hundred years separating us from the Mills: no Darwinism to encourage an unthinking expectation of unilinear progress of mankind through "natural selection" or "selective breeding"; no Freudian theory to belittle women's sexuality and encourage their acceptance as the "second sex"; no functional anthropology or sociology to justify a conservative acceptance of the status quo; no Marxist theory to encourage a narrow concentration on economic variables. What the Mills had as their guide is what we have only begun to recapture in our counterpart efforts to expand the horizons of men and women to fuller realization of their human potential: a blend of compassion and logic and a commitment to the view that liberty cannot exist in the absence of the power to use it.

The closest analogy to Mill's intellectual style is the formal structure of what is known in the behavioral sciences as functional analysis, but with this difference: Mill attempted to probe beneath the surface of social forms to find the latent function served by that form, not, however, to pinpoint its "social utility" but to identify the root cause which must be changed to effect the release of women from their subjection. Thus in analyzing chivalry and its equivalent in modern times, "consideration for women," Mill characterized it as a mask hiding the idea of servitude, the notion that women need protection or help because they are "weak." So in a passage that anticipates Genet's analysis, Mill argued that society can never be organized on merit, or depart from its imposition of the power of the strong over the weak, so long as this right of the strong rules in the family, the heart of society:

The principle can not get hold of men's inmost sentiments until this assumption of superiority of power merely on the ascribed grounds of sex, persists. The selfish propensities, self worship of men, have their source and root in the present constitution of the relation between men and women.

So, too, Mill had a terse and firm answer to the claim that there are "natural" differences between the sexes which preclude full equality for women (by our time amplified by the thousands of psychological and sociological studies which demonstrate differences between the sexes): "No one can know the nature of the sexes as long as they have only been seen in their present relation to each other; . . . what women are is what we have required them to be." Mill left open the possibility that women qua women may have some special type of originality to contribute, though cautious to point out we have no way to predict this until women have had the freedom to develop in an autonomous way, with time to emancipate themselves from the "influence of accepted male models," and strike out on their own.

From Mill's correspondence following the publication of the *Subjection* essay, we can gain some understanding of his reasons for developing the particular arguments he does in the volume, and for excluding certain other topics. There is, for example, little or nothing in the book on marriage and divorce laws. In a letter to Professor John Nichol of Glasgow, Mill wrote:

I thought it best not to discuss the questions of marriage and divorce along with that of the equality of women; not only from the obvious inexpediency of establishing a connection in people's minds between the equality and any particular opinions on the divorce question, but also because I do not think that the conditions of the dissolubility of marriage can be properly determined until women have an equal voice in determining them, nor until there has been experience of the marriage relation as it would exist between equals. Until then I should not like to commit myself to more than the general principle of relief from the contract in extreme cases.[81]

81. Elliot, *The Letters of John Stuart Mill,* vol. 2, p. 212.

Mill's sense of political expediency and timing played a major role in what he felt was useful to discuss in the essay. At the time he wrote, women had no legal right to their own children, and one reader of his essay wrote to suggest that since there was an infinitely closer relationship of children to their mothers than to their fathers, the law should really reflect this reality, and if anything, give legal rights over children to women. Mill answered Mrs. Hooker:

What you so justly say respecting the infinitely closer relationship of a child to its mother than to its father, I have learned . . . to regard as full of important consequences with regard to the future legal position of parents and children. This, however, is a portion of the truth for which the human mind will not, for some time, be sufficiently prepared to make its discussion useful.[82]

The underlying intent behind Mill's argument in the essay comes out most clearly in a letter to his friend and biographer, Alexander Bain. Mill explained that the stress he gave to the capacities of women, which occupy so large a proportion of the essay, was done for two reasons. One was that the principal objection then offered against sex equality was that women were not "fit for or capable of this, that or the other mental achievement." The second reason is perhaps as cogent in 1970 as it was in John Mill's own time:

But there is a still stronger reason. The most important thing women have to do is to stir up the zeal of women themselves. We have to stimulate their aspirations—to bid them not despair of anything, nor think anything beyond their reach, but try their faculties against all difficulties. In no other way can the verdict of experience be fairly collected, and in no other way can we excite the enthusiasm in women which is necessary to break down the old barriers. I believe the point has now been reached at which, the higher we pitch our claims, the more disposition there will be to   concede part of them. . . . Everything I hear strengthens me in the belief, which I at first entertained with a slight mixture of misgiving, that the book has come out at the right time, and that no part of it is premature.[83]

82. Ibid., p. 214.
83. Ibid., p. 210.

It is fitting to note the reaction to the book by an American woman famous in the history of the women's movement, Elizabeth Cady Stanton. This *enfant terrible* of the suffrage cause wrote Mill after reading the *Subjection* essay in 1869:

I lay the book down with a peace and joy I never felt before, for it is the first response from any man to show he is capable of seeing and feeling all the nice shades and degrees of woman's wrongs and the central point of her weakness and degradation.[84]

That Mill was able to achieve this is a tribute to the remarkable blend of compassion and logic both Harriet and Mill himself brought to the analysis of women and the hope for a future equality of the sexes.

When Carrie Chapman Catt wrote her foreword to an American edition of Mill's *The Subjection of Women,* she closed with a few lines that are as relevant in 1970 as they were in 1911:

For some years the book has been out of print, and its pages have grown unfamiliar to those who should know them best. A new edition is a happy incident and its accessibility to the masses will prove of untold value to the movement.[85]

In 1911 the "movement" was the suffrage movement, still some nine years from its victory in securing the vote for American women. In 1970 the movement is much broader and its goals more diffuse, for the women's liberation movement seeks nothing short of full equality of the sexes. In this sense contemporary activists are closer to the perspective of John Mill and Harriet Taylor than of the majority of turn-of-century American suffragists. We can not tell how many years remain until our movement is victorious. The answer lies with those who read and study these pages: all the tens of thousands of women and men who seek to understand the political and ideological

84. Alma Lutz, *Created Equal: A Biography of Elizabeth Cady Stanton* (New York: John Day Company, 1940), pp. 171–72.

85. John Stuart Mill, *The Subjection of Women* (New York: Frederick A. Stokes, 1911), p. xv.

history of the movement to secure equality between the sexes. If these same readers carry their knowledge into a vigorous commitment to scholarship and to political action, at least one small corner of this whirling globe may know full sex equality by the close of the twentieth century.

2

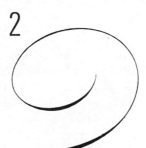

Early Essays on Marriage and Divorce

JOHN STUART MILL
and
HARRIET TAYLOR

Early Essays on Marriage and Divorce

The Essay by John Stuart Mill

he to whom my life is devoted has
wished for written exposition of my
opinions on the subject which, of
all connected with human Institutions,
is nearest to her happiness. Such as
that exposition can be made without
her to suggest and to decide, it is
given in these pages: she, herself, has
not refused to put into writing for
me, what she has thought and felt
on the same subject, and *there* I shall
be taught, all perhaps which I have,
and certainly all which I have
not, found out for myself. In the
investigation of truth, as in all else,
"it is not good for man to be alone."
And more than all, in what concerns

These essays are reprinted with permission
from F. A. Hayek, *John Stuart Mill and Harriet Taylor: Their Correspondence and Subsequent Marriage* (London: Routledge and Kegan
Paul Ltd., 1951). In the Hayek version certain
abbreviations (&, w^d, sh^d, w^h) found in the
original manuscript were preserved. These have
here been expanded. Moreover, Hayek added
several question marks in parentheses to indicate that the reading of the preceding word or
words was doubtful. These queries have been
deleted from the present version.—A.S.R.

the relations of Man with Woman, the law which is to be observed by both should surely be made by both; not, as hitherto, by the stronger only.

How easy would it be for either me or you, to resolve this question for ourselves alone. Its difficulties, for difficulties it has, are such as obstruct the avenues of all great questions which are to be decided for mankind at large, and therefore not for natures resembling each other, but for natures or at least characters tending to all the points of the moral' compass. All popular morality is, as I once said to you, a compromise among conflicting natures; each renouncing a certain portion of what its own desires call for, in order to avoid the evils of a perpetual warfare with all the rest. That is the best popular morality, which attains this general pacification with the least sacrifice of the happiness of the higher natures; who are the greatest, indeed the only real, sufferers by the compromise; for *they* are called upon to give up what would really make them happy; while others are commonly required only to restrain desires the gratification of which would bring no real happiness. In the adjustment, moreover, of the compromise, the higher natures count only in proportion to their number, how small! and to the number of those whom they can influence: while the conditions of the compromise weigh heavily upon them in the state of their greater capacity of happiness, and its natural consequence, their keener sense of *want* and disappointment when the degree of happiness which they know would fall to their lot but for untoward external circumstances, is denied them.

By the higher natures I mean those characters who from the combination of natural and acquired advantages have the greatest capacity of feeling happiness, and of bestowing it. Of bestowing it in two ways: as being beautiful to contemplate, and therefore the natural objects of admiration and love; and also as being fitted, and induced, by their qualities of mind and heart, to promote by their actions, and by all that depends upon their will, the greatest possible happiness of all who are within the sphere of their influence.

If all persons were like these, or even would be guided by these, morality would be very different from what it must now be; or rather it would not exist at all as morality, since morality and inclination would coincide. If all resembled you, my lovely friend, it would be idle to prescribe rules for them: By following their own impulses under the guidance of their own judgment, they would find more happiness, and would confer more, than by obeying any moral principles or maxims whatever; since these cannot possibly be adapted beforehand to every peculiarity of circumstance which can be taken into account by a sound and vigorous intellect *worked* by a strong *will*, and guided by what Carlyle calls "an open loving heart." Where there exists a genuine and strong desire to do that which is most for the happiness of all, general rules are merely aids to prudence, in the choice of means; not peremptory obligations. Let but the desires be right, and the "imagination lofty and refined": and provided there be disdain of all false seeming, "to the pure all things are pure."

It is easy enough to settle to moral bearings of our question upon such characters. The highest natures are of course impassioned natures; to such, marriage is but one continued act of self-sacrifice where strong affection is not; every tie therefore which restrains them from seeking out and uniting themselves with some one whom they can perfectly love, is a yoke to which they cannot be subjected without oppression: and to such a person when found, they would, natural superstition apart, scorn to be united by any other tie than free and voluntary choice. If such natures have been healthily developed in other respects, they will have all other good and worthy feelings strong enough to prevent them from pursuing this happiness at the expense of greater suffering of others: and that is the limit of the forbearance which morality ought in such a case to enjoin.

But will the morality which suits the highest natures, in this matter, be also best for all inferior natures? My conviction is that it will: but this can be only a happy accident. All the difficulties of morality in any of its brands, grow out of

the conflict which continually arises between the highest morality and even the best popular morality which the degree of
development yet achieved by average human nature, will allow
to exist.

If all, or even most persons, in the choice of a companion
of the other sex, were led by any real aspiration towards, or
sense of, the happiness which such companionship in its best
shape is capable of giving to the best natures, there would
never have been any reason why law or opinion should have
set any limits to the most unbounded freedom of uniting and
separating: nor is it probable that popular morality would
ever, in a civilized or refined people, have imposed any restraint upon that freedom. But, as I once said to you, the law
of marriage as it now exists, has been made *by* sensualists,
and *for* sensualists and *to bind* sensualists. The aim and purpose of that law is either to tie up the sense, in the hope by
so doing, of tying up the soul also, or else to tie up the sense
because the soul is not cared about at all. Such purposes never
could have entered into the minds of any to whom nature had
given souls capable of the higher degrees of happiness: nor
could such a law ever have existed but among persons to whose
natures it was in some degree congenial, and therefore more
suitable than at first sight may be supposed by those whose
natures are widely different.

There can, I think, be no doubt that for a long time the
indissolubility of marriage acted powerfully to elevate the social position of women. The state of things to which in almost
all countries it succeeded, was one in which the power of
repudiation existed on one side but not on both: in which the
stronger might cast away the weaker, but the weaker could
not fly from the stronger. To a woman of impassioned character, the difference between this and what now exists, is not
worth much; for she would wish to be repudiated, rather than
to remain united only because she could not be got rid of.
But the aspirations of most women are less high. They would
wish to retain any bond of union they have ever had with a
man to whom they do not prefer any other, and for whom

they have that inferior kind of affection which habits of intimacy frequently produce. Now, assuming what may be assumed of the greater number of men, that they are attracted to women solely by sensuality, or at best by transitory *taste;* it is not deniable, that the irrevocable vow gave to women, when the passing gust had blown over, a permanent hold upon the men who would otherwise have cast them off. Something, indeed *much*, of a community of interest, arose from the mere fact of being indissolubly united: the husband took an interest in the wife as being *his* wife, if he did not from any better feeling: it became essential to his respectability that his wife also should be respected; and commonly when the first revulsion of feeling produced by satiety, went off, the mere fact of continuing together if the woman had anything lovable in her and the man not wholly brutish, could hardly fail to raise up some feeling of regard and attachment. She obtained also, what is often far more precious to her, the certainty of not being separated from the children.

Now if this be all that human life *has* for women, it is little enough: and any woman who feels herself capable of great happiness, and whose aspirations have not been artificially checked, will claim to be set free from *only* this, to seek for more. But women in general, as I have already remarked, are more easily contented, and this I believe to be the cause of the general aversion of women to the idea of facilitating divorce. They have a habitual belief that their power over men is chiefly derived from men's sensuality; and that the same sensuality would go elsewhere in search of gratification, unless restrained by law and opinion. They on their part, mostly seek in marriage, a home, and the state or condition of a married woman, with the addition or not as it may happen, of a splendid establishment etc. etc. These things once obtained, the indissolubility of marriage renders them sure of keeping. And most women, either because these things give them all the happiness they are capable of, or from the artificial barriers which curb all spontaneous movements to seek their greatest felicity, are generally more anxious not to peril the good they have than to go in search of a greater. If marriage were dissoluble, they think they could not retain the position once acquired; or not without practicing upon the attention of men by those arts, disgusting in the extreme to any woman of simplicity, by which a cunning mistress sometimes established and retains her ascendancy.

These considerations are nothing to an impassioned character; but there is something in them, for the characters from which they emanate—is not that so? The only conclusion, however, which can be drawn from them, is one for which there would exist ample grounds even if the law of marriage as it now exists were perfection. This conclusion is, the absurdity and immorality of a state of society and opinion in which a woman is at all dependent for her social position upon the fact of her being or not being married. Surely it is wrong, wrong in every way, and on every view of morality, even the vulgar view—that there should exist any motives to marriage except the happiness which two persons who love one another feel in associating their existence.

The means by which the condition of married women is rendered artificially desirable, are not any superiority of legal rights, for in that respect single women, especially if possessed of property, have the advantage: the civil disabilities are greatest in the case of the married woman. It is not law, but education and custom which make the difference. Woman are so brought up, as not to be able to subsist in the mere physical sense, without a man to keep them: they are so brought up as not to be able to protect themselves against injury or insult, without some man on whom they have a special claim, to protect them: they are so brought up, as to have no vocation or useful office to fulfil in the world, remaining single; for all women who are educated to *be* married, and what little they are taught deserving the name useful, is chiefly what in the ordinary course of things will not come into actual use, unless nor until they are married. A single woman therefore is felt both by herself and others as a kind of excrescence on the surface of society, having no use or function or office there. She is not indeed precluded from useful and honorable exertion of various kinds: but a married woman is *presumed* to be a useful member of society unless there is evidence to the contrary; a single woman must establish what very few either women or men ever do establish, an *individual* claim.

All this, though not the less really absurd and immoral even under the law of marriage which now exists, evidently grows out of that law, and fits into the general state of society of which that law forms a part, nor could continue to exist if the law were changed, and marriage were not a contract at all, or were an easily dissoluble one: The indissolubility of marriage is the keystone of woman's present lot, and the whole comes down and must be reconstructed if that is removed.

And the truth is, that this question of marriage cannot properly be considered by itself alone. The question is not what marriage ought to be, but a far wider question, what woman ought to be. Settle that first, and the other will settle itself. Determine whether marriage is to be a relation between two equal beings, or between a superior and an inferior, between a protector and a dependent; and all other doubts will easily be resolved.

But in this question there is surely no difficulty. There is no natural inequality between the sexes; except perhaps in bodily strength; even that admits of doubt: and if bodily strength is to be the measure of superiority, mankind are no better than savages. Every step in the progress of civilization has tended to diminish the deference paid to bodily strength, until now when that quality confers scarcely any advantages except its natural ones: the strong man has little or no power to employ his strength as a means of acquiring any other advantage over the weaker in body. Every step in the progress of civilization has similarly been marked by a nearer approach to equality in the condition of the sexes; and if they are still far from being equal, the hindrance is not now in the difference of physical strength, but in artificial feelings and prejudices.

If nature has not made men and women unequal, still less ought the law to make them so. It may be assumed, as one of those presuppositions which would almost be made weaker by anything so ridiculous as attempting to prove them, that men and women ought to be perfectly coequal: that a woman ought not to be dependent on a man, more than a man on a woman, except so far as their affections make them so, by a voluntary surrender, renewed and renewing at each instant by free and spontaneous choice.

But this perfect independence of each other for all save affection, cannot be, if there be dependence in pecuniary circumstances; a dependence which in the immense majority of cases must exist, if the woman be not capable, as well as the man, of gaining her own subsistence.

The first and indispensable step, therefore, towards the enfranchisement of woman, is that she be so educated, as not to be dependent either on her father or her husband for subsistence: a position which in nine cases out of ten, makes her either the plaything or the slave of the man who feeds her; and in the tenth case, only his humble friend. Let it not be said that she has an equivalent and compensating advantage in the exemption from toil: men think it base and servile in men to accept food as the price of dependence, and why do they not deem it so in women? solely because they do not desire that women should be their equals. Where there is strong affection, dependence is its own reward: but it must be voluntary dependence; and the more perfectly voluntary it is, the more exclusively each owes every thing to the other's affection and to nothing else,—the greater is the happiness. And where affection is not, the woman who will be dependent for the sake of a maintenance, proves herself as low-minded as a man in the like case—or *would* prove herself so if that resource were not too often the only one her education has given her, and if her education had not also tought her not to consider as degradation, that which is the essence of all prostitution, the act of delivering up her person for bread.

It does not follow that a woman should *actually* support herself because she should be *capable* of doing so: in the natural course of events she will *not*. It is not desirable to burthen the labour market with a double number of competitors. In a healthy state of things, the husband would be able by his single exertions to earn all that is necessary for both: and there would be no need that the wife should take part in the mere providing of what is required to *support* life: it will be for the happiness of both that her occupation should rather be to adorn and beautify it. Except in the class of actual day-labourers, that will be her natural task, if task it can be called, which will in so great a measure be accomplished rather by *being* than by *doing*.

We have all heard the vulgar talk that the proper employment of a wife are household superintendance, and the education of her children. As for household superintendance, if nothing be meant but merely seeing that servants do their duty, that is not an occupation; every woman that is capable of doing it at all can do it without devoting anything like half an hour every day to that purpose peculiarly. It is not like the duty of a head of an office, to whom his subordinates bring their work to be inspected when finished: the defects in the performance of household duties present *themselves* to inspection: skill in superintendance consists in knowing the right way of noticing a fault when it occurs, and giving reasonable advice and instruction how to avoid it: and more depends on establishing a good *system* at first, than upon a perpetual and studious watchfulness. But if it be meant that the mistress of a family shall herself do the work of servants, *that* is good and will naturally take place in the rank in which there do not exist the means of hiring servants; but nowhere else.

Then as to the education of children: if by that term be meant, instructing them in particular arts or particular branches of knowledge, it is absurd to impose that upon mothers: absurd in two ways: absurd to set one-half of the adult human race to perform each on a small scale, what a much smaller number of teachers would accomplish for all, by devoting themselves exclusively to it; and absurd to set all mothers doing that for which some persons must be fitter than others, and for which average mothers cannot possibly be *so* fit as persons trained to the profession. Here again, when the means do not exist for hiring teachers, the mother is the natural teacher: but no special provision needs to be made for that case. Whether she is to teach or not, it is desirable that she should *know*; because knowledge is desirable for its own sake; for its uses, for its pleasures, and for its beautifying influence when not cultivated to the neglect of other gifts. What she knows, she will be able to teach to her children if necessary: but to erect such teaching into her occupation whether she can better employ herself or not, is absurd.

The education which it *does* belong to mothers to give, and which if not imbibed from them is seldom obtained in any perfection at all, is the training of the affections: and through the affections, of the conscience, and the whole moral being. But *this* most precious, and most indispensable part of education, does not take up *time*; it is not a business, an occupation; and a mother does not accomplish it by sitting down with her child for one or two or three hours to a task. She effects it by being with the child; by making it happy, and therefore at peace with all things; by checking bad habits in the commencement and by loving the child and by making the child love her. It is not by particular effects, but imperceptibly and unconsciously that she makes her own character pass into the child; that she makes the child love what she loves, venerate what she venerates and imitate as far as a child can her example. These things cannot be done by a hired teacher; and they are better and greater than all the rest. But to impose upon mothers what hired teachers *can* do, is mere squandering of the glorious existence of a woman fit for a woman's highest destiny. With regard to such things, her part is to see that they are rightly done, not to do them.

The great occupation of woman should be to *beautify* life: to cultivate, for her own sake and that of those who surround her, all her faculties of mind, soul, and body; all her powers of enjoyment, and powers of giving enjoyment; and to diffuse beauty, elegance, and grace, everywhere. If in addition to this the activity of her nature demands more energetic and definite employment, there is never any lack of it in the world: If she loves, her natural impulse will be to associate her existence with him she loves, and to share *his* occupations; in which, if he loves her (with that affection of *equality* which alone deserves to be called love) she will naturally take as strong an interest, and be as thoroughly conversant, as the most perfect confidence on his side can make her.

Such will naturally be the occupations of a woman who has fulfilled what seems to be considered as the end of her existence and attained what is really its happiest state, by uniting herself to a man whom she loves. But whether so united or not, women will never be what they should be, nor their social position what it should be, until women, as universally as men, have the power of gaining their own livelihood: until, therefore, every girl's parents have either provided her with independent means of subsistence, or given her an education qualifying her to provide those means for herself. The only difference between the employments of women and those of men will be, that those which partake most of the beautiful, or which require delicacy and taste rather than muscular exertion, will naturally fall to the share of women: all branches of the fine arts in particular.

In considering, then, what is the best law of marriage, we are to suppose that women already are, what they would be in the best state of society; no less capable of existing independently and respectably without men, than men without women. Marriage, on whatever footing it might be placed, would be wholly a matter of choice, not, as for a woman it now is, something approaching to a matter of necessity; something, at least, which every woman is under strong artificial motives to desire, and which if she attain not, her life is considered to be a failure.

These suppositions being made: and it being no longer any advantage to a woman to be married, merely for the sake of being married: why should any woman cling to the indissolubility of marriage, as if it could be for the good of one party that it should continue when the other party desires that it should be dissolved?

It is not denied by anyone that there are numerous cases in which the happiness of both parties would be greatly promoted by a dissolution of marriage. We will add, that when the social position of the two sexes shall be perfectly equal, a divorce if it be for the happiness of either party, will be for the happiness of both. No one but a sensualist would desire to retain a merely animal connexion with a person of the other sex, unless perfectly assured of being preferred by that person, above all other persons in the world. This certainty never can be quite perfect under the law of marriage as it now exists: it would be nearly absolute, if the tie were merely voluntary.

Not only there are, but it is in vain to hope that there will not always be, innumerable cases, in which the first connexion formed will be one the dissolution of which if it *could be*, certainly would be and ought to be, effected: It has long ago been remarked that of all the more serious acts of the life of a human being, there is not one which is commonly performed with so little of forethought or consideration, as that which is irrevocable, and which is fuller of evil than any other acts of the being's whole life if it turn out ill. And this is not so astonishing as it seems: The imprudence, while the contract remains indissoluble, consists in marrying at all: If you do marry there is little wisdom shewn by a very anxious and careful deliberation beforehand: Marriage is really, what it has been sometimes called, a lottery: and whoever is in a state of mind to calculate chances calmly and value them correctly, is not at all likely to purchase a ticket. Those who marry after taking great pains about the matter, generally do but buy their disappointment dearer. Then the failures in marriage are such as are naturally incident to a first trial: the parties are inexperienced and cannot judge. Nor does this evil seem to be remediable. A woman is allowed to give herself away for life, at an age at which she is not allowed to dispose of the most inconsiderable landed estate: what then? if people are not to marry until they have learnt prudence, they will seldom marry before thirty: can this be expected, or is it to be desired? To direct the immature judgment, there is the advice of parents and guardians: a precious security! The only thing which a young girl can do, worse than marrying to please herself, is marrying to please any other person. However paradoxical it may sound to the ears of those who are reputed to have grown wise as wine grows good, by *keeping*, it is yet true, that A, an average person can better know what is for his own happiness, than B, an average person can know what is for A's happiness. Fathers and mothers as the world is constituted, do not judge more wisely than sons and daughters, they only judge differently: and the judgments of both being of the ordinary strength, or rather of the ordinary weakness, a person's own self has the advantage of a considerable greater number of *data* to judge from, and the further one of a stronger interest in the subject. Foolish people will say, that being interested in the subject is a disqualification: strange that they should not distinguish between being interested in a cause as a party before a judge, i.e. interested in deciding one way, right or wrong— and being interested as a person is in the management of his own property, interested in deciding right. The parties themselves are only interested in doing what is most for their happiness; but their relatives may have all sorts of selfish interests to promote by inducing them to marry or not to marry.

The first choice, therefore, is made under very complicated disadvantages. By the facts of its being the *first* the parties are necessarily inexperienced in the particular matter: they are commonly young (especially the party who is in the greatest peril from a mistake) and therefore inexperienced in the knowledge and judgment of mankind and of themselves generally: and finally they have seldom had so much as an opportunity offered them of gaining any real knowledge of each other, since in nine cases out of ten they have never been once in each other's society completely unconstrained, or without consciously or unconsciously acting a part.

The chances therefore are many to one against the supposition that a person who requires, or is capable of, great happiness, will find that happiness in a first choice: and in a very large proportion of cases the first choice is such that if it cannot be recalled, it only embitters existence. The reasons, then, are most potent for allowing a subsequent change.

What there is to be said in favor of the indissolubility, superstition apart, resolves itself into this that it is highly desirable that changes should not be frequent, and desirable that the first choice should be, even if not compulsorily, yet very generally, persevered in: That consequently we ought to beware lest in giving facilities for retracting a bad choice, we hold out greater encouragement than at present for making such a choice as there will probably be occasion to retract.

It is proper to state as strongly as possible the arguments which may be advanced in support of this view in question.

Repeated trials for happiness, and repeated failures, have the most mischievous effects on all minds. The finer spirits are broken down, and disgusted with all things: their susceptibilities are deadened, or converted into sources of bitterness, and they lose the power of being ever *contented*. On the commoner natures the effects produced are not the less deplorable. Not only is their capacity for happiness worn out, but their morality is depraved: all refinement and delicacy of character is extinguished; all sense of any peculiar duties or of any peculiar sacredness attaching to the relation between the sexes is worn away: and such alliances come to be looked upon with the very same kind of feelings which are now connected with a passing intrigue.

Thus much as to the parties themselves: but besides the parties there are also to be considered their children: beings who are wholly dependent both for happiness and for excellence upon their parents: and who in all but the extreme causes of actual profligacy, or perpetual bickering and discussion, *must* be better cared for in both points if their parents remain together.

So much importance is due to this last consideration, that I am convinced, if marriages were easily dissoluble, two persons of opposite sexes who unite their destinies would generally, if they were wise, think it their duty to avoid having children until they had lived together for a considerable length of time, and found in each other a happiness adequate to their aspirations. If this principle of morality were observed, how many of the difficulties of the subject we are considering would be smoothed down! To be jointly the parents of a human being, should be the very last pledge of the deepest, holiest, and most desirable affection: for *that* is a tie which independently of convention, is indeed indissoluble: an additional and external tie, most precious where the souls are already indissolubly united, but simply burthensome while it appears possible to either that they should ever desire to separate.

It can hardly be anticipated, however, that such a course will be followed by any but those who to the greatest loftiness and delicacy of feeling, unite the power of the most deliberate reflexion. If the feelings be obtuse, the force of these considerations will not be felt; and if the judgment be weak or hasty, whether from inherent defect or inexperience, people will fancy themselves in love for their whole lives with a perfect being, when the case is far otherwise, and will suppose they risk nothing by creating a new relationship with that being, which can no longer be got rid of. It will therefore most commonly happen that when circumstances arise which induce the parents to separate, there will be children to suffer by the separation: nor do I see how this difficulty can be entirely got over, until the habits of society allow of a regulated community of living, among persons intimately acquainted, which would prevent the necessity of a total separation between the parents even when they had ceased to be connected by any nearer tie than mutual goodwill, and a common interest in their children.

There is yet another argument which may be urged against facility of divorce. It is this. Most persons have but a very moderate capacity of happiness; but no person ever finds this out without experience, very few even with experience: and most persons are constantly wreaking that discontent which has its source internally, upon outward things. Expecting therefore in marriage a far greater degree of happiness than they commonly find: and knowing not that the fault is in their own scanty capabilities of happiness—they fancy they should have been happier with some one else: or at all events the disappointment becomes associated in their minds with the being in whom they had placed their hopes—and so they dislike one another for a time—and during that time they would feel inclined to separate: but if they remain united, the feeling of disappointment after a time goes off, and they pass their lives together with fully as much happiness as they could find either singly or in any other union, without having undergone the wearing of repeated and unsuccessful experiments.

Such are the arguments for adhering to the indissolubility of the contract: and for such characters as compose the great majority of the human race, it is not deniable that these arguments have considerable weight.

That weight however is not so great as it appears. In all the above arguments it is tacitly assumed, that the choice lies between the absolute interdiction of divorce, and a state of things in which the parties would separate on the most passing feeling of dissatisfaction. Now this is not really the alternative. Were divorce ever so free, it would be resorted to under the same sense of moral responsibility and under the same restraints from opinion, as any other of the acts of our lives. In no state of society but one in which opinions sanctions almost promiscuous intercourse (and in which therefore even the indissoluble bond is not practically regarded), would it be otherwise than disreputable to either party, the woman especially, to change frequently or on light grounds. My belief is that—in a tolerably moral state of society, the first choice would almost always, especially where it had produced children, be adhered to, unless in case of such uncongeniality of disposition as rendered it positively uncomfortable to one or both of the parties to live together, or in case of a strong passion conceived by one of them for a third person. Now in either of these cases I can conceive no argument strong enough to convince me, that the first connexion ought to be forcibly preserved.

I see not why opinion should not act with as great efficacy, to enforce the true rules of morality in these matters, as the false. Robert Owen's definitions of chastity and prostitution, are quite as simple and take as firm a hold of the mind as the vulgar ones which connect the ideas of virtue and vice with the performance or non-performance of an arbitrary ceremonial.

The arguments, therefore, in favour of the indissolubility of marriage, are as nothing in comparison with the far more potent arguments for leaving this like the other relations voluntarily contracted by human beings, to depend for its continuance upon the wishes of the contracting parties. The strongest of all these arguments is that by no other means can the condition and character of women become what it ought to be.

When women are merely slaves, to give them a permanent hold upon their masters was a first step towards their evolution. That step is now complete: and in the progress of civilization, the time has come when women may aspire to something more than merely to find a protector. The position of a single woman has ceased to be dangerous and precarious; and the law, and general opinion, suffice without any more special guardianship, to shield her in ordinary circumstances from insult or inquiry: woman in short is no longer a mere property, but a person who is counted not solely on her husband's or father's account but on her own. She is now ripe for equality. But it is absurd to talk of equality while marriage is an indissoluble tie. It was a change greatly for the better, from a state in which all the obligation was on the side of the weaker, all the rights on the side of the physically stronger, to even the present condition of an obligation nominally equal on both. But this nominal equality is not real equality. The stronger is always able to relieve himself wholly or in great measure, from as much of the obligation as he finds burthensome: the weaker cannot. The husband can ill-use his wife, neglect her, and seek other women, not perhaps altogether with impunity, but what are the penalties which opinion imposes on him compared with those which fall upon the wife who even with that provocation retaliates upon her husband? It is true perhaps that if divorce were permitted, opinion would with like injustice, try the wife who resorted to that remedy by a harder measure than the husband. But this would be of less consequence: Once separated she would be comparatively independent of opinion: but so long as she is forcibly united to one of those who *make* the opinion, she must to a great extent be its slave.

The Essay by Harriet Taylor

If I could be Providence for the world for a time, for the express purpose of raising the condition of women, I should come to you to know the *means*—the *purpose* would be to remove all interference with affection, or with anything which is, or which even might be supposed to be, demonstrative of affection. In the present state of women's mind, perfectly uneducated, and with whatever of timidity and dependence is natural to them increased a thousand fold by their habit of utter dependence, it would probably be mischievous to remove at once all restraints, they would buy themselves protectors at a dearer cost than even at present—but without raising their natures at all. It seems to me that once give women the desire to raise their social condition, and they have a power which in the present state of civilization and of men's characters, might be made of tremendous effect. Whether nature made a difference in the nature of men and women or not, it seems now that all men, with the exception of a few lofty minded, are sensualists more or less—women on the contrary are quite exempt from this trait, however it may appear otherwise in the cases of some. It seems strange that it should be so, unless it was meant to be a source of power in semi-civilized states such as the present—or it may not be so—it may be only that the habits of freedom and low indulgence on which boys grow up and the contrary notion of what is called purity in girls may have produced the appearance of different natures in the two sexes. As certain it is that there is equality in nothing now—

all the pleasures such as they are being men's, and all the disagreeables and pains being women's, as that every pleasure would be infinitely heightened both in kind and degree by the perfect equality of the sexes. Women are educated for one single object, to gain their living by marrying—(some poor souls get it without the churchgoing. It's the same way—they do not seem to be a bit worse than their honoured sisters). To be married is the object of their existence and that object being gained they do really cease to exist as to anything worth calling life or any useful purpose. One observes very few marriages where there is any real sympathy or enjoyment or companionship between the parties. The woman knows what her power is and gains by it what she has been taught to consider "proper" to her state. The woman who would gain power by such means is unfit for power, still they do lose this power for paltry advantages and I am astonished it has never occurred to them to gain some large purpose; but their minds are degenerated by habits of dependance. I should think that 500 years hence none of the follies of their ancestors will so excite wonder and contempt as the fact of legislative restraints as to matters of feeling—or rather in the expression of feeling. When once the law undertakes to say which demonstration of feeling shall be given to which, it seems quite consistent not to legislate for *all*, and to say how many shall be seen and how many heard, and what kind and degree of feeling allows of shaking hands. The Turks' is the only consistent mode. I have no doubt that when the whole community is really educated, though the present laws of marriage were to continue they would be perfectly disregarded, because no one would marry. The wisest and perhaps the quickest means to do away with its evils is to be found in promoting education—as it is the means of all good—but meanwhile it is hard that those who suffer most from its evils and who are always the best people, should be left without remedy. Would not the best plan be divorce which could be attained by any *without any reason assigned*, and at small expence, but which could only be finally pronounced after a long period? not *less* time than two years should elapse between suing for divorce and permission to contract again—but what the decision will be must be certain at the moment of asking for it—unless during that time the suit should be withdrawn.

(I feel like a lawyer in talking of it only! O how absurd and little it all is!)

In the present system of habits and opinions, girls enter into what is called a contract perfectly ignorant of the conditions of it, and that they should be so is considered absolutely essential to their fitness for it!

But after all the one argument of the matter which I think might be said so as to strike both high and low natures is— who would wish to have the person without inclination? Whoever would take the benefit of a law of divorce must be those whose inclination is to separate and who on earth would wish another to remain with them against their inclination—I should think no one—people sophisticate about the matter now and will not believe that one *really would wish to go*"! Suppose instead of calling it a "law of divorce" it were to be called "proof of affection"—they would like it better then.

At this present time, in this state of civilization, what evil could be caused by, first placing women on the most entire equality with men, as to all rights and privileges, civil and political, and then doing away with all laws whatever relating to marriage? Then if a woman had children she must take charge of them, women could not then have children without considering how to maintain them. Women would have no more reason to barter person for bread, or for anything else, than have men. Public offices being open to them alike, all occupations would be divided between the sexes in their natural arrangements. Fathers would provide for their daughters in the same manner as for their sons.

All the difficulties about divorce seem to be in the consideration for the children—but on this plan it would be the women's *interest* not to have children—now it is thought to be the woman's interest to have children as so many ties to the man who feeds her.

Love in its true and finest meaning, seems to be the way in which is manifested all that is highest best and beautiful in the nature of human beings—none but poets have approached to the perception of the beauty of the material world—still less of the spiritual—and hence never yet existed a poet, except by inspiration of that feeling which is the perception of beauty in all forms and by all means which are given us, as well as by *sight*. Are we not born with the *five* senses, merely as a foundation for others which we may make by them—and who extends and refines those material senses to the highest—into infinity—best fulfils the end of creation—that is only saying, *who enjoys most is most* virtuous. It is for *you*—the most worthy to be the apostle of all the highest virtues to teach such as may be tought, that the higher the *kind* of enjoyment, the *greater* the *degree*, perhaps there is but one class to whom this *can* be *tought*—the poetic nature struggling with superstition: you are fitted to be the saviour of such.

3

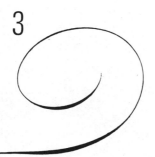

Enfranchisement of Women

HARRIET TAYLOR MILL

PORTRAIT OF HARRIET TAYLOR AROUND 1834
From F. A. Hayek, *John Stuart Mill and Harriet Taylor,*
Routledge and Kegan Paul Ltd., 1951.

Enfranchisement
of Women

ll the more recent of these papers
were joint productions of myself and
of one whose loss, even in a merely
intellectual point of view, can never
be repaired or alleviated. But the
following Essay is hers in a peculiar
sense, my share in it being little more
than that of an editor and amanuensis.
Its authorship having been known
at the time, and publicly attributed
to her, it is proper to state, that she
never regarded it as a complete
discussion of the subject which it treats
of: and, highly as I estimate it, I would
rather it remained unacknowledged,
than that it should be read with the
idea that even the faintest image can
be found in it of a mind and heart
which in their union of the rarest, and
what are deemed the most conflicting
excellences, were unparalleled in any
human being that I have known or
read of. While she was the light, life,
and grace of every society in which
she took part, the foundation of her
character was a deep seriousness,
resulting from the combination of the

Originally printed in *Westminster Review,*
July 1851.

91

strongest and most sensitive feelings with the highest principles.
All that excites admiration when found separately in others,
seemed brought together in her: a conscience at once healthy
and tender; a generosity, bounded only by a sense of justice
which often forgot its own claims, but never those of others; a
heart so large and loving, that whoever was capable of making
the smallest return of sympathy, always received tenfold; and in
the intellectual department, a vigour and truth of imagination,
a delicacy of perception, an accuracy and nicety of observation, only equalled by her profundity of speculative thought,
and by a practical judgment and discernment next to infallible. So elevated was the general level of her faculties, that
the highest poetry, philosophy, oratory, or art, seemed trivial
by the side of her, and equal only to expressing some small
part of her mind. And there is no one of those modes of
manifestation in which she could not easily have taken the
highest rank, had not her inclination led her for the most part
to content herself with being the inspirer, prompter, and un-
avowed coadjutor of others.

The present paper was written to promote a cause which
she had deeply at heart, and though appealing only to the
severest reason, was meant for the general reader. The question, in her opinion, was in a stage in which no treatment but
the most calmly argumentative could be useful, while many
of the strongest arguments were necessarily omitted, as being
unsuited for popular effect. Had she lived to write out all
her thoughts on this great question, she would have produced
something as far transcending in profundity the present Essay,
as, had she not placed a rigid restraint on her feelings, she
would have excelled it in fervid eloquence. Yet nothing which
even she could have written on any single subject, would have
given an adequate idea of the depth and compass of her mind.
As during life she continually detected, before any one else
had seemed to perceive them, those changes of times and circumstances which ten or twelve years later became subjects of
general remark, so I venture to prophecy that if mankind continue to improve, their spiritual history for ages to come will

be the progressive working out of her thoughts, and realization of her conceptions.

Most of our readers will probably learn from these pages for the first time, that there has arisen in the United States, and in the most civilized and enlightened portion of them, an organized agitation on a new question—new, not to thinkers, nor to any one by whom the principles of free and popular government are felt as well as acknowledged, but new, and even unheard-of, as a subject for public meetings and practical political action. This question is, the enfranchisement of women; their admission, in law and in fact, to equality in all rights, political, civil, and social, with the male citizens of the community.

It will add to the surprise with which many will receive this intelligence, that the agitation which has commenced is not a pleading by male writers and orators for women, those who are professedly to be benefited remaining either indifferent or ostensibly hostile. It is a political movement, practical in its objects, carried on in a form which denotes an intention to persevere. And it is a movement not merely *for* women, but *by* them. Its first public manifestation appears to have been a Convention of Women, held in the State of Ohio, in the spring of 1850. Of this meeting we have seen no report. On the 23rd and 24th of October last, a succession of public meetings was held at Worcester in Massachusetts, under the name of a "Women's Rights Convention," of which the president was a woman, and nearly all the chief speakers women: numerously reinforced, however, by men, among whom were some of the most distinguished leaders in the kindred cause of negro emancipation. A general and four special committees were nominated, for the purpose of carrying on the undertaking until the next annual meeting.

According to the report in the *New York Tribune,* above a thousand persons were present throughout, and "if a larger place could have been had, many thousands more would have attended." The place was described as "crowded from the beginning with attentive and interested listeners." In regard to the quality of the speaking, the proceedings bear an advantageous comparison with those of any popular movement with which we are acquainted, either in this country or in America. Very rarely in the oratory of public meetings is the part of verbiage and declamation so small, that of calm good sense and reason so considerable. The result of the Convention was in every respect encouraging to those by whom it was summoned: and it is probably destined to inaugurate one of the most important of the movements towards political and social reform, which are the best characteristics of the present age.

That the promoters of this new agitation take their stand on principles, and do not fear to declare these in their widest extent, without time-serving or compromise, will be seen from the resolutions adopted by the Convention, part of which we transcribe.

Resolved—That every human being, of full age, and resident for a proper length of time on the soil of the nation, who is required to obey the law, is entitled to a voice in its enactment; that every such person, whose property or labour is taxed for the support of the government, is entitled to a direct share in such government; therefore,

Resolved—That women are entitled to the right of suffrage, and to be considered eligible to office, . . . and that every party which claims to represent the humanity, the civilization, and the progress of the age, is bound to inscribe on its banners equality before the law, without distinction of sex or colour.

Resolved—That civil and political rights acknowledge no sex, and therefore the word "male" should be struck from every State Constitution.

Resolved—That, since the prospect of honourable and useful employment in after-life is the best stimulus to the use of educational advantages, and since the best education is that we give ourselves, in the struggles, employments, and discipline of life; therefore it is impossible that women should make full use of the instruction already accorded to them, or that their career should do justice to their faculties, until the avenues to the various civil and professional employments are thrown open to them.

Resolved—That every effort to educate women, without according to them their rights, and arousing their conscience by the weight of their responsibilities, is futile, and a waste of labour.

Resolved—That the laws of property, as affecting married persons, demand a thorough revisal, so that all rights be equal between them; that the wife have, during life, an equal control over the property gained by their mutual toil and sacrifices, and be heir to her husband precisely to that extent that he is heir to her, and entitled at her death to dispose by will of the same share of the joint property as he is.

The following is a brief summary of the principal demands.

1. *Education* in primary and high schools, universities, medical, legal, and theological institutions.

2. *Partnership* in the labours and gains, risks and remunerations, of productive industry.

3. *A coequal share* in the formation and administration of laws —municipal, state, and national—through legislative assemblies, courts, and executive offices.

It would be difficult to put so much true, just, and reasonable meaning into a style so little calculated to recommend it as that of some of the resolutions. But whatever objection may be made to some of the expressions, none, in our opinion, can be made to the demands themselves. As a question of justice, the case seems to us too clear for dispute. As one of expediency, the more thoroughly it is examined the stronger it will appear.

That women have as good a claim as men have, in point of personal right, to the suffrage, or to a place in the jury-box, it would be difficult for any one to deny. It cannot certainly be denied by the United States of America, as a people or as a community. Their democratic institutions rest avowedly on the inherent right of every one to a voice in the government. Their Declaration of Independence, framed by the men who are still their great constitutional authorities—that document which has been from the first, and is now, the acknowledged basis of their polity, commences with this express statement:

We hold these truths to be self-evident: that all men are created equal; that they are endowed by their Creator with certain inalienable rights; that among these are life, liberty, and the pursuit of happiness; that to secure these rights, governments are instituted among men, deriving their just powers from the consent of the governed.

We do not imagine that any American democrat will evade the force of these expressions by the dishonest or ignorant subterfuge, that "men," in this memorable document, does not stand for human beings, but for one sex only; that "life, liberty, and the pursuit of happiness" are "inalienable rights" of only one moiety of the human species; and that "the governed," whose consent is affirmed to be the only source of just power, are meant for that half of mankind only, who, in relation to the other, have hitherto assumed the character of governors. The contradiction between principle and practice cannot be explained away. A like dereliction of the fundamental maxims of their political creed has been committed by the Americans in the flagrant instance of the negroes; of this they are learning to recognise the turpitude. After a struggle which, by many of its incidents, deserves the name of heroic, the abolitionists are now so strong in numbers and in influence that they hold the balance of parties in the United States. It was fitting that the men whose names will remain associated with the extirpation, from the democratic soil of America, of the aristocracy of colour, should be among the originators, for America and for the rest of the world, of the first collective protest against the aristocracy of sex; a distinction as accidental as that of colour, and fully as irrelevant to all questions of government.

Not only to the democracy of America, the claim of women to civil and political equality makes an irresistible appeal, but also to those Radicals and Chartists in the British islands, and democrats on the Continent, who claim what is called universal suffrage as an inherent right, unjustly and oppressively withheld from them. For with what truth or rationality could the suffrage be termed universal, while half the human species remained excluded from it? To declare that a voice in the government is the right of all, and demand it only for a part —the part, namely, to which the claimant himself belongs— is to renounce even the appearance of principle. The Chartist who denies the suffrage to women, is a Chartist only because he is not a lord: he is one of those levellers who would level only down to themselves.

Even those who do not look upon a voice in the government as a matter of personal right, nor profess principles which require that it should be extended to all, have usually traditional maxims of political justice with which it is impossible to reconcile the exclusion of all women from the common rights of citizenship. It is an axiom of English freedom that taxation and representation should be co-extensive. Even under the laws which give the wife's property to the husband, there are many unmarried women who pay taxes. It is one of the fundamental doctrines of the British Constitution, that all persons should be tried by their peers: yet women, whenever tried, are tried by male judges and a male jury. To foreigners the law accords the privilege of claiming that half the jury should be composed of themselves; not so to women. Apart from maxims of detail, which represent local and national rather than universal ideas; it is an acknowledged dictate of justice to make no degrading distinctions without necessity. In all things the presumption ought to be on the side of equality. A reason must be given why anything should be permitted to one person and interdicted to another. But when that which is interdicted includes nearly everything which those to whom it is permitted most prize, and to be deprived of which they feel to be most insulting; when not only political liberty but personal freedom of action is the prerogative of a caste; when even in the exercise of industry, almost all employments which task the higher faculties in an important field, which lead to distinction, riches, or even pecuniary independence, are fenced round as the exclusive domain of the predominant section, scarcely any doors being left open to the dependent class, except such as all who can enter elsewhere disdainfully pass by; the miserable expediencies which are advanced as excuses for so grossly partial a dispensation, would not be sufficient, even if they were real, to render it other than a flagrant injustice. While, far from being expedient, we are firmly convinced that the division of mankind into two castes, one born to rule over the other, is in this case, as in all cases, an unqualified mischief; a source of perversion and demoralization, both to the favoured class and to those at whose expense they are favoured; producing none of the good which it is the custom to ascribe to it, and forming a bar, almost insuperable while it lasts, to any really vital improvement, either in the character or in the social condition of the human race.

These propositions it is now our purpose to maintain. But before entering on them, we would endeavour to dispel the preliminary objections which, in the minds of persons to whom the subject is new, are apt to prevent a real and conscientious examination of it. The chief of these obstacles is that most formidable one, custom. Women never have had equal rights with men. The claim in their behalf, of the common rights of mankind, is looked upon as barred by universal practice. This strongest of prejudices, the prejudice against what is new and unknown, has, indeed, in an age of changes like the present, lost much of its force; if it had not, there would be little hope of prevailing against it. Over three-fourths of the habitable world, even at this day, the answer, "it has always been so," closes all discussion. But it is the boast of modern Europeans, and of their American kindred, that they know and do many things which their forefathers neither knew nor did; and it is perhaps the most unquestionable point of superiority in the present above former ages, that habit is not now the tyrant it formerly was over opinions and modes of action, and that the worship of custom is a declining idolatry. An uncustomary thought, on a subject which touches the greater interests of life, still startles when first presented; but if it can be kept before the mind until the impression of strangeness wears off, it obtains a hearing, and as rational a consideration as the intellect of the hearer is accustomed to bestow on any other subject.

In the present case, the prejudice of custom is doubtless on the unjust side. Great thinkers, indeed, at different times, from Plato to Condorcet, besides some of the most eminent names of the present age, have made emphatic protests in favour of the equality of women. And there have been voluntary societies, religious or secular, of which the Society of Friends is the most known, by whom that principle was recognised. But there has been no political community or nation in which, by law and usage, women have not been in a state of political and civil inferiority. In the ancient world the same fact was alleged, with equal truth, in behalf of slavery. It might have been alleged in favour of the mitigated form of slavery, serfdom, all through the middle ages. It was urged against freedom of industry, freedom of conscience, freedom of the press; none of these liberties were thought compatible with a well-ordered state, until they had proved their possibility by actually existing as facts. That an institution or a practice is customary is no presumption of its goodness, when any other sufficient cause can be assigned for its existence. There is no difficulty in understanding why the subjection of women has been a custom. No other explanation is needed than physical force.

That those who were physically weaker should have been made legally inferior, is quite conformable to the mode in which the world has been governed. Until very lately, the rule of physical strength was the general law of human affairs. Throughout history, the nations, races, classes, which found themselves the strongest, either in muscles, in riches, or in military discipline, have conquered and held in subjection the rest. If, even in the most improved nations, the law of the sword is at last discountenanced as unworthy, it is only since the calumniated eighteenth century. Wars of conquest have only ceased since democratic revolutions began. The world is very young, and has but just begun to cast off injustice. It is only now getting rid of negro slavery. It is only now getting rid of monarchical despotism. It is only now getting rid of hereditary feudal nobility. It is only now getting rid of disabilities on the ground of religion. It is only beginning to treat any *men* as citizens, except the rich and a favoured portion of the middle class. Can we wonder that it has not yet done as much for women? As society was constituted until the last few generations, inequality was its very basis; association grounded on equal rights scarcely existed; to be equals was to be enemies; two persons could hardly co-operate in anything, or meet in any amicable relation, without the law's appointing that one of them should be the superior of the other. Mankind have outgrown this state, and all things now tend to substitute, as the general principle of human relations, a just equality, instead of the dominion of the strongest. But of all relations, that between men and women being the nearest and most intimate, and connected with the greatest number of strong emotions, was sure to be the last to throw off the old rule and receive the new: for in proportion to the strength of a feeling, is the tenacity with which it clings to the forms and circumstances with which it has even accidentally become associated.

When a prejudice, which has any hold on the feelings, finds itself reduced to the unpleasant necessity of assigning reasons, it thinks it has done enough when it has re-asserted the very point in dispute, in phrases which appeal to the pre-existing feeling. Thus, many persons think they have sufficiently justified the restrictions on women's field of action, when they have said that the pursuits from which women are excluded are *unfeminine,* and that the *proper sphere* of women is not politics or publicity, but private and domestic life.

We deny the right of any portion of the species to decide for another portion, or any individual for another individual, what is and what is not their "proper sphere." The proper sphere for all human beings is the largest and highest which they are able to attain to. What this is, cannot be ascertained, without complete liberty of choice. The speakers at the Convention in America have therefore done wisely and right, in refusing to entertain the question of the peculiar aptitudes either of women or of men, or the limits within this or that occupation may be supposed to be more adapted to the one or to the other. They justly maintain, that these questions can only be satisfactorily answered by perfect freedom. Let every occupation be open to all, without favour or discouragement to any, and employments will fall into the hands of those men or women who are found by experience to be most

capable of worthily exercising them. There need be no fear
that women will take out of the hands of men any occupation
which men perform better than they. Each individual will
prove his or her capacities, in the only way in which capacities can be proved—by trial; and the world will have the
benefit of the best faculties of all its inhabitants. But to interfere beforehand by an arbitrary limit, and declare that whatever be the genius, talent, energy, or force of mind of an
individual of a certain sex or class, those faculties shall not
be exerted, or shall be exerted only in some few of the many
modes in which others are permitted to use theirs, is not only
an injustice to the individual, and a detriment to society, which
loses what it can ill spare, but is also the most effectual mode
of providing that, in the sex or class so fettered, the qualities
which are not permitted to be exercised shall not exist.

We shall follow the very proper example of the Convention,
in not entering into the question of the alleged differences in
physical or mental qualities between the sexes; not because
we have nothing to say, but because we have too much; to
discuss this one point tolerably would need all the space we
have to bestow on the entire subject.[1] But if those who assert

1. An excellent passage on this part of the subject, from one of
Sydney Smith's contributions to the Edinburgh Review, we will not
refrain from quoting: "A great deal has been said of the original
difference of capacity between men and women, as if women were
more quick and men more judicious—as if women were more remarkable for delicacy of association, and men for stronger powers of attention. All this, we confess, appears to us very fanciful. That there is
a difference in the understandings of the men and the women we every
day meet with, everybody, we suppose, must perceive; but there is
none surely which may not be accounted for by the difference of circumstances in which they have been placed, without referring to any
conjectural difference of original conformation of mind. As long as
boys and girls run about in the dirt, and trundle hoops together, they
are both precisely alike. If you catch up one-half of these creatures,
and train them to a particular set of actions and opinions, and the
other half to a perfectly opposite set, of course their understandings
will differ, as one or the other sort of occupations has called this or
that talent into action. There is surely no occasion to go into any
deeper or more abstruse reasoning, in order to explain so very simple
a phenomenon." (*Sydney Smith's Works*, vol. i. p. 200.)

that the "proper sphere" for women is the domestic, mean by
this that they have not shown themselves qualified for any
other, the assertion evinces great ignorance of life and of history. Women have shown fitness for the highest social functions, exactly in proportion as they have been admitted to
them. By a curious anomaly, though ineligible to even the lowest offices of State, they are in some countries admitted to the
highest of all, the regal; and if there is any one function for
which they have shown a decided vocation, it is that of reigning. Not to go back to ancient history, we look in vain for
abler or firmer rulers than Elizabeth; than Isabella of Castile;
than Maria Teresa; than Catherine of Russia; than Blanche,
mother of Louis IX of France; than Jeanne d'Albret, mother
of Henri Quatre. There are few kings on record who contended
with more difficult circumstances, or overcame them more tri-
umphantly, than these. Even in semi-barbarous Asia, princesses
who have never been seen by men, other than those of their
own family, or ever spoken with them unless from behind a
curtain, have as regents, during the minority of their sons,
exhibited many of the most brilliant examples of just and vigorous administration. In the middle ages, when the distance
between the upper and lower ranks was greater than even between women and men, and the women of the privileged class,
however subject to tyranny from the men of the same class,
were at a less distance below them than any one else was,
and often in their absence represented them in their functions
and authority—numbers of heroic châtelaines, like Jeanne de
Montfort, or the great Countess of Derby as late even as the
time of Charles I, distinguished themselves not only by their
political but their military capacity. In the centuries immediately before and after the Reformation, ladies of royal houses,
as diplomatists, as governors of provinces, or as the confi-
dential advisers of kings, equalled the first statesmen of their
time: and the treaty of Cambray, which gave peace to Europe,
was negotiated in conferences where no other person was
present, by the aunt of the Emperor Charles the Fifth, and the
mother of Francis the First.

Concerning the fitness, then, of women for politics, there can be no question: but the dispute is more likely to turn upon the fitness of politics for women. When the reasons alleged for excluding women from active life in all its higher departments are stripped of their garb of declamatory phrases, and reduced to the simple expression of a meaning, they seem to be mainly three: first, the incompatibility of active life with maternity, and with the cares of a household; secondly; its alleged hardening effect on the character; and thirdly, the inexpediency of making an addition to the already excessive pressure of competition in every kind of professional or lucrative employment.

The first, the maternity argument, is usually laid most stress upon: although (it needs hardly be said) this reason, if it be one, can apply only to mothers. It is neither necessary nor just to make imperative on women that they shall be either mothers or nothing; or that if they have been mothers once, they shall be nothing else during the whole remainder of their lives. Neither women nor men need any law to exclude them from an occupation, if they have undertaken another which is incompatible with it. No one proposes to exclude the male sex from Parliament because a man may be a soldier or sailor in active service, or a merchant whose business requires all his time and energies. Nine-tenths of the occupations of men exclude them *de facto* from public life, as effectually as if they were excluded by law; but that is no reason for making laws to exclude even the nine-tenths, much less the remaining tenth. The reason of the case is the same for women as for men. There is no need to make provision by law that a woman shall not carry on the active details of a household, or of the education of children, and at the same time practise a profession, or be elected to parliament. Where incompatibility is real, it will take care of itself: but there is gross injustice in making the incompatibility a pretence for the exclusion of those in whose case it does not exist. And these, if they were free to choose, would be a very large proportion. The maternity argument deserts its supporters in the case of single women, a large and increasing class of the population; a fact which, it is not irrelevant to remark, by tending to diminish the excessive competition of numbers, is calculated to assist greatly the prosperity of all. There is no inherent reason or necessity that all women should voluntarily choose to devote their lives to one animal function and its consequences. Numbers of women are wives and mothers only because there is no other career open to them, no other occupation for their feelings or their activities. Every improvement in their education, and enlargement of their faculties, everything which renders them more qualified for any other mode of life, increases the number of those to whom it is an injury and an oppression to be denied the choice. To say that women must be excluded from active life because maternity disqualifies them for it, is in fact to say, that every other career should be forbidden them in order that maternity may be their only resource.

But secondly, it is urged, that to give the same freedom of occupation to women as to men, would be an injurious addition to the crowd of competitors, by whom the avenues to almost all kinds of employment are choked up, and its remuneration depressed. This argument, it is to be observed, does not reach the political question. It gives no excuse for withholding from women the rights of citizenship. The suffrage, the jury-box, admission to the legislature and to office, it does not touch. It bears only on the industrial branch of the subject. Allowing it, then, in an economical point of view, its full force; assuming that to lay open to women the employments now monopolized by men, would tend, like the breaking down of other monopolies, to lower the rate of remuneration in those employments; let us consider what is the amount of this evil consequence, and what the compensation for it. The worst ever asserted, much worse than is at all likely to be realized, is that if women competed with men, a man and a woman could not together earn more than is now earned by the man alone. Let us make this supposition, the most unfavourable supposition possible: the joint income of the two would be the same as before, while the woman would be raised from the position of a servant to that of a partner. Even if every woman, as matters now stand, had a claim on some man for support, how infinitely preferable is it that part of the income should be of the woman's earning, even if the aggregate sum were but little increased by it, rather than that she should be compelled to stand aside in order that men may be the sole earners, and the sole dispensers of what is earned. Even under the present laws respecting the property of women, a woman who contributes materially to the support of the family, cannot be treated in the same contemptuously tyrannical manner as one who, however she may toil as a domestic drudge, is a dependent on the man for subsistence.[2] As for the depression of wages by increase of competition, remedies will be found for it in time. Palliatives might be applied immediately; for instance, a more rigid exclusion of children from industrial employment, during the years in which they ought to be working only to strengthen their bodies and minds for after-life. Children are necessarily dependent, and under the power of others; and their labour, being not for themselves but for the gain of their parents, is a proper subject for legislative regulation. With respect to the future, we neither believe that improvident multiplication, and the consequent excessive difficulty of gaining a subsistence, will always continue, nor that the division of mankind into capitalists and hired labourers, and the regulation of the reward of labourers mainly by demand and supply, will be for ever, or even much longer, the rule of the world. But so long as competition is the general law of human life, it is tyranny to shut out one-half of the competitors. All who have attained the age of self-government have an equal claim to be permitted to sell whatever kind of useful labour they are capable of, for the price which it will bring.

2. The truly horrible effects of the present state of the law among the lowest of the working population, is exhibited in those cases of hideous maltreatment of their wives by working men, with which every newspaper, every police report, teems. Wretches unfit to have the smallest authority over any living thing, have a helpless woman for their household slave. These excesses could not exist if women both earned, and had the right to possess, a part of the income of the family.

The third objection to the admission of women to political or professional life, its alleged hardening tendency, belongs to an age now past, and is scarcely to be comprehended by people of the present time. There are still, however, persons who say that the world and its avocations render men selfish and unfeeling; that the struggles, rivalries, and collisions of business and of politics make them harsh and unamiable; that if half the species must unavoidably be given up to these things, it is the more necessary that the other half should be kept free from them; that to preserve women from the bad influences of the world, is the only chance of preventing men from being wholly given up to them.

There would have been plausibility in this argument when the world was still in the age of violence; when life was full of physical conflict, and every man had to redress his injuries or those of others, by the sword or by the strength of his arm. Women, like priests, by being exempted from such responsibilities, and from some part of the accompanying dangers, may have been enabled to exercise a beneficial influence. But in the present condition of human life, we do not know where those hardening influences are to be found, to which men are subject and from which women are at present exempt. Individuals now-a-days are seldom called upon to fight hand to hand, even with peaceful weapons; personal enmities and rivalities count for little in worldly transactions; the general pressure of circumstances, not the adverse will of individuals, is the obstacle men now have to make head against. That pressure, when excessive, breaks the spirit, and cramps and sours the feelings, but not less of women than of men, since they suffer certainly not less from its evils. There are still quarrels and dislikes, but the sources of them are changed. The feudal chief once found his bitterest enemy in his powerful neighbour, the minister or courtier in his rival for place: but opposition of interest in active life, as a cause of personal animosity, is out of date; the enmities of the present day arise not from great things but small, from what people say of one another, more than from what they do; and if there are hatred, malice, and all uncharitableness, they are to be found among women fully as much as among men. In the present state of civilization, the notion of guarding women from the hardening influences of the world, could only be realized by secluding them from society altogether. The common duties of common life, as at present constituted, are incompatible with any other softness in women than weakness. Surely weak minds in weak bodies must ere long cease to be even supposed to be either attractive or amiable.

But, in truth, none of these arguments and considerations touch the foundations of the subject. The real question is, whether it is right and expedient that one-half of the human race should pass through life in a state of forced subordination to the other half. If the best state of human society is that of being divided into two parts, one consisting of persons with a will and a substantive existence, the other of humble companions to these persons, attached, each of them to one, for the purpose of bringing up *his* children, and making *his* home pleasant to him; if this is the place assigned to women, it is but kindness to educate them for this; to make them believe that the greatest good fortune which can befal them, is to be chosen by some man for this purpose; and that every other career which the world deems happy or honourable, is closed to them by the law, not of social institutions, but of nature and destiny.

When, however, we ask why the existence of one-half the species should be merely ancillary to that of the other—why each woman should be a mere appendage to a man, allowed to have no interests of her own, that there may be nothing to compete in her mind with his interests and his pleasure; the only reason which can be given is, that men like it. It is agreeable to them that men should live for their own sake, women for the sake of men: and the qualities and conduct in subjects which are agreeable to rulers, they succeed for a long time in making the subjects themselves consider as their appropriate virtues. Helvetius has met with much obloquy for asserting, that persons usually mean by virtues the qualities which are useful or convenient to themselves. How truly this is said of mankind in general, and how wonderfully the ideas of virtue set afloat by the powerful, are caught and imbibed by those under their dominion, is exemplified by the manner in which the world were once persuaded that the supreme virtue of subjects was loyalty to kings, and are still persuaded that the paramount virtue of womanhood is loyalty to men. Under a nominal recognition of a moral code common to both, in practice self-will and self-assertion form the type of what are designated as manly virtues, while abnegation of self, patience, resignation, and submission to power, unless when resistance is commanded by other interests than their own, have been stamped by general consent as pre-eminently the duties and graces required of women. The meaning being merely, that power makes itself the centre of moral obligation, and that a man likes to have his own will, but does not like that his domestic companion should have a will different from his.

We are far from pretending that in modern and civilized times, no reciprocity of obligation is acknowledged on the part of the stronger. Such an assertion would be very wide of the truth. But even this reciprocity, which has disarmed tyranny, at least in the higher and middle classes, of its most revolting features, yet when combined with the original evil of the dependent condition of women, has introduced in its turn serious evils.

In the beginning, and among tribes which are still in a primitive condition, women were and are the slaves of men for purposes of toil. All the hard bodily labour devolves on them. The Australian savage is idle, while women painfully dig up the roots on which he lives. An American Indian, when he has killed a deer, leaves it, and sends a woman to carry it home. In a state somewhat more advanced, as in Asia, women were and are the slaves of men for purposes of sensuality. In Europe there early succeeded a third and milder dominion, secured not by blows, nor by locks and bars, but by sedulous inculcation on the mind; feelings also of kindness, and ideas of duty, such as a superior owes to inferiors under his protection, became more and more involved in the relation. But it did not, for many ages, become a relation of companionship, even between unequals. The lives of the two persons were apart. The wife was part of the furniture of home—of the resting-place to which the man returned from business or pleasure. His occupations were, as they still are, among men; his pleasures and excitements also were, for the most part, among men—among his equals. He was a patriarch and a despot within four walls, and irresponsible power had its effect, greater or less according to his disposition, in rendering him domineering, exacting, self-worshipping, when not capriciously or brutally tyrannical. But if the moral part of his nature suffered, it was not necessarily so, in the same degree, with the intellectual or the active portion. He might have as much vigour of mind and energy of character as his nature enabled him, and as the circumstances of his times allowed. He might write the *Paradise Lost,* or win the battle of Marengo. This was the condition of the Greeks and Romans, and of the moderns until a recent date. Their relations with their domestic subordinates occupied a mere corner, though a cherished one, of their lives. Their education as men, the formation of their character and faculties, depended mainly on a different class of influences.

It is otherwise now. The progress of improvement has imposed on all possessors of power, and of domestic power among the rest, an increased and increasing sense of correlative obligation. No man now thinks that his wife has no claim upon his actions but such as he may accord to her. All men of any conscience believe that their duty to their wives is one of the most binding of their obligations. Nor is it supposed to consist solely in protection, which, in the present state of civilization, women have almost ceased to need: it involves care for their happiness and consideration of their wishes, with a not unfrequent sacrifice of their own to them. The power of husbands has reached the stage which the power of kings had arrived at, when opinion did not yet question the rightfulness of arbitrary power, but in theory, and to a certain extent in practice, condemned the selfish use of it. This improvement in the moral sentiments of mankind, and increased sense of the consideration due by every man to those who have no one but himself to look to, has tended to make home more and more the centre of interest, and domestic circumstances and society a larger and larger part of life, and of its pursuits and pleasures. The tendency has been strengthened by the changes of tastes and manners which have so remarkably distinguished the last two or three generations. In days not far distant, men found their excitement and filled up their time in violent bodily exercises, noisy merriment, and intemperance. They have now, in all but the very poorest classes, lost their inclination for these things, and for the coarser pleasures generally; they have now scarcely any tastes but those which they have in common with women, and, for the first time in the world, men and women are really companions. A most beneficial change, if the companionship were between equals; but being between unequals, it produces, what good observers have noticed, though without perceiving its cause, a progressive deterioration among men in what had hitherto been considered the masculine excellences. Those who are so careful that women should not become men, do not see that men are becoming, what they have decided that women should be—are falling into the feebleness which they have so long cultivated in their companions. Those who are associated in their lives, tend to become assimilated in character. In the present closeness of association between the sexes, men cannot retain manliness unless women acquire it.

There is hardly any situation more unfavourable to the maintenance of elevation of character or force of intellect, than to live in the society, and seek by preference the sympathy, of inferiors in mental endowments. Why is it that we constantly see in life so much of intellectual and moral promise followed by such inadequate performance, but because the aspirant has compared himself only with those below himself, and has not sought improvement or stimulus from measuring himself with

his equals or superiors. In the present state of social life, this
is becoming the general condition of men. They care less and
less for any sympathies, and are less and less under any personal influences, but those of the domestic roof. Not to be
misunderstood, it is necessary that we should distinctly disclaim the belief, that women are even now inferior in intellect
to men. There are women who are the equals in intellect of
any men who ever lived; and comparing ordinary women with
ordinary men, the varied though petty details which compose
the occupation of most women, call forth probably as much
of mental ability, as the uniform routine of the pursuits which
are the habitual occupation of a large majority of men. It is
from nothing in the faculties themselves, but from the petty
subjects and interests on which alone they are exercised, that
the companionship of women, such as their present circumstances make them, so often exercises a dissolvent influence
on high faculties and aspirations in men. If one of the two
has no knowledge and no care about the great ideas and purposes which dignify life, or about any of its practical concerns
save personal interests and personal vanities, her conscious,
and still more her unconscious influence, will, except in rare
cases, reduce to a secondary place in his mind, if not entirely
extinguish, those interests which she cannot or does not
share.

Our argument here brings us into collision with what may
be termed the moderate reformers of the education of women;
a sort of persons who cross the path of improvement on all
great questions; those who would maintain the old bad principles, mitigating their consequences. These say, that women
should be, not slaves, nor servants, but companions; and educated for that office (they do not say that men should be
educated to be the companions of women). But since uncul-
tivated women are not suitable companions for cultivated men,
and a man who feels interest in things above and beyond the
family circle wishes that his companion should sympathize
with him in that interest; they therefore say, let women improve their understanding and taste, acquire general knowledge,

cultivate poetry, art, even coquet with science, and some stretch
their liberality so far as to say, inform themselves on politics;
not as pursuits, but sufficiently to feel an interest in the subjects, and to be capable of holding a conversation on them
with the husband, or at least of understanding and imbibing
his wisdom. Very agreeable to him, no doubt, but unfortunately the reverse of improving. It is from having intellectual
communion only with those to whom they can lay down the
law, that so few men continue to advance in wisdom beyond
the first stages. The most eminent men cease to improve, if
they associate only with disciples. When they have overtopped
those who immediately surround them, if they wish for further
growth, they must seek for others of their own stature to con-
sort with. The mental companionship which is improving, is
communion between active minds, not mere contact between
an active mind and a passive. This inestimable advantage is
even now enjoyed, when a strong-minded man and a strong-
minded woman are, by a rare chance, united: and would be
had far oftener, if education took the same pains to form
strong-minded women which it takes to prevent them from
being formed. The modern, and what are regarded as the improved and enlightened modes of education of women, abjure,
as far as words go, an education of mere show, and profess to
aim at solid instruction, but mean by that expression, superficial information on solid subjects. Except accomplishments,
which are now generally regarded as to be taught well if
taught at all, nothing is taught to women thoroughly. Small
portions only of what it is attempted to teach thoroughly to
boys, are the whole of what it is intended or desired to teach
to women. What makes intelligent beings is the power of
thought: the stimuli which call forth that power are the interest
and dignity of thought itself, and a field for its practical application. Both motives are cut off from those who are told from
infancy that thought, and all its greater applications, are other
people's business, while theirs is to make themselves agreeable to other people. High mental powers in women will be
but an exceptional accident, until every career is open to them,

and until they, as well as men, are educated for themselves and for the world—not one sex for the other.

In what we have said on the effect of the inferior position of women, combined with the present constitution of married life, we have thus far had in view only the most favourable cases, those in which there is some real approach to that union and blending of characters and of lives, which the theory of the relation contemplates as its ideal standard. But if we look to the great majority of cases, the effect of womens' legal inferiority, on the character both of women and of men, must be painted in far darker colours. We do not speak here of the grosser brutalities, nor of the man's power to seize on the woman's earnings, or compel her to live with him against her will. We do not address ourselves to any one who requires to have it proved that these things should be remedied. We suppose average cases, in which there is neither complete union nor complete disunion of feelings and character; and we affirm that in such cases the influence of the dependence on the woman's side, is demoralizing to the character of both.

The common opinion is, that whatever may be the case with the intellectual, the moral influence of women over men is almost salutary. It is, we are often told, the great counteractive of selfishness. However the case may be as to personal influence, the influence of the position tends eminently to promote selfishness. The most insignificant of men, the man who can obtain influence or consideration nowhere else, finds one place where he is chief and head. There is one person, often greatly his superior in understanding, who is obliged to consult him, and whom he is not obliged to consult. He is judge, magistrate, ruler, over their joint concerns; arbiter of all differences between them. The justice or conscience to which her appeal must be made, is his justice and conscience: it is his to hold the balance and adjust the scales between his own claims or wishes and those of another. His is now the only tribunal, in civilized life, in which the same person is judge and party. A generous mind, in such a situation, makes the balance incline against its own side, and gives the other not less, but more, than a fair equality; and thus the weaker side may be enabled to turn the very fact of dependence into an instrument of power, and in default of justice, take an ungenerous advantage of generosity; rendering the unjust power, to those who make an unselfish use of it, a torment and a burthen. But how is it when average men are invested with this power, without reciprocity and without responsibility? Give such a man the idea that he is first in law and in opinion —that to will is his part, and hers to submit; it is absurd to suppose that this idea merely glides over his mind, without sinking into it, or having any effect on his feelings and practice. The propensity to make himself the first object of consideration, and others at most the second, is not so rare as to be wanting where everything seems purposely arranged for encouraging its indulgence. If there is any self-will in the man, he becomes either the conscious or unconscious despot of his household. The wife, indeed, often succeeds in gaining her objects, but it is by some of the many various forms of indirectness and management.

Thus the position is corrupting equally to both; in the one it produces the vices of power, in the other those of artifice. Women, in their present physical and moral state, having stronger impulses, would naturally be franker and more direct than men; yet all the old saws and traditions represent them as artful and dissembling. Why? Because their only way to their objects is by indirect paths. In all countries where women have strong wishes and active minds, this consequence is inevitable: and if it is less conspicuous in England than in some other places, it is because Englishwomen, saving occasional exceptions, have ceased to have either strong wishes or active minds.

We are not now speaking of cases in which there is anything deserving the name of strong affection on both sides. That, where it exists, is too powerful a principle not to modify greatly the bad influences of the situation; it seldom, however, destroys them entirely. Much oftener the bad influences are too strong for the affection, and destroy it. The highest order of durable and happy attachments would be a hundred times more frequent than they are, if 'the affection which the two sexes sought from one another were that genuine friendship, which only exists between equals in privileges as in faculties. But with regard to what is commonly called affection in married life—the habitual and almost mechanical feeling of kindliness, and pleasure in each other's society, which generally grows up between persons who constantly live together, unless there is actual dislike—there is nothing in this to contradict or qualify the mischievous influence of the unequal relation. Such feelings often exist between a sultan and his favourites, between a master and his servants; they are merely examples of the pliability of human nature, which accommodates itself in some degree even to the worst circumstances, and the commonest natures always the most easily.

With respect to the influence personally exercised by women over men, it, no doubt, renders them less harsh and brutal; in ruder times, it was often the only softening influence to which they were accessible. But the assertion, that the wife's influence renders the man less selfish, contains, as things now are, fully as much error as truth. Selfishness towards the wife herself, and towards those in whom she is interested, the children, though favoured by her dependence, the wife's influence, no doubt, tends to counteract. But the general effect on him of her character, so long as her interests are concentrated in the family, tends but to substitute for individual selfishness a family selfishness, wearing an amiable guise, and putting on the mask of duty. How rarely is the wife's influence on the side of public virtue; how rarely does it do otherwise than discourage any effort of principle by which the private interests or worldly vanities of the family can be expected to suffer. Public spirit, sense of duty towards the public good, is of all virtues, as women are now educated and situated, the most rarely to be found among them; they have seldom even, what in men is often a partial substitute for public spirit, a sense of personal honour connected with any public duty. Many a man, whom no money or personal flattery would have bought, has bartered his political opinions against a title or invitations for his wife; and a still greater number are made mere hunters after the puerile vanities of society, because their wives value them. As for opinions; in Catholic countries, the wife's influence is another name for that of the priest; he gives her, in the hopes and emotions connected with a future life, a consolation for the sufferings and disappointments which are her ordinary lot in this. Elsewhere, her weight is thrown into the scale either of the most commonplace, or of the most outwardly prosperous opinions: either those by which censure will be escaped, or by which worldly advancement is likeliest to be procured. In England, the wife's influence is usually on the illiberal and anti-popular side: this is generally the gaining side for personal interest and vanity; and what to her is the democracy or liberalism in which she has no part—which leaves her the Pariah it found her? The man himself, when he marries, usually declines into Conservatism; begins to sympathize with the holders of power, more than with its victims, and thinks it his part to be on the side of authority. As to mental progress, except those vulgar attainments by which vanity or ambition are promoted, there is generally an end to it in a man who marries a woman mentally his inferior; unless, indeed, he is unhappy in marriage, or becomes indifferent. From a man of twenty-five or thirty, after he is married, an experienced observer seldom expects any further progress in mind or feelings. It is rare that the progress already made is maintained. Any spark of the *mens divinior* which might otherwise have spread and become a flame, seldom survives for any length of time unextinguished. For a mind which learns to be satisfied with what it already is—which does not incessantly look forward to a degree of improvement not yet reached— becomes relaxed, self-indulgent, and loses the spring and the tension which maintain it even at the point already attained. And there is no fact in human nature to which experience bears more invariable testimony than to this—that all social or sympathetic influences which do not raise up, pull down; if they do not tend to stimulate and exalt the mind, they tend to vulgarize it.

For the interest, therefore, not only of women but of men, and of human improvement in the widest sense, the emancipation of women, which the modern world often boasts of having effected, and for which credit is sometimes given to civilization, and sometimes to Christianity, cannot stop where it is. If it were either necessary or just that one portion of mankind should remain mentally and spiritually only half developed, the development of the other portion ought to have been made, as far as possible, independent of their influence. Instead of this, they have become the most intimate, and it may now be said, the only intimate associates of those to whom yet they are sedulously kept inferior; and have been raised just high enough to drag the others down to themselves.

We have left behind a host of vulgar objections, either as not worthy of an answer, or as answered by the general course of our remarks. A few words, however, must be said on one plea, which in England is made much use of for giving an unselfish air to the upholding of selfish privileges, and which, with unobserving, unreflecting people, passes for much more than it is worth. Women, it is said, do not desire—do not seek, what is called their emancipation. On the contrary, they generally disown such claims when made in their behalf, and fall with *acharnement* upon any one of themselves who identifies herself with their common cause.

Supposing the fact to be true in the fullest extent ever asserted, if it proves that European women ought to remain as they are, it proves exactly the same with respect to Asiatic women; for they too, instead of murmuring at their seclusion, and at the restraint imposed upon them, pride themselves on it, and are astonished at the effrontery of women who receive visits from male acquaintances, and are seen in the streets unveiled. Habits of submission make men as well as women servile-minded. The vast population of Asia do not desire or value, probably would not accept, political liberty, nor the savages of the forest, civilization; which does not prove that either of those things is undesirable for them, or that they will not, at some future time, enjoy it. Custom hardens human beings to any kind of degradation, by deadening the part of their nature which would resist it. And the case of women is, in this respect, even a peculiar one, for no other inferior caste that we have heard of have been taught to regard their degradation as their honour. The argument, however, implies a secret consciousness that the alleged preference of women for their dependent state is merely apparent, and arises from their being allowed no choice; for if the preference be natural, there can be no necessity for enforcing it by law. To make laws compelling people to follow their inclination, has not hitherto been thought necessary by any legislator. The plea that women do not desire any change, is the same that has been urged, times out of mind, against the proposal of abolishing any social evil—"there is no complaint"; which is generally not true, and when true, only so because there is not that hope of success, without which complaint seldom makes itself audible to unwilling ears. How does the objector know that women do not desire equality and freedom? He never knew a woman who did not, or would not, desire it for herself individually. It would be very simple to suppose, that if they do desire it they will say so. Their position is like that of the tenants or labourers who vote against their own political interests to please their landlords or employers; with the unique addition, that submission is inculcated on them from childhood, as the peculiar attraction and grace of their character. They are taught to think, that to repel actively even an admitted injustice done to themselves, is somewhat unfeminine, and had better be left to some male friend or protector. To be accused of rebelling against anything which admits of being called an ordinance of society, they are taught to regard as an imputation of a serious offence, to say the least, against the proprieties of their sex. It requires unusual moral courage as well as disinterestedness in a woman, to express opinions favourable to women's enfranchisement, until, at least, there is some prospect of obtaining it. The comfort of her individual life, and her social consideration, usually depend on the good-will of those who hold the undue power; and to possessors of power any complaint, however bitter, of the misuse of it, is a less flagrant act of insubordination than to protest against the power itself. The professions of women in this matter remind us of the State offenders of old, who, on the point of execution, used to protest their love and devotion to the sovereign by whose un-just mandate they suffered. Griselda herself might be matched from the speeches put by Shakespeare into the mouths of male victims of kingly caprice and tyranny: the Duke of Bucking-ham, for example, in *Henry the Eighth,* and even Wolsey. The literary class of women, especially in England, are osten-tatious in disclaiming the desire for equality or citizenship, and proclaiming their complete satisfaction with the place which society assigns to them; exercising in this, as in many other respects, a most noxious influence over the feelings and opinions of men, who unsuspectingly accept the servilities of toadyism as concessions to the force of truth, not considering that it is the personal interest of these women to profess what-ever opinions they expect will be agreeable to men. It is not among men of talent, sprung from the people, and patronized and flattered by the aristocracy, that we look for the leaders of a democratic movement. Successful literary women are just as unlikely to prefer the cause of women to their own social consideration. They depend on men's opinion for their literary as well as for their feminine successes; and such is their bad opinion of men, that they believe there is not more than one in ten thousand who does not dislike and fear strength, sin-cerity, or high spirit in a woman. They are therefore anxious to earn pardon and toleration for whatever of these qualities their writings may exhibit on other subjects, by a studied dis-play of submission on this: that they may give no occasion for vulgar men to say (what nothing will prevent vulgar men from saying), that learning makes women unfeminine, and that literary ladies are likely to be bad wives.

But enough of this; especially as the fact which affords the occasion for this notice, makes it impossible any longer to assert the universal acquiescence of women (saving individual exceptions) in their dependent condition. In the United States, at least, there are women, seemingly numerous, and now organized for action on the public mind, who demand equality in the fullest acceptation of the word, and demand it by a straightforward appeal to men's sense of justice, not plead for it with a timid deprecation of their displeasure.

Like other popular movements, however, this may be seriously retarded by the blunders of its adherents. Tried by the ordinary standard of public meetings, the speeches at the Convention are remarkable for the preponderance of the rational over the declamatory element; but there are some exceptions; and things to which it is impossible to attach any rational meaning, have found their way into the resolutions. Thus, the resolution which sets forth the claims made in behalf of women, after claiming equality in education, in industrial pursuits, and in political rights, enumerates as a fourth head of demand something under the name of "social and spiritual union," and "a medium of expressing the highest moral and spiritual views of justice," with other similar verbiage, serving only to mar the simplicity and rationality of the other demands; resembling those who would weakly attempt to combine nominal equality between men and women, with enforced distinctions in their privileges and functions. What is wanted for women is equal rights, equal admission to all social privileges; not a position apart, a sort of sentimental priesthood. To this, the only just and rational principle, both the resolutions and the speeches, for the most part, adhere. They contain so little which is akin to the nonsensical paragraph in question, that we suspect it not to be the work of the same hands as most of the other resolutions. The strength of the cause lies in the support of those who are influenced by reason and principle; and to attempt to recommend it by sentimentalities, absurd in reason, and inconsistent with the principle on which the movement is founded, is to place a good cause on a level with a bad one.

There are indications that the example of America will be followed on this side of the Atlantic; and the first step has been taken in that part of England where every serious move-

ment in the direction of political progress has its commencement—the manufacturing districts of the North. On the 13th
of February 1851, a petition of women, agreed to by a public
meeting at Sheffield, and claiming the elective franchise, was
presented to the House of Lords by the Earl of Carlisle.

4

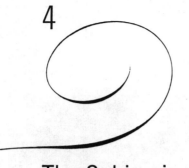

The Subjection
of Women

JOHN STUART MILL

CAMEO OF JOHN STUART MILL
From Hugh S. R. Elliot, ed., *The Letters of John Stuart Mill*,
Longmans, Green and Co., 1910

The Subjection of Women

1

The object of this Essay is to explain as clearly as I am able, the grounds of an opinion which I have held from the very earliest period when I had formed any opinions at all on social or political matters, and which, instead of being weakened or modified, has been constantly growing stronger by the progress of reflection and the experience of life: That the principle which regulates the existing social relations between the two sexes—the legal subordination of one sex to the other—is wrong in itself, and now one of the chief hindrances to human improvement; and that it ought to be replaced by a principle of perfect equality, admitting no power or privilege on the one side, nor disability on the other.

The very words necessary to express the task I have undertaken, show how arduous it is. But it would be a mistake to suppose that the difficulty of the case must lie in the insufficiency or obscurity of the grounds of reason on which my conviction rests. The difficulty is that which exists in all cases in which there is a mass of feeling to be contended against. So long as an opinion is strongly rooted in the feelings, it gains rather than loses in stability by having a preponderating weight of argument against it. For if it were accepted as a result of argument, the refutation of the argument might shake the solidity of the conviction; but when it rests solely on feeling, the worse it fares in argumentative contest, the more persuaded its adherents are that their feeling must have some deeper ground, which the arguments do not reach; and while the feeling remains, it is always throwing up fresh intrenchments of argument to repair any breach made in the old. And there are so many causes tending to make the feelings connected with this subject the most intense and most deeply-rooted of all those which gather round and protect old institutions and customs, that we need not wonder to find them as yet less undermined and loosened than any of the rest by the progress of the great modern spiritual and social transition; nor suppose that the barbarisms to which men cling longest must be less barbarisms than those which they earlier shake off.

In every respect the burthen is hard on those who attack an almost universal opinion. They must be very fortunate as well as unusually capable if they obtain a hearing at all. They have more difficulty in obtaining a trial, than any other litigants have in getting a verdict. If they do extort a hearing, they are subjected to a set of logical requirements totally different from those exacted from other people. In all other cases, the burthen of proof is supposed to lie with the affirmative. If a person is charged with a murder, it rests with those who accuse him to give proof of his guilt, not with himself to prove his innocence. If there is a difference of opinion about the reality of any alleged historical event, in which the feelings of men in general are not much interested, as the Siege of Troy for example, those who maintain that the event took place are expected to produce their proofs, before those who take the other side can be required to say anything; and at no time are these required to do more than show that the evidence produced by the others is of no value. Again, in practical matters, the burthen of proof is supposed to be with those who are against liberty; who contend for any restriction or prohibition; either any limitation of the general freedom of human action, or any disqualification or disparity of privilege affecting one person or kind of persons, as compared with others. The *a priori* presumption is in favour of freedom and impartiality. It is held that there should be no restraint not required by the general good, and that the law should be no respecter of persons, but should treat all alike, save where dissimilarity of treatment is required by positive reasons, either of justice or of policy. But of none of these rules of evidence will the benefit be allowed to those who maintain the opinion I profess. It is useless for me to say that those who maintain the doctrine that men have a right to command and women are under an obligation to obey, or that men are fit for government and women unfit, are on the affirmative side of the question, and that they are bound to show positive evidence for the assertions, or submit to their rejection. It is equally unavailing for me to say that those who deny to women any freedom or privilege rightly allowed to men, having the double presumption against them that they are opposing freedom and recommending partiality, must be held to the strictest proof of their case, and unless their success be such as to exclude all doubt, the judgment ought to go against them. These would be thought good pleas in any common case; but they will not be thought so in this instance. Before I could hope to make any impression, I should be expected not only to answer all that has ever been said by those who take the other side of the question, but to imagine all that could be said by them—to find them in reasons, as well as answer all I find: and besides refuting all arguments for the affirmative, I shall be called upon for invincible positive arguments to prove a negative. And even if I could do all this, and leave the opposite party with a host of unanswered arguments against them, and not a single unrefuted one on their side, I should be thought to have done little; for a cause supported on the one hand by universal usage, and on the other by so great a preponderance of popular sentiment, is supposed to have a presumption in its favour, superior to any conviction which an appeal to reason has power to produce in any intellects but those of a high class.

I do not mention these difficulties to complain of them; first, because it would be useless; they are inseparable from having to contend through people's understandings against the hostility of their feelings and practical tendencies: and truly the understandings of the majority of mankind would need to be much better cultivated than has ever yet been the case, before they can be asked to place such reliance in their own power of estimating arguments, as to give up practical principles in which they have been born and bred and which are the basis of much of the existing order of the world, at the first argumentative attack which they are not capable of logically resisting. I do not therefore quarrel with them for having too little faith in argument, but for having too much faith in custom and the general feeling. It is one of the characteristic prejudices of the reaction of the nineteenth century against the eighteenth, to accord to the unreasoning elements in human nature the infallibility which the eighteenth century is supposed to have ascribed to the reasoning elements. For the apotheosis of Reason we have substituted that of Instinct; and we call everything instinct which we find in ourselves and for which we cannot trace any rational foundation. This idolatry, infinitely more degrading than the other, and the most pernicious of the false worships of the present day, of all of which it is now the main support, will probably hold its ground until it gives way before a sound psychology, laying bare the real root of much that is bowed down to as the intention of Nature and the ordinance of God. As regards the present question, I am willing to accept the unfavourable conditions which the prejudice assigns to me. I consent that established custom, and the general feeling, should be deemed conclusive against me, unless that custom and feeling from age to age can be shown to have owed their existence to other causes than their soundness, and to have derived their power from the worse rather than the better parts of human nature. I am willing that judg-

ment should go against me, unless I can show that my judge
has been tampered with. The concession is not so great as it
might appear; for to prove this, is by far the easiest portion
of my task.

The generality of a practice is in some cases a strong presumption that it is, or at all events once was, conducive to
laudable ends. This is the case, when the practice was first
adopted, or afterwards kept up, as a means to such ends, and
was grounded on experience of the mode in which they could
be most effectually attained. If the authority of men over
women, when first established, had been the result of a conscientious comparison between different modes of constituting
the government of society; if, after trying various other modes
of social organization—the government of women over men,
equality between the two, and such mixed and divided modes
of government as might be invented—it had been decided, on
the testimony of experience, that the mode in which women
are wholly under the rule of men, having no share at all in
public concerns, and each in private being under the legal
obligation of obedience to the man with whom she has associated her destiny, was the arrangement most conducive to the
happiness and well being of both; its general adoption might
then be fairly thought to be some evidence that, at the time
when it was adopted, it was the best: though even then the
considerations which recommended it may, like so many other
primeval social facts of the greatest importance, have subsequently, in the course of ages, ceased to exist. But the state
of the case is in every respect the reverse of this. In the first
place, the opinion in favour of the present system, which entirely subordinates the weaker sex to the stronger, rests upon
theory only; for there never has been trial made of any other:
so that experience, in the sense in which it is vulgarly opposed
to theory, cannot be pretended to have pronounced any verdict. And in the second place, the adoption of this system of
inequality never was the result of deliberation, or forethought,
or any social ideas, or any notion whatever of what conduced
to the benefit of humanity or the good order of society. It arose

simply from the fact that from the very earliest twilight of human society, every woman (owing to the value attached to her by men, combined with her inferiority in muscular strength) was found in a state of bondage to some man. Laws and systems of polity always begin by recognising the relations they find already existing between individuals. They convert what was a mere physical fact into a legal right, give it the sanction of society, and principally aim at the substitution of public and organized means of asserting and protecting these rights, instead of the irregular and lawless conflict of physical strength. Those who had already been compelled to obedience became in this manner legally bound to it. Slavery, from being a mere affair of force between the master and the slave, became regularized and a matter of compact among the masters, who, binding themselves to one another for common protection, guaranteed by their collective strength the private possessions of each, including his slaves. In early times, the great majority of the male sex were slaves, as well as the whole of the female. And many ages elapsed, some of them ages of high cultivation, before any thinker was bold enough to question the rightfulness, and the absolute social necessity, either of the one slavery or of the other. By degrees such thinkers did arise: and (the general progress of society assisting) the slavery of the male sex has, in all the countries of Christian Europe at least (though, in one of them, only within the last few years) been at length abolished, and that of the female sex has been gradually changed into a milder form of dependence. But this dependence, as it exists at present, is not an original institution, taking a fresh start from considerations of justice and social expediency—it is the primitive state of slavery lasting on, through successive mitigations and modifications occasioned by the same causes which have softened the general manners, and brought all human relations more under the control of justice and the influence of humanity. It has not lost the taint of its brutal origin. No presumption in its favour, therefore, can be drawn from the fact of its existence. The only such presumption which it could be supposed to have, must be grounded on its having lasted till now, when so many other things which came down from the same odious source have been done away with. And this, indeed, is what makes it strange to ordinary ears, to hear it asserted that the inequality of rights between men and women has no other source than the law of the strongest.

That this statement should have the effect of a paradox, is in some respects creditable to the progress of civilization, and the improvement of the moral sentiments of mankind. We now live—that is to say, one or two of the most advanced nations of the world now live—in a state in which the law of the strongest seems to be entirely abandoned as the regulating principle of the world's affairs: nobody professes it, and, as regards most of the relations between human beings, nobody is permitted to practise it. When any one succeeds in doing so, it is under cover of some pretext which gives him the semblance of having some general social interest on his side. This being the ostensible state of things, people flatter themselves that the rule of mere force is ended; that the law of the strongest cannot be the reason of existence of anything which has remained in full operation down to the present time. However any of our present institutions may have begun, it can only, they think, have been preserved to this period of advanced civilization by a well-grounded feeling of its adaptation to human nature, and conduciveness to the general good. They do not understand the great vitality and durability of institutions which place right on the side of might; how intensely they are clung to; how the good as well as the bad propensities and sentiments of those who have power in their hands, become identified with retaining it; how slowly these bad institutions give way, one at a time, the weakest first, beginning with those which are least interwoven with the daily habits of life; and how very rarely those who have obtained legal power because they first had physical, have ever lost their hold of it until the physical power had passed over to the other side. Such shifting of the physical force not having taken place in the case of women; this fact, combined with all the peculiar and characteristic features of the particular case, made it certain from the first that this branch of the system of right founded on might, though softened in its most atrocious features at an earlier period than several of the others, would be the very last to disappear. It was inevitable that this one case of a social relation grounded on force, would survive through generations of institutions grounded on equal justice, an almost solitary exception to the general character of their laws and customs; but which, so long as it does not proclaim its own origin, and as discussion has not brought out its true character, is not felt to jar with modern civilization, any more than domestic slavery among the Greeks jarred with their notion of themselves as a free people.

The truth is, that people of the present and the last two or three generations have lost all practical sense of the primitive condition of humanity; and only the few who have studied history accurately, or have much frequented the parts of the world occupied by the living representatives of ages long past, are able to form any mental picture of what society then was. People are not aware how entirely, in former ages, the law of superior strength was the rule of life; how publicly and openly it was avowed, I do not say cynically or shamelessly— for these words imply a feeling that there was something in it to be ashamed of, and no such notion could find a place in the faculties of any person in those ages, except a philosopher or a saint. History gives a cruel experience of human nature, in shewing how exactly the regard due to the life, possessions, and entire earthly happiness of any class of persons, was measured by what they had the power of enforcing; how all who made any resistance to authorities that had arms in their hands, however dreadful might be the provocation, had not only the law of force but all other laws, and all the notions of social obligation against them; and in the eyes of those whom they resisted, were not only guilty of crime, but of the worst of all crimes, deserving the most cruel chastisement which human beings could inflict. The first small vestige of a feeling of obligation in a superior to acknowledge any

right in inferiors, began when he had been induced, for convenience, to make some promise to them. Though these prom-
ises, even when sanctioned by the most solemn oaths, were
for many ages revoked or violated on the most trifling provocation or temptation, it is probable that this, except by persons of still worse than the average morality, was seldom done
without some twinges of conscience. The ancient republics,
being mostly grounded from the first upon some kind of mutual compact, or at any rate formed by an union of persons
not very unequal in strength, afforded, in consequence, the
first instance of a portion of human relations fenced round,
and placed under the dominion of another law than that of
force. And though the original law of force remained in full
operation between them and their slaves, and also (except
so far as limited by express compact) between a commonwealth and its subjects, or other independent commonwealths;
the banishment of that primitive law even from so narrow a
field, commenced the regeneration of human nature, by giving
birth to sentiments of which experience soon demonstrated the
immense value even for material interests, and which thence-
forward only required to be enlarged, not created. Though
slaves were no part of the commonwealth, it was in the free
states that slaves were first felt to have rights as human beings. The Stoics were, I believe, the first (except so far as the
Jewish law constitutes an exception) who taught as a part of
morality that men were bound by moral obligations to their
slaves. No one, after Christianity became ascendant, could
ever again have been a stranger to this belief, in theory; nor,
after the rise of the Catholic Church, was it ever without persons to stand up for it. Yet to enforce it was the most arduous
task which Christianity ever had to perform. For more than
a thousand years the Church kept up the contest, with hardly
any perceptible success. It was not for want of power over
men's minds. Its power was prodigious. It could make kings
and nobles resign their most valued possessions to enrich the
Church. It could make thousands, in the prime of life and the
height of worldly advantages, shut themselves up in convents

to work out their salvation by poverty, fasting, and prayer. It could send hundreds of thousands across land and sea, Europe and Asia, to give their lives for the deliverance of the Holy Sepulchre. It could make kings relinquish wives who were the object of their passionate attachment, because the Church declared that they were within the seventh (by our calculation the fourteenth) degree of relationship. All this it did; but it could not make men fight less with one another, nor tyrannize less cruelly over the serfs, and when they were able, over burgesses. It could not make them renounce either of the applications of force; force militant, or force triumphant. This they could never be induced to do until they were themselves in their turn compelled by superior force. Only by the growing power of kings was an end put to fighting except between kings or competitors for kingship; only by the growth of a wealthy and warlike bourgeoisie in the fortified towns, and of a plebeian infantry which proved more powerful in the field than the undisciplined chivalry, was the insolent tyranny of the nobles over the bourgeoisie and peasantry brought within some bounds. It was persisted in not only until, but long after, the oppressed had obtained a power enabling them often to take conspicuous vengeance; and on the Continent much of it continued to the time of the French Revolution, though in England the earlier and better organization of the democratic classes put an end to it sooner, by establishing equal laws and free national institutions.

If people are mostly so little aware how completely, during the greater part of the duration of our species, the law of force was the avowed rule of general conduct, any other being only a special and exceptional consequence of peculiar ties—and from how very recent a date it is that the affairs of society in general have been even pretended to be regulated according to any moral law; as little do people remember or consider, how institutions and customs which never had any ground but the law of force, last on into ages and states of general opinion which never would have permitted their first establishment. Less than forty years ago, Englishmen might still by law hold human beings in bondage as saleable property: within the present century they might kidnap them and carry them off, and work them literally to death. This absolutely extreme case of the law of force, condemned by those who can tolerate almost every other form of arbitrary power, and which, of all others, presents features the most revolting to the feelings of all who look at it from an impartial position, was the law of civilized and Christian England within the memory of persons now living: and in one half of Anglo-Saxon America three or four years ago, not only did slavery exist, but the slave trade, and the breeding of slaves expressly for it, was a general practice between slave states. Yet not only was there a greater strength of sentiment against it, but, in England at least, a less amount either of feeling or of interest in favour of it, than of any other of the customary abuses of force: for its motive was the love of gain, unmixed and undisguised; and those who profited by it were a very small numerical fraction of the country, while the natural feeling of all who were not personally interested in it, was unmitigated abhorrence. So extreme an instance makes it almost superfluous to refer to any other: but consider the long duration of absolute monarchy. In England at present it is the almost universal conviction that military despotism is a case of the law of force, having no other origin or justification. Yet in all the great nations of Europe except England it either still exists, or has only just ceased to exist, and has even now a strong party favourable to it in all ranks of the people, especially among persons of station and consequence. Such is the power of an established system, even when far from universal; when not only in almost every period of history there have been great and well-known examples of the contrary system, but these have almost invariably been afforded by the most illustrious and most prosperous communities. In this case, too, the possessor of the undue power, the person directly interested in it, is only one person, while those who are subject to it and suffer from it are literally all the rest. The yoke is naturally and necessarily humiliating to all persons, except the one who is on the throne, together with, at most, the one who expects to succeed to it. How different are these cases from that of the power of men over women! I am not now prejudging the question of its justifiableness. I am showing how vastly more permanent it could not but be, even if not justifiable, than these other dominations which have nevertheless lasted down to our own time. Whatever gratification of pride there is in the possession of power, and whatever personal interest in its exercise, is in this case not confined to a limited class, but common to the whole male sex. Instead of being, to most of its supporters, a thing desirable chiefly in the abstract, or, like the political ends usually contended for by factious, of little private importance to any but the leaders; it comes home to the person and hearth of every male head of a family, and of every one who looks forward to being so. The clodhopper exercises, or is to exercise, his share of the power equally with the highest nobleman. And the case is that in which the desire of power is the strongest: for every one who desires power, desires it most over those who are nearest to him, with whom his life is passed, with whom he has most concerns in common, and in whom any independence of his authority is oftenest likely to interfere with his individual preferences. If, in the other cases specified, power manifestly grounded only on force, and having so much less to support them, are so slowly and with so much difficulty got rid of, much more must it be so with this, even if it rests on no better foundation than those. We must consider, too, that the possessors of the power have facilities in this case, greater than in any other, to prevent any uprising against it. Every one of the subjects lives under the very eye, and almost, it may be said, in the hands, of one of the masters—in closer intimacy with him than with any of her fellow-subjects; with no means of combining against him, no power of even locally overmastering him, and, on the other hand, with the strongest motives for seeking his favour and avoiding to give him offence. In struggles for political emancipation, everybody knows how often its champions are bought off by bribes, or daunted by terrors. In the case of women, each individual of the subject-class is in a chronic state of bribery and intimidation combined. In setting up the standard of resistance, a large number of the leaders, and still more of the followers, must make an almost complete sacrifice of the pleasures or the alleviations of their own individual lot. If ever any system of privilege and enforced subjection had its yoke tightly riveted on the necks of those who are kept down by it, this has. I have not yet shown that it is a wrong system: but every one who is capable of thinking on the subject must see that even if it is, it was certain to outlast all other forms of unjust authority. And when some of the grossest of the other forms still exist in many civilized countries, and have only recently been got rid of in others, it would be strange if that which is so much the deepest-rooted had yet been perceptibly shaken anywhere. There is more reason to wonder that the protests and testimonies against it should have been so numerous and so weighty as they are.

Some will object, that a comparison cannot fairly be made between the government of the male sex and the forms of unjust power which I have adduced in illustration of it, since these are arbitrary, and the effect of mere usurpation, while it on the contrary is natural. But was there ever any domination which did not appear natural to those who possessed it? There was a time when the division of mankind into two classes, a small one of masters and a numerous one of slaves, appeared, even to the most cultivated minds, to be a natural, and the only natural, condition of the human race. No less an intellect, and one which contributed no less to the progress of human thought, than Aristotle, held this opinion without doubt or misgiving; and rested it on the same premises on which the same assertion in regard to the dominion of men over women is usually based, namely that there are different natures among mankind, free natures, and slave natures; that the Greeks were of a free nature, the barbarian races of Thracians and Asiatics of a slave nature. But why need I go back to Aristotle? Did not the slaveowners of the Southern United States maintain the same doctrine, with all the fanaticism with which men cling to the theories that justify their passions and legitimate their personal interests? Did they not call heaven and earth to witness that the dominion of the white man over the black is natural, that the black race is by nature incapable of freedom, and marked out for slavery? some even going so far as to say that the freedom of manual labourers is an unnatural order of things anywhere. Again, the theorists of absolute monarchy have always affirmed it to be the only natural form of government; issuing from the patriarchal, which was the primitive and spontaneous form of society, framed on the model of the paternal, which is anterior to society itself, and, as they contend, the most natural authority of all. Nay, for that matter, the law of force itself, to those who could not plead any other, has always seemed the most natural of all grounds for the exercise of authority. Conquering races hold it to be Nature's own dictate that the conquered should obey the conquerors, or, as they euphoniously paraphrase it, that the feebler and more unwarlike races should submit to the braver and manlier. The smallest acquaintance with human life in the middle ages, shows how supremely natural the dominion of the feudal nobility over men of low condition appeared to the nobility themselves, and how unnatural the conception seemed, of a person of the inferior class claiming equality with them, or exercising authority over them. It hardly seemed less so to the class held in subjection. The emancipated serfs and burgesses, even in their most vigorous struggles, never made any pretension to a share of authority; they only demanded more or less of limitation to the power of tyrannizing over them. So true is it that unnatural generally means only uncustomary, and that everything which is usual appears natural. The subjection of women to men being a universal custom, any departure from it quite naturally appears unnatural. But how entirely, even in this case, the feeling is dependent on custom, appears by ample experience. Nothing so much astonishes the people of distant parts of the world, when they first learn anything about England, as to be told that it is under a queen: the thing seems to them so unnatural as to be almost incredible. To Englishmen this does not seem in the least degree unnatural, because they are used to it; but they do feel it unnatural that women should be soldiers or members of parliament. In the feudal ages, on the contrary, war and politics were not thought unnatural to women, because not unusual; it seemed natural that women of the privileged classes should be of manly character, inferior in nothing but bodily strength to their husbands and fathers. The independence of women seemed rather less unnatural to the Greeks than to other ancients, on account of the fabulous Amazons (whom they believed to be historical), and the partial example afforded by the Spartan women; who, though no less subordinate by law than in other Greek states, were more free in fact, and being trained to bodily exercises in the same manner with men, gave ample proof that they were not naturally disqualified for them. There can be little doubt that Spartan experience suggested to Plato, among many other of his doctrines, that of the social and political equality of the two sexes.

But, it will be said, the rule of men over women differs from all these others in not being a rule of force: it is accepted voluntarily; women make no complaint, and are consenting parties to it. In the first place, a great number of women do not accept it. Ever since there have been women able to make their sentiments known by their writings (the only mode of publicity which society permits to them), an increasing number of them have recorded protests against their present social condition: and recently many thousands of them, headed by the most eminent women known to the public, have petitioned Parliament for their admission to the Parliamentary Suffrage. The claim of women to be educated as solidly, and in the same branches of knowledge, as men, is urged with growing intensity, and with a great prospect of success; while the demand for their admission into professions and occupations hitherto closed against them, becomes every year more urgent. Though there are not in this country, as there are in the United States, periodical Conventions and an organized party to agitate for the Rights of Women, there is a numerous and active Society organized and managed by women, for the more limited object of obtaining the political franchise. Nor is it only in our own country and in America that women are beginning to protest, more or less collectively, against the disabilities under which they labour. France, and Italy, and Switzerland, and Russia now afford examples of the same thing. How many more women there are who silently cherish similar aspirations, no one can possibly know; but there are abundant tokens how many *would* cherish them, were they not so strenuously taught to repress them as contrary to the proprieties of their sex. It must be remembered, also, that no enslaved class ever asked for complete liberty at once. When Simon de Montfort called the deputies of the commons to sit for the first time in Parliament, did any of them dream of demanding that an assembly, elected by their constituents, should make and destroy ministries, and dictate to the king in affairs of state? No such thought entered into the imagination of the most ambitious of them. The nobility had already these pretensions; the commons pretended to nothing but to be exempt from arbitrary taxation, and from the gross individual oppression of the king's officers. It is a political law of nature that those who are under any power of ancient origin, never begin by complaining of the power itself, but only of its oppressive exercise. There is never any want of women who complain of ill usage by their husbands. There would be infinitely more, if complaint were not the greatest of all provocatives to a repetition and increase of the ill usage. It is this which frustrates all attempts to maintain the power but protect the woman against its abuses. In no other case (except that of a child) is the person who has been proved judicially to have suffered an injury, replaced under the physical power of the culprit who inflicted it. Accordingly wives, even in the most extreme and protracted cases of bodily ill usage, hardly ever dare avail themselves of the laws made for their protection: and if, in a moment of irrepressible indignation, or by the interference of neighbours, they are induced to do so, their whole effort afterwards is to disclose as little as they can, and to beg off their tyrant from his merited chastisement.

All causes, social and natural, combine to make it unlikely that women should be collectively rebellious to the power of men. They are so far in a position different from all other subject classes, that their masters require something more from them than actual service. Men do not want solely the obedience of women, they want their sentiments. All men, except the most brutish, desire to have, in the woman most nearly connected with them, not a forced slave but a willing one, not a slave merely, but a favourite. They have therefore put everything in practice to enslave their minds. The masters of all other slaves rely, for maintaining obedience, on fear; either fear of themselves, or religious fears. The masters of women wanted more than simple obedience, and they turned the whole force of education to effect their purpose. All women are brought up from the very earliest years in the belief that their ideal of character is the very opposite to that of men; not self-will, and government by self-control, but submission, and yielding to the control of others. All the moralities tell them that it is the duty of women, and all the current sentimentalities that it is their nature, to live for others; to make complete abnegation of themselves, and to have no life but in their affections. And by their affections are meant the only ones they are allowed to have—those to the men with whom they are connected, or to the children who constitute an additional and indefeasible tie between them and a man. When we put together three things—first, the natural attraction between opposite sexes; secondly, the wife's entire dependence on the husband, every privilege or pleasure she has being either his gift, or depending entirely on his will; and lastly, that the principal object of human pursuit, consideration, and all objects of social ambition, can in general be sought or obtained by her only through him, it would be a miracle if the object of being attractive to men had not become the polar star of feminine education and formation of character. And, this great means of influence over the minds of women having been acquired, an instinct of selfishness made men avail themselves of it to the utmost as a means of holding women in subjection, by representing to them meekness, submissiveness, and resignation of all individual will into the hands of a man, as an essential part of sexual attractiveness. Can it be doubted that any of the other yokes which mankind have succeeded in breaking, would have subsisted till now if the same means had existed, and had been as sedulously used, to bow down their minds to it? If it had been made the object of the life of every young plebeian to find personal favour in the eyes of some patrician, of every young serf with some seigneur; if domestication with him, and a share of his personal affections, had been held out as the prize which they all should look out for, the most gifted and aspiring being able to reckon on the most desirable prizes; and if, when this prize had been obtained, they had been shut out by a wall of brass from all interests not centering in him, all feelings and desires but those which he shared or inculcated; would not serfs and seigneurs, plebeians and patricians, have been as broadly distinguished at this day as men and women are? and would not all but a thinker here and there, have believed the distinction to be a fundamental and unalterable fact in human nature?

The preceding considerations are amply sufficient to show that custom, however universal it may be, affords in this case no presumption, and ought not to create any prejudice, in favour of the arrangements which place women in social and political subjection to men. But I may go farther, and maintain that the course of history, and the tendencies of progressive human society, afford not only no presumption in favour of this system of inequality of rights, but a strong one against it; and that, so far as the whole course of human improvement up to this time, the whole stream of modern tendencies, warrants any inference on the subject, it is, that this relic of the past is discordant with the future, and must necessarily disappear.

For, what is the peculiar character of the modern world—the difference which chiefly distinguishes modern institutions, modern social ideas, modern life itself, from those of times long past? It is, that human beings are no longer born to their place in life, and chained down by an inexorable bond to the place they are born to, but are free to employ their faculties, and such favourable chances as offer, to achieve the lot which may appear to them most desirable. Human society of old was constituted on a very different principle. All were born to a fixed social position, and were mostly kept in it by law, or interdicted from any means by which they could emerge from it. As some men are born white and others black, so some were born slaves and others freemen and citizens; some were born patricians, others plebeians; some were born feudal nobles, others commoners and *roturiers*. A slave or serf could never make himself free, nor, except by the will of his master, become so. In most European countries it was not till towards the close of the middle ages, and as a consequence of the growth of regal power, that commoners could be ennobled. Even among nobles, the eldest son was born the exclusive heir to the paternal possessions, and a long time elapsed before it was fully established that the father could disinherit him. Among the industrious classes, only those who were born members of a guild, or were admitted into it by its members, could lawfully practise their calling within its local limits; and nobody could practise any calling deemed important, in any but the legal manner—by processes authoritatively prescribed. Manufacturers have stood in the pillory for presuming to carry on their business by new and improved methods. In modern Europe, and most in those parts of it which have participated most largely in all other modern improvements, diametrically opposite doctrines now prevail. Law and government do not undertake to prescribe by whom any social or industrial operation shall or shall not be conducted, or what modes of conducting them shall be lawful. These things are left to the unfettered choice of individuals. Even the laws which required that workmen should serve an apprenticeship, have in this country been repealed: there being ample assurance that in all cases in which an apprenticeship is necessary, its necessity will suffice to enforce it. The old theory was, that the least possible should be left to the choice of the individual agent; that all he had to do should, as far as practicable, be laid down for him by superior wisdom. Left to himself he was sure to go wrong. The modern conviction, the fruit of a thousand years of experience, is, that things in which the individual is the person directly interested, never go right but as they are left to his own discretion; and that any regulation of them by authority, except to protect the rights of others, is sure to be mischievous. This conclusion, slowly arrived at, and not adopted until almost every possible application of the contrary theory had been made with disastrous result, now (in the industrial department) prevails universally in the most advanced countries, almost universally in all that have pretensions to any sort of advancement. It is not that all processes are supposed to be equally good, or all persons to be equally qualified for everything; but that freedom of individual choice is now known to be the only thing which procures the adoption of the best processes, and throws each operation into the hands of those who are best qualified for it. Nobody thinks it necessary to make a law that only a strong-armed man shall be a blacksmith. Freedom and competition suffice to make blacksmiths strong-armed men, because the weak-armed can earn more by engaging in occupations for which they are more fit. In consonance with this doctrine, it is felt to be an overstepping of the proper bounds of authority to fix beforehand, on some general presumption, that certain persons are not fit to do certain things. It is now thoroughly known and admitted that if some such presumptions exist, no such presumption is infallible. Even if it be well grounded in a majority of cases, which it is very likely not to be, there will be a minority of exceptional cases in which it does not hold: and in those it is both an injustice to the individuals, and a detriment to society, to place barriers in the way of their using their faculties for their own benefit and for that of others. In the cases, on the other hand, in which the unfitness is real, the ordinary motives of human conduct will on the whole suffice to prevent the incompetent person from making, or from persisting in, the attempt.

If this general principle of social and economical science is not true; if individuals, with such help as they can derive from the opinion of those who know them, are not better judges than the law and the government, of their own capacities and vocation; the world cannot too soon abandon this principle, and return to the old system of regulations and disabilities. But if the principle is true, we ought to act as if we believed it, and not to ordain that to be born a girl instead of a boy, any more than to be born black instead of white, or a commoner instead of a nobleman, shall decide the person's position through all life—shall interdict people from all the more elevated social positions, and from all, except a few, respectable occupations. Even were we to admit the utmost that is ever pretended as to the superior fitness of men for all the functions now reserved to them, the same argument applies which forbids a legal qualification for members of Parliament. If only once in a dozen years the conditions of eligibility exclude a fit person, there is a real loss, while the exclusion of thousands of unfit persons is no gain; for if the constitution of the electoral body disposes them to choose unfit persons, there are always plenty of such persons to choose from. In all things of any difficulty and importance, those who can do them well are fewer than the need, even with the most unrestricted latitude of choice: and any limitation of the field of selection deprives society of some chances of being served by the competent, without ever saving it from the incompetent.

At present, in the more improved countries, the disabilities of women are the only case, save one, in which laws and institutions take persons at their birth, and ordain that they shall never in all their lives be allowed to compete for certain things. The one exception is that of royalty. Persons still are born to the throne; no one, not of the reigning family, can ever occupy it, and no one even of that family can, by any means but the course of hereditary succession, attain it. All other dignities and social advantages are open to the whole male sex: many indeed are only attainable by wealth, but wealth may be striven for by any one, and is actually obtained by many men of the very humblest origin. The difficulties, to the majority, are indeed insuperable without the aid of fortunate accidents; but no male human being is under any legal ban: neither law nor opinion superadd artificial obstacles to the natural ones. Royalty, as I have said, is excepted: but in this case every one feels it to be an exception—an anomaly in the modern world, in marked opposition to its customs and principles, and to be justified only by extraordinary special expediencies, which, though individuals and nations differ in estimating their weight, unquestionably do in fact exist. But in this exceptional case, in which a high social function is, for important reasons, bestowed on birth instead of being put up to competition, all free nations contrive to adhere in substance to the principle from which they nominally derogate; for they circumscribe this high function by conditions avowedly intended to prevent the person to whom it ostensibly belongs from really performing it; while the person by whom it is performed, the responsible minister, does obtain the post by a competition from which no full-grown citizen of the male sex is legally excluded. The disabilities, therefore, to which women are subject from the mere fact of their birth, are the solitary examples of the kind in modern legislation. In no instance except this, which comprehends half the human race, are the higher social functions closed against any one by a fatality of birth which no exertions, and no change of circumstances, can overcome; for even religious disabilities (besides that in England and in Europe they have practically almost ceased to exist) do not close any career to the disqualified person in case of conversion.

The social subordination of women thus stands out an isolated fact in modern social institutions; a solitary breach of what has become their fundamental law; a single relic of an old world of thought and practice exploded in everything else, but retained in the one thing of most universal interest; as if a gigantic dolmen, or a vast temple of Jupiter Olympius, occupied the site of St. Paul's and received daily worship, while the surrounding Christian churches were only resorted to on fasts and festivals. This entire discrepancy between one social fact and all those which accompany it, and the radical opposition between its nature and the progressive movement which is the boast of the modern world, and which has successively swept away everything else of an analogous character, surely affords, to a conscientious observer of human tendencies, serious matter for reflection. It raises a prima facie presumption on the unfavourable side, far outweighing any which custom and usage could in such circumstances create on the favourable; and should at least suffice to make this, like the choice between republicanism and royalty, a balanced question.

The least that can be demanded is, that the question should not be considered as prejudged by existing fact and existing opinion, but open to discussion on its merits, as a question of justice and expediency: the decision on this, as on any of the other social arrangements of mankind, depending on what an enlightened estimate of tendencies and consequences may show to be most advantageous to humanity in general, without distinction of sex. And the discussion must be a real discussion, descending to foundations, and not resting satisfied with vague and general assertions. It will not do, for instance, to assert in general terms, that the experience of mankind has pronounced in favour of the existing system. Experience cannot possibly have decided between two courses, so long as there has only been experience of one. If it be said that the doctrine of the equality of the sexes rests only on theory, it must be remembered that the contrary doctrine also has only theory to rest upon. All that is proved in its favour by direct experience, is that mankind have been able to exist under it, and to attain the degree of improvement and prosperity which we now see; but whether that prosperity has been attained sooner, or is now greater, than it would have been under the other system, experience does not say. On the other hand, experience does say, that every step in improvement has been so invariably accompanied by a step made in raising the social position of women, that historians and philosophers have been led to adopt their elevation or debasement as on the whole the surest test and most correct measure of the civilization of a people or an age. Through all the progressive period of human history, the condition of women has been approaching nearer to equality with men. This does not of itself prove that the assimilation must go on to complete equality; but it assuredly affords some presumption that such is the case.

Neither does it avail anything to say that the *nature* of the two sexes adapts them to their present functions and position, and renders these appropriate to them. Standing on the ground of common sense and the constitution of the human mind, I deny that any one knows, or can know, the nature of the two sexes, as long as they have only been seen in their present relation to one another. If men had ever been found in society without women, or women without men, or if there had been a society of men and women in which the women were not under the control of the men, something might have been positively known about the mental and moral differences which may be inherent in the nature of each. What is now called the nature of women is an eminently artificial thing—the result of forced repression in some directions, unnatural stimulation in others. It may be asserted without scruple, that no other class of dependents have had their character so entirely distorted from its natural proportions by their relation with their masters; for, if conquered and slave races have been, in some respects, more forcibly repressed, whatever in them has not been crushed down by an iron heel has generally been let alone, and if left with any liberty of development, it has developed itself according to its own laws; but in the case of women, a hot-house and stove cultivation has always been carried on of some of the capabilities of their nature, for the benefit and pleasure of their masters. Then, because certain products of the general vital force sprout luxuriantly and reach a great development in this heated atmosphere and under this active nurture and watering, while other shoots from the same root, which are left outside in the wintry air, with ice purposely heaped all round them, have a stunted growth, and some are burnt off with fire and disappear; men, with that inability to recognise their own work which distinguishes the unanalytic mind, indolently believe that the tree grows of itself in the way they have made it grow, and that it would die if one half of it were not kept in a vapour bath and the other half in the snow.

Of all difficulties which impede the progress of thought, and the formation of well-grounded opinions on life and social arrangements, the greatest is now the unspeakable ignorance and inattention of mankind in respect to the influences which form human character. Whatever any portion of the human species now are, or seem to be, such, it is supposed, they have a natural tendency to be: even when the most elementary knowledge of the circumstances in which they have been placed, clearly points out the causes that made them what they are. Because a cottier deeply in arrears to his landlord is not industrious, there are people who think that the Irish are naturally idle. Because constitutions can be overthrown when the authorities appointed to execute them turn their arms against them, there are people who think the French incapable of free government. Because the Greeks cheated the Turks, and the Turks only plundered the Greeks, there are persons who think that the Turks are naturally more sincere: and because women, as is often said, care nothing about politics except their personalities, it is supposed that the general good is naturally less interesting to women than to men. History, which is now so much better understood than formerly, teaches another lesson: if only by showing the extraordinary susceptibility of human nature to external influences, and the extreme variableness of those of its manifestations which are supposed to be most universal and uniform. But in history, as in travelling, men usually see only what they already had in their own minds; and few learn much from history, who do not bring much with them to its study.

Hence, in regard to that most difficult question, what are the natural differences between the two sexes—a subject on which it is impossible in the present state of society to obtain complete and correct knowledge—while almost everybody dogmatizes upon it, almost all neglect and make light of the only means by which any partial insight can be obtained into it. This is, an analytic study of the most important department of psychology, the laws of the influence of circumstances on character. For, however great and apparently ineradicable the moral and intellectual differences between men and women might be, the evidence of their being natural differences could only be negative. Those only could be inferred to be natural which could not possibly be artificial—the residuum, after deducting every characteristic of either sex which can admit of being explained from education or external circumstances. The profoundest knowledge of the laws of the formation of character is indispensable to entitle any one to affirm even that there is any difference, much more what the difference is, between the two sexes considered as moral and rational beings; and since no one, as yet, has that knowledge, (for there is hardly any subject which, in proportion to its importance, has been so little studied), no one is thus far entitled to any positive opinion on the subject. Conjectures are all that can at present be made; conjectures more or less probable, according as more or less authorized by such knowledge as we yet have of the laws of psychology, as applied to the formation of character.

Even the preliminary knowledge, what the differences between the sexes now are, apart from all questions as to how they are made what they are, is still in the crudest and most incomplete state. Medical practitioners and physiologists have ascertained, to some extent, the differences in bodily constitution; and this is an important element to the psychologist: but hardly any medical practitioner is a psychologist. Respecting the mental characteristics of women; their observations are of no more worth than those of common men. It is a subject on which nothing final can be known, so long as those who alone can really know it, women themselves, have given but little testimony, and that little, mostly suborned. It is easy to know stupid women. Stupidity is much the same all the world over. A stupid person's notions and feelings may confidently be inferred from those which prevail in the circle by which the person is surrounded. Not so with those whose opinions and feelings are an emanation from their own nature and faculties. It is only a man here and there who has any tolerable knowledge of the character even of the women of his own family. I do not mean, of their capabilities; these nobody knows, not even themselves, because most of them have never been called out. I mean their actually existing thoughts and feelings. Many a man thinks he perfectly understands women, because he has had amatory relations with several, perhaps with many of them. If he is a good observer, and his experience extends to quality as well as quantity, he may have learnt something of one narrow department of their nature—an important department, no doubt. But of all the rest of it, few persons are generally more ignorant, because there are few from whom it is so carefully hidden. The most favourable case which a man can generally have for studying the character of a woman, is that of his own wife: for the opportunities are greater, and the cases of complete sympathy not so unspeakably rare. And in fact, this is the source from which any knowledge worth having on the subject has, I believe, generally come. But most men have not had the opportunity of studying in this way more than a single case: accordingly one can, to an almost laughable degree, infer what a man's wife is like, from his opinions about women in general. To make even this one case yield any result, the woman must be worth knowing, and the man not only a competent judge, but of a character so sympathetic in itself, and so well adapted to hers, that he can either read her mind by sympathetic intuition, or has nothing in himself which makes her shy of disclosing it. Hardly anything, I believe, can be more rare than this conjunction. It often happens that there is the most complete unity of feeling and community of interests as to all external things, yet the one has as little admission into the internal life of the other as if they were common acquaintance. Even with true affection, authority on the one side and subordination on the other prevent perfect confidence. Though nothing may be intentionally withheld, much is not shown. In the analogous relation of parent and child, the corresponding phenomenon must have been in the observation of every one. As between father and son, how many are the cases in which the father, in spite of real affection on both sides, obviously to all the world does not know, nor suspect, parts of the son's character familiar to his companions and equals. The truth is, that the position of looking up to another is extremely unpropitious to complete sincerity and openness with him. The fear of losing ground in his opinion or in his feelings is so strong, that even in an upright character, there is an unconscious tendency to show only the best side, or the side which, though not the best, is that which he most likes to see: and it may be confidently said that thorough knowledge of one another hardly ever exists, but between persons who, besides being intimates, are equals. How much more true, then, must all this be, when the one is not only under the authority of the other, but has it inculcated on her as a duty to reckon everything else subordinate to his comfort and pleasure, and to let him neither see nor feel anything coming from her, except what is agreeable to him. All these difficulties stand in the way of a man's obtaining any thorough knowledge even of the one woman whom alone, in general, he has sufficient opportunity of studying. When we further consider that to understand one woman is not necessarily to understand any other woman; that even if he could study many women of one rank, or of one country, he would not thereby understand women of other ranks or countries; and even if he did, they are still only the women of a single period of history; we may safely assert that the knowledge which men can acquire of women, even as they have been and are, without reference to what they might be, is wretchedly imperfect and superficial, and always will be so, until women themselves have told all that they have to tell.

And this time has not come; nor will it come otherwise than gradually. It is but of yesterday that women have either been qualified by literary accomplishments, or permitted by society, to tell anything to the general public. As yet very few of them dare tell anything, which men, on whom their literary success depends, are unwilling to hear. Let us remember in what manner, up to a very recent time, the expression, even by a male author, of uncustomary opinions, or what are deemed eccentric feelings, usually was, and in some degree still is, received; and we may form some faint conception under what impediments a woman, who is brought up to think custom and opinion her sovereign rule, attempts to express in books anything drawn from the depths of her own nature. The greatest woman who has left writings behind her sufficient to give her an eminent rank in the literature of her country, thought it necessary to prefix as a motto to her boldest work, "Un homme peut braver l'opinion; une femme doit s'y soumettre."[1] The greater part of what women write about women is mere sycophancy to men. In the case of unmarried women, much of it seems only intended to increase their chance of a husband. Many, both married and unmarried, overstep the mark, and inculcate a servility beyond what is desired or relished by any man, except the very vulgarest. But this is not so often the case as, even at a quite late period, it still was. Literary women are becoming more freespoken, and more willing to express their real sentiments. Unfortunately, in this country especially, they are themselves such artificial products, that their sentiments are compounded of a small element of individual observation and consciousness, and a very large one of acquired associations. This will be less and less the case, but it will remain true to a great extent, as long as social institutions do not admit the same free development of originality in women which is possible to men. When that time comes, and not before, we shall see, and not merely hear, as much as it is necessary to know of the nature of women, and the adaptation of other things to it.

I have dwelt so much on the difficulties which at present

1. Title page of Mme. de Stael's "Delphine."

obstruct any real knowledge by men of the true nature of women, because in this as in so many other things "opinio copiæ inter maximas causas inopiæ est"; and there is little chance of reasonable thinking on the matter, while people flatter themselves that they perfectly understand a subject of which most men know absolutely nothing, and of which it is at present impossible that any man, or all men taken together, should have knowledge which can qualify them to lay down the law to women as to what is, or is not, their vocation. Happily, no such knowledge is necessary for any practical purpose connected with the position of women in relation to society and life. For, according to all the principles involved in modern society, the question rests with women themselves —to be decided by their own experience, and by the use of their own faculties. There are no means of finding what either one person or many can do, but by trying—and no means by which any one else can discover for them what it is for their happiness to do or leave undone.

One thing we may be certain of—that what is contrary to women's nature to do, they never will be made to do by simply giving their nature free play. The anxiety of mankind to interfere in behalf of nature, for fear lest nature should not succeed in effecting its purpose, is an altogether unnecessary solicitude. What women by nature cannot do, it is quite superfluous to forbid them from doing. What they can do, but not so well as the men who are their competitors, competition suffices to exclude them from; since nobody asks for protective duties and bounties in favour of women; it is only asked that the present bounties and protective duties in favour of men should be recalled. If women have a greater natural inclination for some things than for others, there is no need of laws or social inculcation to make the majority of them do the former in preference to the latter. Whatever women's services are most wanted for, the free play of competition will hold out the strongest inducements to them to undertake. And, as the words imply, they are most wanted for the things for which they are most fit; by the apportionment of which to them, the collective faculties of the two sexes can be applied on the whole with the greatest sum of valuable result.

The general opinion of men is supposed to be, that the natural vocation of a woman is that of a wife and mother. I say, is supposed to be, because, judging from acts—from the whole of the present constitution of society—one might infer that their opinion was the direct contrary. They might be supposed to think that the alleged natural vocation of women was of all things the most repugnant to their nature; insomuch that if they are free to do anything else—if any other means of living, or occupation of their time and faculties, is open, which has any chance of appearing desirable to them—there will not be enough of them who will be willing to accept the condition said to be natural to them. If this is the real opinion of men in general, it would be well that it should be spoken out. I should like to hear somebody openly enunciating the doctrine (it is already implied in much that is written on the subject)— "It is necessary to society that women should marry and produce children. They will not do so unless they are compelled. Therefore it is necessary to compel them." The merits of the case would then be clearly defined. It would be exactly that of the slaveholders of South Carolina and Louisiana. "It is necessary that cotton and sugar should be grown. White men cannot produce them. Negroes will not, for any wages which we choose to give. *Ergo* they must be compelled." An illustration still closer to the point is that of impressment. Sailors must absolutely be had to defend the country. It often happens that they will not voluntarily enlist. Therefore there must be the power of forcing them. How often has this logic been used! and, but for one flaw in it, without doubt it would have been successful up to this day. But it is open to the retort— First pay the sailors the honest value of their labour. When you have made it as well worth their while to serve you, as to work for other employers, you will have no more difficulty than others have in obtaining their services. To this there is no logical answer except "I will not": and as people are now not only ashamed, but are not desirous, to rob the labourer of his hire, impressment is no longer advocated. Those who attempt to force women into marriage by closing all other doors against them, lay themselves open to a similar retort. If they mean what they say, their opinion must evidently be, that men do not render the married condition so desirable to women, as to induce them to accept it for its own recommendations. It is not a sign of one's thinking the boon one offers very attractive, when one allows only Hobson's choice, "that or none." And here, I believe, is the clue to the feelings of those men, who have a real antipathy to the equal freedom of women. I believe they are afraid, not lest women should be unwilling to marry, for I do not think that any one in reality has that apprehension; but lest they should insist that marriage should be on equal conditions; lest all women of spirit and capacity should prefer doing almost anything else, not in their own eyes degrading, rather than marry, when marrying is giving themselves a master, and a master too of all their earthly possessions. And truly, if this consequence were necessarily incident to marriage, I think that the apprehension would be very well founded. I agree in thinking it probable that few women, capable of anything else, would, unless under an irresistible *entrainement,* rendering them for the time insensible to anything but itself, choose such a lot, when any other means were open to them of filling a conventionally honourable place in life: and if men are determined that the law of marriage shall be a law of despotism, they are quite right, in point of mere policy, in leaving to women only Hobson's choice. But, in that case, all that has been done in the modern world to relax the chain on the minds of women, has been a mistake. They never should have been allowed to receive a literary education. Women who read, much more women who write, are, in the existing constitution of things, a contradiction and a disturbing element: and it was wrong to bring women up with any acquirements but those of an odalisque, or of a domestic servant.

2

t will be well to commence the detailed
discussion of the subject by the
particular branch of it to which the
course of our observations has led us:
the conditions which the laws of this
and all other countries annex to the
marriage contract. Marriage being the
destination appointed by society
for women, the prospect they are
brought up to, and the object which
it is intended should be sought by all
of them, except those who are too
little attractive to be chosen by any
man as his companion; one might have
supposed that everything would have
been done to make this condition
as eligible to them as possible, that
they might have no cause to regret
being denied the option of any other.
Society, however, both in this, and,
at first, in all other cases, has preferred
to attain its object by foul rather than
fair means: but this is the only case
in which it has substantially persisted
in them even to the present day.
Originally women were taken by force,
or regularly sold by their father to
the husband. Until a late period in
European history, the father had the

power to dispose of his daughter in marriage at his own will
and pleasure, without any regard to hers. The Church, indeed,
was so far faithful to a better morality as to require a formal
"yes" from the woman at the marriage ceremony; but there
was nothing to shew that the consent was other than com-
pulsory; and it was practically impossible for the girl to refuse
compliance if the father persevered, except perhaps when she
might obtain the protection of religion by a determined resolution to take monastic vows. After marriage, the man had
anciently (but this was anterior to Christianity) the power
of life and death over his wife. She could invoke no law
against him; he was her sole tribunal and law. For a long
time he could repudiate her, but she had no corresponding
power in regard to him. By the old laws of England, the husband was called the *lord* of the wife; he was literally regarded
as her sovereign, inasmuch that the murder of a man by his
wife was called treason (*petty* as distinguished from *high* treason), and was more cruelly avenged than was usually the case
with high treason, for the penalty was burning to death. Because the various enormities have fallen into disuse (for most
of them were never formally abolished, or not until they had
long ceased to be practised) men suppose that all is now as it
should be in regard to the marriage contract; and we are continually told that civilization and Christianity have restored to
the woman her just rights. Meanwhile the wife is the actual
bond-servant of her husband: no less so, as far as legal obligation goes, than slaves commonly so called. She vows a life-
long obedience to him at the altar, and is held to it all through
her life by law. Casuists may say that the obligation of obedience stops short of participation in crime, but it certainly
extends to everything else. She can do no act whatever but
by his permission, at least tacit. She can acquire no property
but for him; the instant it becomes hers, even if by inheritance,
it becomes *ipso facto* his. In this respect the wife's position
under the common law of England is worse than that of slaves
in the laws of many countries: by the Roman law, for example, a slave might have his peculium, which to a certain

extent the law guaranteed to him for his exclusive use. The higher classes in this country have given an analogous advantage to their women, through special contracts setting aside the law, by conditions of pin-money, etc.: since parental feeling being stronger with fathers than the class feeling of their own sex, a father generally prefers his own daughter to a son-in-law who is a stranger to him. By means of settlements, the rich usually contrive to withdraw the whole or part of the inherited property of the wife from the absolute control of the husband: but they do not succeed in keeping it under her own control; the utmost they can do only prevents the husband from squandering it, at the same time debarring the rightful owner from its use. The property itself is out of the reach of both; and as to the income derived from it, the form of settlement most favourable to the wife (that called "to her separate use") only precludes the husband from receiving it instead of her: it must pass through her hands, but if he takes it from her by personal violence as soon as she receives it, he can neither be punished, nor compelled to restitution. This is the amount of the protection which, under the laws of this country, the most powerful nobleman can give to his own daughter as respects her husband. In the immense majority of cases there is no settlement: and the absorption of all rights, all property, as well as all freedom of action, is complete. The two are called "one person in law," for the purpose of inferring that whatever is hers is his, but the parallel inference is never drawn that whatever is his is hers; the maxim is not applied against the man, except to make him responsible to third parties for her acts, as a master is for the acts of his slaves or of his cattle. I am far from pretending that wives are in general no better treated than slaves; but no slave is a slave to the same lengths, and in so full a sense of the word, as a wife is. Hardly any slave, except one immediately attached to the master's person, is a slave at all hours and all minutes; in general he has, like a soldier, his fixed task, and when it is done, or when he is off duty, he disposes, within certain limits, of his own time, and has a family life into which the master rarely intrudes. "Uncle Tom" under his first master had his own life in his "cabin," almost as much as any man whose work takes him away from home, is able to have in his own family. But it cannot be so with the wife. Above all, a female slave has (in Christian countries) an admitted right, and is considered under a moral obligation, to refuse to her master the last familiarity. Not so the wife: however brutal a tyrant she may unfortunately be chained to—though she may know that he hates her, though it may be his daily pleasure to torture her, and though she may feel it impossible not to loathe him—he can claim from her and enforce the lowest degradation of a human being, that of being made the instrument of an animal function contrary to her inclinations. While she is held in this worst description of slavery as to her own person, what is her position in regard to the children in whom she and her master have a joint interest? They are by law *his* children. He alone has any legal rights over them. Not one act can she do towards or in relation to them, except by delegation from him. Even after he is dead she is not their legal guardian, unless he by will has made her so. He could even send them away from her, and deprive her of the means of seeing or corresponding with them, until this power was in some degree restricted by Serjeant Talfourd's Act. This is her legal state. And from this state she has no means of withdrawing herself. If she leaves her husband, she can take nothing with her, neither her children nor anything which is rightfully her own. If he chooses, he can compel her to return, by law, or by physical force; or he may content himself with seizing for his own use anything which she may earn, or which may be given to her by her relations. It is only legal separation by a decree of a court of justice, which entitles her to live apart, without being forced back into the custody of an exasperated jailer—or which empowers her to apply any earnings to her own use, without fear that a man whom perhaps she has not seen for twenty years will pounce upon her some day and carry all off. This legal separation, until lately, the courts of justice would only give at an expense which made it inaccessible to any one out of the higher ranks. Even now it is only given in cases of desertion, or of the extreme of cruelty; and yet complaints are made every day that it is granted too easily. Surely, if a woman is denied any lot in life but that of being the personal body-servant of a despot, and is dependent for everything upon the chance of finding one who may be disposed to make a favourite of her instead of merely a drudge, it is a very cruel aggravation of her fate that she should be allowed to try this chance only once. The natural sequel and corollary from this state of things would be, that since her all in life depends upon obtaining a good master, she should be allowed to change again and again until she finds one. I am not saying that she ought to be allowed this privilege. That is a totally different consideration. The question of divorce, in the sense involving liberty of remarriage, is one into which it is foreign to my purpose to enter. All I now say is, that to those to whom nothing but servitude is allowed, the free choice of servitude is the only, though a most insufficient, alleviation. Its refusal completes the assimilation of the wife to the slave—and the slave under not the mildest form of slavery: for in some slave codes the slave could, under certain circumstances of ill usage, legally compel the master to sell him. But no amount of ill usage, without adultery superadded, will in England free a wife from her tormentor.

I have no desire to exaggerate, nor does the case stand in any need of exaggeration. I have described the wife's legal position, not her actual treatment. The laws of most countries are far worse than the people who execute them, and many of them are only able to remain laws by being seldom or never carried into effect. If married life were all that it might be expected to be, looking to the laws alone, society would be a hell upon earth. Happily there are both feelings and interests which in many men exclude, and in most, greatly temper, the impulses and propensities which lead to tyranny: and of those feelings, the tie which connects a man with his wife affords, in a normal state of things, incomparably the strongest example. The only tie which at all approaches to it, that between him and his children, tends, in all save exceptional cases, to strengthen, instead of conflicting with, the first. Because this is true; because men in general do not inflict, nor women suffer, all the misery which could be inflicted and suffered if the full power of tyranny with which the man is legally invested were acted on; the defenders of the existing form of the institution think that all its iniquity is justified, and that any complaint is merely quarrelling with the evil which is the price paid for every great good. But the mitigations in practice, which are compatible with maintaining in full legal force this or any other kind of tyranny, instead of being any apology for despotism, only serve to prove what power human nature possesses of reacting against the vilest institutions, and with what vitality the seeds of good as well as those of evil in human character diffuse and propagate themselves. Not a word can be said for despotism in the family which cannot be said for political despotism. Every absolute king does not sit at his window to enjoy the groans of his tortured subjects, nor strips them of their last rag and turns them out to shiver in the road. The despotism of Louis XVI was not the despotism of Philippe le Bel, or of Nadir Shah, or of Caligula; but it was bad enough to justify the French Revolution, and to palliate even its horrors. If an appeal be made to the intense attachments which exist between wives and their husbands, exactly as much may be said of domestic slavery. It was quite an ordinary fact in Greece and Rome for slaves to submit to death by torture rather than betray their masters. In the proscriptions of the Roman civil wars it was remarked that wives and slaves were heroically faithful, sons very commonly treacherous. Yet we know how cruelly many Romans treated their slaves. But in truth these intense individual feelings nowhere rise to such a luxuriant height as under the most atrocious institutions. It is part of the irony of life, that the strongest feelings of devoted gratitude of which human nature seems to be susceptible, are called forth in human beings towards those who, having the power entirely to crush their earthly existence, voluntarily refrain from using that power. How great a place in most men this sentiment fills, even in religious devotion, it would be cruel to inquire. We daily see how much their gratitude to Heaven appears to be stimulated by the contemplation of fellow-creatures to whom God has not been so merciful as he has to themselves.

Whether the institution to be defended is slavery, political absolution, or the absolutism of the head of a family, we are always expected to judge of it from its best instances; and we are presented with pictures of loving exercise of authority on one side, loving submission to it on the other—superior wisdom ordering all things for the greatest good of the dependents, and surrounded by their smiles and benedictions. All this would be very much to the purpose if any one pretended that there are no such things as good men. Who doubts that there may be great goodness, and great happiness, and great affection, under the absolute government of a good man? Meanwhile, laws and institutions require to be adapted, not to good men, but to bad. Marriage is not an institution designed for a select few. Men are not required, as a preliminary to the marriage ceremony, to prove by testimonials that they are fit to be trusted with the exercise of absolute power. The tie of affection and obligation to a wife and children is very strong with those whose general social feelings are strong, and with many who are little sensible to any other social ties; but there are all degrees of sensibility and insensibility to it, as there are all grades of goodness and wickedness in men, down to those whom no ties will bind, and on whom society has no action but through its *ultima ratio,* the penalties of the law. In every grade of this descending scale are men to whom are committed all the legal powers of a husband. The vilest malefactor has some wretched woman tied to him, against whom he can commit any atrocity except killing her, and, if tolerably cautious, can do that without much danger of the legal penalty. And how many thousands are there among the lowest classes in every country, who, without being in a legal sense malefactors in any other respect, because in every other quarter their aggressions meet with resistance, indulge the utmost habitual excesses of bodily violence towards the unhappy wife, who alone, at least of grown persons, can neither repel nor escape from their brutality; and towards whom the excess of dependence inspires their mean and savage natures, not with a generous forbearance, and a point of honour to behave well to one whose lot in life is trusted entirely to their kindness, but on the contrary with a notion that the law has delivered her to them as their thing, to be used at their pleasure, and that they are not expected to practise the consideration towards her which is required from them towards everybody else. The law, which till lately left even these atrocious extremes of domestic oppression practically unpunished, has within these few years made some feeble attempts to repress them. But its attempts have done little, and cannot be expected to do much, because it is contrary to reason and experience to suppose that there can be any real check to brutality, consistent with leaving the victim still in the power of the executioner. Until a conviction for personal violence, or at all events a repetition of it after a first conviction, entitles the woman *ipso facto* to a divorce, or at least to a judicial separation, the attempt to repress these "aggravated assaults" by legal penalties will break down for want of a prosecutor, or for want of a witness.

When we consider how vast is the number of men, in any great country, who are little higher than brutes, and that this never prevents them from being able, through the law of marriage, to obtain a victim, the breadth and depth of human misery caused in this shape alone by the abuse of the institution swells to something appalling. Yet these are only the extreme cases. They are the lowest abysses, but there is a sad succession of depth after depth before reaching them. In domestic as in political tyranny the case of absolute monsters chiefly illustrates the institution by showing that there is scarcely any horror which may not occur under it if the despot pleases, and thus setting in a strong light what must be the terrible frequency of things only a little less atrocious. Absolute fiends are as rare as angels, perhaps rarer: ferocious savages, with occasional touches of humanity, are however very frequent: and in the wide interval which separates these from any worthy representatives of the human species, how many are the forms and gradations of animalism and selfishness, often under an outward varnish of civilization and even cultivation, living at peace with the law, maintaining a creditable appearance to all who are not under their power, yet sufficient often to make the lives of all who are so, a torment and a burthen to them! It would be tiresome to repeat the commonplaces about the unfitness of men in general for power, which, after the political discussions of centuries, every one knows by heart, were it not that hardly any one thinks of applying these maxims to the case in which above all others they are applicable, that of power, not placed in the hands of a man here and there, but offered to every adult male, down to the basest and most ferocious. It is not because a man is not known to have broken any of the Ten Commandments, or because he maintains a respectable character in his dealings with those whom he cannot compel to have intercourse with him, or because he does not fly out into violent bursts of ill-temper against those who are not obliged to bear with him, that it is possible to surmise of what sort his conduct will be in the unrestraint of home. Even the commonest men reserve the violent, the sulky, the undisguisedly selfish side of their character for those who have no power to withstand it. The relation of superiors to dependents is the nursery of these vices of character, which, wherever else they exist, are an overflowing from that source. A man who is morose or violent to his equals, is sure to be one who has lived among inferiors, whom he could frighten or worry into submission. If the family in its best forms is, as it is often said to be, a school of sympathy, tenderness, and loving forgetfulness of self, it is still oftener, as respects its chief, a school of wilfulness, overbearingness, unbounded self-indulgence, and a double-dyed and idealized selfishness, of which sacrifice itself is only a particular form: the care for the wife and children being only care for them as parts of the man's own interests and belongings, and their individual happiness being immolated in every shape to his smallest preferences. What better is to be looked for under the existing form of the institution? We know that the bad propensities of human nature are only kept within bounds when they are allowed no scope for their indulgence. We know that from impulse and habit, when not from deliberate purpose, almost every one to whom others yield, goes on encroaching upon them, until a point is reached at which they are compelled to resist. Such being the common tendency of human nature; the almost unlimited power which present social institutions give to the man over at least one human being—the one with whom he resides, and whom he has always present—this power seeks out and evokes the latent germs of selfishness in the remotest corners of his nature—fans its faintest sparks and smouldering embers—offers to him a license for the indulgence of those points of his original character which in all other relations he would have found it necessary to repress and conceal, and the repression of which would in time have become a second nature. I know that there is another side to the question. I grant that the wife, if she cannot effectually resist, can at least retaliate; she, too, can make the man's life extremely uncomfortable, and by that power is able to carry many points which she ought, and many which she ought not, to prevail in. But this instrument of self-protection—which may be called the power of the scold, or the shrewish sanction—has the fatal defect, that it avails most against the least tyrannical superiors, and in favour of the least deserving dependents. It is the weapon of irritable and self-willed women; of those who would make the worst use of power if they themselves had it, and who generally turn this power to a bad use. The amiable cannot use such an instrument, the highminded disdain it. And on the other hand, the husbands against whom it is used most effectively are the gentler and more inoffensive; those who cannot be induced, even by provocation, to resort to any very

harsh exercise of authority. The wife's power of being disagreeable generally only establishes a counter-tyranny, and
makes victims in their turn chiefly of those husbands who are
least inclined to be tyrants.

What is it, then, which really tempers the corrupting effects
of the power, and makes it compatible with such amount of
good as we actually see? Mere feminine blandishments, though
of great effect in individual instances, have very little effect
in modifying the general tendencies of the situation; for their
power only lasts while the woman is young and attractive,
often only while her charm is new, and not dimmed by familiarity; and on many men they have not much influence at any
time. The real mitigating causes are, the personal affection
which is the growth of time, in so far as the man's nature is
susceptible of it, and the woman's character sufficiently congenial with his to excite it; their common interests as regards
the children, and their general community of interest as concerns third persons (to which however there are very great
limitations); the real importance of the wife to his daily comforts and enjoyments, and the value he consequently attaches
to her on his personal account, which, in a man capable of
feeling for others, lays the foundation of caring for her on
her own; and lastly, the influence naturally acquired over almost all human beings by those near to their persons (if not
actually disagreeable to them): who, both by their direct
entreaties, and by the insensible contagion of their feelings
and dispositions, are often able, unless counteracted by some
equally strong personal influence, to obtain a degree of command over the conduct of the superior, altogether excessive
and unreasonable. Through these various means, the wife frequently exercises even too much power over the man; she is
able to affect his conduct in things in which she may not be
qualified to influence it for good—in which her influence may
be not only unenlightened, but employed on the morally wrong
side; and in which he would act better if left to his own prompt-
ing. But neither in the affairs of families nor in those of states
is power a compensation for the loss of freedom. Her power

often gives her what she has no right to, but does not enable her to assert her own rights. A Sultan's favourite slave has slaves under her, over whom she tyrannizes; but the desirable thing would be that she should neither have slaves nor be a slave. By entirely sinking her own existence in her husband; by having no will (or persuading him that she has no will) but his, in anything which regards their joint relation, and by making it the business of her life to work upon his sentiments, a wife may gratify herself by influencing, and very probably perverting, his conduct, in those of his external relations which she has never qualified herself to judge of, or in which she is herself wholly influenced by some personal or other partiality or prejudice. Accordingly, as things now are, those who act most kindly to their wives, are quite as often made worse, as better, by the wife's influence, in respect to all interests extending beyond the family. She is taught that she has no business with things out of that sphere; and accordingly she seldom has any honest and conscientious opinion on them; and therefore hardly ever meddles with them for any legitimate purpose, but generally for an interested one. She neither knows nor cares which is the right side in politics, but she knows what will bring in money or invitations, give her husband a title, her son a place, or her daughter a good marriage.

But how, it will be asked, can any society exist without government? In a family, as in a state, some one person must be the ultimate ruler. Who shall decide when married people differ in opinion? Both cannot have their way, yet a decision one way or the other must be come to.

It is not true that in all voluntary association between two people, one of them must be absolute master: still less that the law must determine which of them it shall be. The most frequent case of voluntary association, next to marriage, is partnership in business: and it is not found or thought necessary to enact that in every partnership, one partner shall have entire control over the concern, and the others shall be bound to obey his orders. No one would enter into partnership on terms which would subject him to the responsibilities of a principal, with only the powers and privileges of a clerk or agent. If the law dealt with other contracts as it does with marriage, it would ordain that one partner should administer the common business as if it was his private concern; that the others should have only delegated powers; and that this one should be designated by some general presumption of law, for example as being the eldest. The law never does this: nor does experience show it to be necessary that any theoretical inequality of power should exist between the partners, or that the partnership should have any other conditions than what they may themselves appoint by their articles of agreement. Yet it might seem that the exclusive power might be conceded with less danger to the rights and interests of the inferior, in the case of partnership than in that of marriage, since he is free to cancel the power by withdrawing from the connexion. The wife has no such power, and even if she had, it is almost always desirable that she should try all measures before resorting to it.

It is quite true that things which have to be decided every day, and cannot adjust themselves gradually, or wait for a compromise, ought to depend on one will: one person must have their sole control. But it does not follow that this should always be the same person. The natural arrangement is a division of powers between the two; each being absolute in the executive branch of their own department, and any change of system and principle requiring the consent of both. The division neither can nor should be pre-established by the law, since it must depend on individual capacities and suitabilities. If the two persons chose, they might pre-appoint it by the marriage contract, as pecuniary arrangements are now often pre-appointed. There would seldom be any difficulty in deciding such things by mutual consent, unless the marriage was one of those unhappy ones in which all other things as well as this, become subjects of bickering and dispute. The division of rights would naturally follow the division of duties and functions; and that is already made by consent, or at all events not by law, but by general custom, modified and modifiable at the pleasure of the persons concerned.

The real practical decision of affairs, to whichever may be given the legal authority, will greatly depend, as it even now does, upon comparative qualifications. The mere fact that he is usually the eldest, will in most cases give the preponderance to the man; at least until they both attain a time of life at which the difference in their years is of no importance. There will naturally also be a more potential voice on the side, whichever it is, that brings the means of support. Inequality from this source does not depend on the law of marriage, but on the general conditions of human society, as now constituted. The influence of mental superiority, either general or special, and of superior decision of character, will necessarily tell for much. It always does so at present. And this fact shows how little foundation there is for the apprehension that the powers and responsibilities of partners in life (as of partners in business), cannot be satisfactorily apportioned by agreement between themselves. They always are so apportioned, except in cases in which the marriage institution is a failure. Things never come to an issue of downright power on one side, and obedience on the other, except where the connexion altogether has been a mistake, and it would be a blessing to both parties to be relieved from it. Some may say that the very thing by which an amicable settlement of differences becomes possible, is the power of legal compulsion known to be in reserve; as people submit to an arbitration because there is a court of law in the background, which they know that they can be forced to obey. But to make the cases parallel, we must suppose that the rule of the court of law was, not to try the cause, but to give judgment always for the same side, suppose the defendant. If so, the amenability to it would be a motive with the plaintiff to agree to almost any arbitration, but it would be just the reverse with the defendant. The despotic power which the law gives to the husband may be a reason to make the wife assent to any compromise by which power is practically shared between the two, but it cannot be the reason why the husband does. That there is always among decently conducted people a practical compromise, though one of them at least is under no physical or moral necessity of making it, shows that the natural motives which lead to a voluntary adjustment of the united life of two persons in a manner acceptable to both, do on the whole, except in unfavourable cases, prevail. The matter is certainly not improved by laying down as an ordinance of law, that the superstructure of free government shall be raised upon a legal basis of despotism on one side and subjection on the other, and that every concession which the despot makes may, at his mere pleasure, and without any warning, be recalled. Besides that no freedom is worth much when held on so precarious a tenure, its conditions are not likely to be the most equitable when the law throws so prodigious a weight into one scale; when the adjustment rests between two persons one of whom is declared to be entitled to everything, the other not only entitled to nothing except during the good pleasure of the first, but under the strongest moral and religious obligation not to rebel under any excess of oppression.

A pertinacious adversary, pushed to extremities, may say, that husbands indeed are willing to be reasonable, and to make fair concessions to their partners without being compelled to it, but that wives are not: that if allowed any rights of their own, they will acknowledge no rights at all in any one else, and never will yield in anything, unless they can be compelled, by the man's mere authority, to yield in everything. This would have been said by many persons some generations ago, when satires on women were in vogue, and men thought it a clever thing to insult women for being what men made them. But it will be said by no one now who is worth replying to. It is not the doctrine of the present day that women are less susceptible of good feeling, and consideration for those with whom they are united by the strongest ties, than men are. On the contrary, we are perpetually told that women are better than men, by those who are totally opposed to treating them as if they were as good; so that the saying has passed into a piece of tiresome cant, intended to put a complimentary face upon an injury, and resembling those celebrations of royal clemency which, according to Gulliver, the king of Lilliput always prefixed to his most sanguinary decrees. If women are better than men in anything, it surely is in individual self-sacrifice for those of their own family. But I lay little stress on this, so long as they are universally taught that they are born and created for self-sacrifice. I believe that equality of rights would abate the exaggerated self-abnegation which is the present artificial ideal of feminine character, and that a good woman would not be more self-sacrificing than the best man: but on the other hand, men would be much more un-selfish and self-sacrificing than at present, because they would no longer be taught to worship their own will as such a grand thing that it is actually the law for another rational being. There is nothing which men so easily learn as this self-worship: all privileged persons, and all privileged classes, have had it. The more we descend in the scale of humanity, the intenser it is; and most of all in those who are not, and can never ex-pect to be, raised above any one except an unfortunate wife and children. The honourable exceptions are proportionally fewer than in the case of almost any other human infirmity. Philosophy and religion, instead of keeping it in check, are generally suborned to defend it; and nothing controls it but that practical feeling of the equality of human beings, which is the theory of Christianity, but which Christianity will never practically teach, while it sanctions institutions grounded on an arbitrary preference of one human being over another.

There are, no doubt, women, as there are men, whom equal-ity of consideration will not satisfy; with whom there is no peace while any will or wish is regarded but their own. Such persons are a proper subject for the law of divorce. They are only fit to live alone, and no human beings ought to be com-pelled to associate their lives with them. But the legal sub-ordination tends to make such characters among women more, rather than less, frequent. If the man exerts his whole power, the woman is of course crushed: but if she is treated with indulgence, and permitted to assume power, there is no rule to set limits to her encroachments. The law, not determining her rights, but theoretically allowing her none at all, practically declares that the measure of what she has a right to, is what she can contrive to get.

The equality of married persons before the law, is not only the sole mode in which that particular relation can be made consistent with justice to both sides, and conducive to the happiness of both, but it is the only means of rendering the daily life of mankind, in any high sense, a school of moral cultivation. Though the truth may not be felt or generally acknowledged for generations to come, the only school of genuine moral sentiment is society between equals. The moral education of mankind has hitherto emanated chiefly from the law of force, and is adapted almost solely to the relations which force creates. In the less advanced states of society, people hardly recognise any relation with their equals. To be an equal is to be an enemy. Society, from its highest place to its lowest, is one long chain, or rather ladder, where every individual is either above or below his nearest neighbour, and wherever he does not command he must obey. Existing moralities accordingly, are mainly fitted to a relation of command and obedience. Yet command and obedience are but unfortunate necessities of human life: society in equality is its normal state. Already in modern life, and more and more as it progressively improves, command and obedience become exceptional facts in life, equal association its general rule. The morality of the first ages rested on the obligation to submit to power; that of the ages next following, on the right of the weak to the forbearance and protection of the strong. How much longer is one form of society and life to content itself with the morality made for another? We have had the morality of submission, and the morality of chivalry and generosity; the time is now come for the morality of justice. Whenever, in former ages, any approach has been made to society in equality, Justice has asserted its claims as the foundation of virtue. It was thus in the free republics of antiquity. But even in the best of these, the equals were limited to the free male citizens; slaves, women, and the unenfranchised residents were under the law of force. The joint influence of Roman civilization and of Christianity obliterated these distinctions, and in theory (if only partially in practice) declared the claims of the human being, as such, to be paramount to those of sex, class, or social position. The barriers which had begun to be levelled were raised again by the northern conquests; and the whole of modern history consists of the slow process by which they have since been wearing away. We are entering into an order of things in which justice will again be the primary virtue; grounded as before on equal, but now also on sympathetic association; having its root no longer in the instinct of equals for self-protection, but in a cultivated sympathy between them; and no one being now left out, but an equal measure being extended to all. It is no novelty that mankind do not distinctly foresee their own changes, and that their sentiments are adapted to past, not to coming ages. To see the futurity of the species has always been the privilege of the intellectual élite, or of those who have learnt from them; to have the feelings of that futurity has been the distinction, and usually the martyrdom, of a still rarer élite. Institutions, books, education, society, all go on training human beings for the old, long after the new has come; much more when it is only coming. But the true virtue of human beings is fitness to live together as equals; claiming nothing for themselves but what they as freely concede to every one else; regarding command of any kind as an exceptional necessity, and in all cases a temporary one; and preferring, whenever possible, the society of those with whom leading and following can be alternate and reciprocal. To these virtues, nothing in life as at present constituted gives cultivation by exercise. The family is a school of despotism, in which the virtues of despotism, but also its vices, are largely nourished. Citizenship, in free countries, is partly a school of society in equality; but citizenship fills only a small place in modern life, and does not come near the daily habits or inmost sentiments. The family, justly constituted, would be the real school of the virtues of freedom. It is sure to be a sufficient one of everything else. It will always be a school of obedience for the children, of command for the parents. What is needed is, that it should be a school of sympathy in equality, of living together in love, without power on one side or obedience on the other. This it ought to be between the parents. It would then be an exercise of those virtues which each requires to fit them for all other association, and a model to the children of the feelings and conduct which their temporary training by means of obedience is designed to render habitual, and therefore natural, to them. The moral training of mankind will never be adapted to the conditions of the life for which all other human progress is a preparation, until they practise in the family the same moral rule which is adapted to the normal constitution of human society. Any sentiment of freedom which can exist in a man whose nearest and dearest intimacies are with those of whom he is absolute master, is not the genuine or Christian love of freedom, but, what the love of freedom generally was in the ancients and in the middle ages—an intense feeling of the dignity and importance of his own personality; making him disdain a yoke for himself, of which he has no abhorrence whatever in the abstract, but which he is abundantly ready to impose on others for his own interest or glorification.

I readily admit (and it is the very foundation of my hopes) that numbers of married people even under the present law, (in the higher classes of England probably a great majority), live in the spirit of a just law of equality. Laws never would be improved, if there were not numerous persons whose moral sentiments are better than the existing laws. Such persons ought to support the principles here advocated; of which the only object is to make all other married couples similar to what these are now. But persons even of considerable moral worth, unless they are also thinkers, are very ready to believe that laws or practices, the evils of which they have not personally experienced, do not produce any evils, but (if seeming to be generally approved of) probably do good, and that it is wrong to object to them. It would, however, be a great mistake in such married people to suppose, because the legal conditions of the tie which unites them do not occur to their thoughts once in a twelvemonth, and because they live and feel in all respects as if they were legally equals, that the same is the case with all other married couples, wherever the husband is not a notorious ruffian. To suppose this, would be to show equal ignorance of human nature and of fact. The less fit a man is for the possession of power—the less likely to be allowed to exercise it over any person with that person's voluntary consent—the more 'does he hug himself in the consciousness of the power the law gives him, exact its legal rights to the utmost point which custom (the custom of men like himself) will tolerate, and take pleasure in using the power, merely to enliven the agreeable sense of possessing it. What is more; in the most naturally brutal and morally uneducated part of the lower classes, the legal slavery of the woman, and something in the merely physical subjection to their will as an instrument, causes them to feel a sort of disrespect and contempt towards their own wife which they do not feel towards any other woman, or any other human being, with whom they come in contact; and which makes her seem to them an appropriate subject for any kind of indignity. Let an acute observer of the signs of feeling, who has the requisite opportunities, judge for himself whether this is not the case: and if he finds that it is, let him not wonder at any amount of disgust and indignation that can be felt against institutions which lead naturally to this depraved state of the human mind.

We shall be told, perhaps, that religion imposes the duty of obedience; as every established fact which is too bad to admit of any other defence, is always presented to us as an injunction of religion. The Church, it is very true, enjoins it in her formularies, but it would be difficult to derive any such injunction from Christianity. We are told that St. Paul said, "Wives, obey your husbands:" but he also said, "Slaves, obey your masters." It was not St. Paul's business, nor was it consistent with his object, the propagation of Christianity, to incite any one to rebellion against existing laws. The apostle's acceptance of all social institutions as he found them, is no more to be construed as a disapproval of attempts to improve them at the proper time, than his declaration, "The powers that be are ordained of God," gives his sanction to military despotism, and to that alone, as the Christian form of political government, or commands passive obedience to it. To pretend that Christianity was intended to stereotype existing forms of government and society, and protect them against change, is to reduce it to the level of Islamism or of Brahminism. It is precisely because Christianity has not done this, that it has been the religion of the progressive portion of mankind, and Islamism, Brahminism, etc., have been those of the stationary portions; or rather (for there is no such thing as a really stationary society) of the declining portions. There have been abundance of people, in all ages of Christianity, who tried to make it something of the same kind; to convert us into a sort of Christian Mussulmans, with the Bible for a Koran, prohibiting all improvement: and great has been their power, and many have had to sacrifice their lives in resisting them. But they have been resisted, and the resistance has made us what we are, and will yet make us what we are to be.

After what has been said respecting the obligation of obedience, it is almost superfluous to say anything concerning the more special point included in the general one—a woman's right to her own property; for I need not hope that this treatise can make any impression upon those who need anything to convince them that a woman's inheritance or gains ought to be as much her own after marriage as before. The rule is simple: whatever would be the husband's or wife's if they were not married, should be under their exclusive control during marriage; which need not interfere with the power to tie up property by settlement, in order to preserve it for children. Some people are sentimentally shocked at the idea of a separate interest in money matters, as inconsistent with the ideal fusion of two lives into one. For my own part, I am one of the strongest supporters of community of goods, when resulting from an entire unity of feeling in the owners, which makes all things common between them. But I have no relish for a community of goods resting on the doctrine, that what is mine is yours but what is yours is not mine; and I should prefer to decline entering into such a compact with any one, though I were myself the person to profit by it.

This particular injustice and oppression to women, which is, to common apprehensions, more obvious than all the rest, admits of remedy without interfering with any other mischiefs: and there can be little doubt that it will be one of the earliest remedied. Already, in many of the new and several of the old States of the American Confederation, provisions have been inserted even in the written Constitutions, securing to women equality of rights in this respect: and thereby improving materially the position, in the marriage relation, of those women at least who have property, by leaving them one instrument of power which they have not signed away; and preventing also the scandalous abuse of the marriage institution, which is perpetrated when a man entraps a girl into marrying him without a settlement, for the sole purpose of getting possession of her money. When the support of the family depends, not on property, but on earnings, the common arrangement, by which the man earns the income and the wife superintends the domestic expenditure, seems to me in general the most suitable division of labour between the two persons. If, in addition to the physical suffering of bearing children, and the whole responsibility of their care and education in early years, the wife undertakes the careful and economical application of the husband's earnings to the general comfort of the family; she takes not only her fair share, but usually the larger share, of the bodily and mental exertion required by their joint existence. If she undertakes any additional portion, it seldom relieves her from this, but only prevents her from performing it properly. The care which she is herself disabled from taking of the children and the household, nobody else takes; those of the children who do not die, grow up as they best can, and the management of the household is likely to be so bad, as even in point of economy' to be a great drawback from the value of the wife's earnings. In an otherwise just state of things, it is not, therefore, I think, a desirable custom, that the wife should contribute by her labour to the income of the family. In an unjust state of things, her doing so may be useful to her, by making her of more value in the eyes of the man who is legally her master; but, on the other hand, it enables him still farther to abuse his power, by forcing her to work, and leaving the support of the family to her exertions, while he spends most of his time in drinking and idleness. The *power* of earning is essential to the dignity of a woman, if she has not independent property. But if marriage were an equal contract, not implying the obligation of obedience; if the connexion were no longer enforced to the oppression of those to whom it is purely a mischief, but a separation, on just terms (I do not now speak of a divorce), could be obtained by any woman who was morally entitled to it; and if she would then find all honourable employments as freely open to her as to men; it would not be necessary for her protection, that during marriage she should make this particular use of her faculties. Like a man when he chooses a profession, so, when a woman marries, it may in general be understood that she makes choice of the management of a household, and the bringing up of a family, as the first call upon her exertions, during as many years of her life as may be required for the purpose; and that she renounces, not all other objects and occupations, but all which are not consistent with the requirements of this. The actual exercise, in a habitual or systematic manner, of outdoor occupations, or such as cannot be carried on at home, would by this principle be practically interdicted to the greater number of married women. But the utmost latitude ought to exist for the adaptation of general rules to individual suitabilities; and there ought to be nothing to prevent faculties exceptionally adapted to any other pursuit, from obeying their vocation notwithstanding marriage: due provision being made for supplying otherwise any falling-short which might become inevitable, in her full performance of the ordinary functions of mistress of a family. These things, if once opinion were rightly directed on the subject, might with perfect safety be left to be regulated by opinion, without any interference of law.

3

On the other point which is involved in the just equality of women, their admissibility to all the functions and occupations hitherto retained as the monopoly of the stronger sex, I should anticipate no difficulty in convincing any one who has gone with me on the subject of the equality of women in the family. I believe that their disabilities elsewhere are only clung to in order to maintain their subordination in domestic life; because the generality of the male sex cannot yet tolerate the idea of living with an equal. Were it not for that, I think that almost every one, in the existing state of opinion in politics and political economy, would admit the injustice of excluding half the human race from the greater number of lucrative occupations, and from almost all high social functions; ordaining from their birth either that they are not, and cannot by any possibility become, fit for employments which are legally open to the stupidest and basest of the other sex, or else that however fit they may be, those employments shall be interdicted to them, in order to be preserved for the exclusive benefit of males. In the last two centuries, when (which was seldom the case) any reason beyond the mere existence of the fact was thought to be required to justify the disabilities of women, people seldom assigned as a reason their inferior mental capacity; which, in times when there was a real trial of personal faculties (from which all women were not excluded) in the struggles of public life, no one really believed in. The reason given in those days was not women's unfitness, but the interest of society, by which was meant the interest of men: just as the *raison d'état,* meaning the convenience of the government, and the support of existing authority, was deemed a sufficient explanation and excuse for the most flagitious crimes. In the present day, power holds a smoother language, and whomsoever it oppresses, always pretends to do so for their own good: accordingly, when anything is forbidden to women, it is thought necessary to say, and desirable to believe, that they are incapable of doing it, and that they depart from their real path of success and happiness when they aspire to it. But to make this reason plausible (I do not say valid), those by whom it is urged must be prepared to carry it to a much greater length than any one ventures to do in the face of present experience. It is not sufficient to maintain that women on the average are less gifted than men on the average, with certain of the higher mental faculties, or that a smaller number of women than of men are fit for occupations and functions of the highest intellectual character. It is necessary to maintain that no women at all are fit for them, and that the most eminent women are inferior in mental faculties to the most mediocre of the men on whom those functions at present devolve. For if the performance of the function is decided either by competition, or by any mode of choice which secures regard to the public interest, there needs to be no apprehension that any important employments will fall into the hands of women inferior to average men, or to the average of their male competitors. The only result would be that there would be fewer women than men in such employments; a result certain to happen in any case,

if only from the preference always likely to be felt by the
majority of women for the one vocation in which there is
nobody to compete with them. Now, the most determined
depreciator of women will not venture to deny, that when we
add the experience of recent times to that of ages past, women,
and not a few merely, but many women, have proved themselves capable of everything, perhaps without a single exception, which is done by men, and of doing it successfully and
creditably. The utmost that can be said is, that there are
many things which none of them have succeeded in doing as
well as they have been done by some men—many in which
they have not reached the very highest rank. But there are
extremely few, dependent only on mental faculties, in which
they have not attained the rank next to the highest. Is not
this enough, and much more than enough, to make it a tyranny
to them, and a detriment to society, that they should not be
allowed to compete with men for the exercise of these functions? Is it not a mere truism to say, that such functions are
often filled by men far less fit for them than numbers of
women, and who would be beaten by women in any fair field
of competition? What difference does it make that there may
be men somewhere, fully employed about other things, who
may be still better qualified for the things in question than
these women? Does not this take place in all competitions?
Is there so great a superfluity of men fit for high duties, that
society can afford to reject the service of any competent person? Are we so certain of always finding a man made to our
hands for any duty or function of social importance which
falls vacant, that we lose nothing by putting a ban upon one-
half of mankind, and refusing beforehand to make their faculties available, however distinguished they may be? And even
if we could do without them, would it be consistent with justice to refuse to them their fair share of honour and distinction, or to deny to them the equal moral right of all
human beings to choose their occupation (short of injury to
others) according to their own preferences, at their own risk?
Nor is the injustice confined to them: it is shared by those

who are in a position to benefit by their services. To ordain that any kind of persons shall not be physicians, or shall not be advocates, or shall not be members of parliament, is to injure not them only, but all who employ physicians or advocates, or elect members of parliament, and who are deprived of the stimulating effect of greater competition on the exertions of the competitors, as well as restricted to a narrower range of individual choice.

It will perhaps be sufficient if I confine myself, in the details of my argument, to functions of a public nature: since, if I am successful as to those, it probably will be readily granted that women should be admissible to all other occupations to which it is at all material whether they are admitted or not. And here let me begin by marking out one function, broadly distinguished from all others, their right to which is entirely independent of any question which can be raised concerning their faculties. I mean the suffrage, both parliamentary and municipal. The right to share in the choice of those who are to exercise a public trust, is altogether a distinct thing from that of competing for the trust itself. If no one could vote for a member of parliament who was not fit to be a candidate, the government would be a narrow oligarchy indeed. To have a voice in choosing those by whom one is to be governed, is a means of self-protection due to every one, though he were to remain for ever excluded from the function of governing: and that women are considered fit to have such a choice, may be presumed from the fact, that the law already gives it to women in the most important of all cases to themselves: for the choice of the man who is to govern a woman to the end of life, is always supposed to be voluntarily made by herself. In the case of election to public trusts, it is the business of constitutional law to surround the right of suffrage with all needful securities and limitations; but whatever securities are sufficient in the case of the male sex, no others need be required in the case of women. Under whatever conditions, and within whatever limits, men are admitted to the suffrage, there is not a shadow of justification for not admitting women under the same. The majority of the women of any class are not likely to differ in political opinion from the majority of the men of the same class, unless the question be one in which the interests of women, as such, are in some way involved; and if they are so, women require the suffrage, as their guarantee of just and equal consideration. This ought to be obvious even to those who coincide in no other of the doctrines for which I contend. Even if every woman were a wife, and if every wife ought to be a slave, all the more would these slaves stand in need of legal protection: and we know what legal protection the slaves have, where the laws are made by their masters.

With regard to the fitness of women, not only to participate in elections, but themselves to hold offices or practise professions involving important public responsibilities; I have already observed that this consideration is not essential to the practical question in dispute: since any woman, who succeeds in an open profession, proves by that very fact that she is qualified for it. And in the case of public offices, if the political system of the country is such as to exclude unfit men, it will equally exclude unfit women: while if it is not, there is no additional evil in the fact that the unfit persons whom it admits may be either women or men. As long therefore as it is acknowledged that even a few women may be fit for these duties, the laws which shut the door on those exceptions cannot be justified by any opinion which can be held respecting the capacities of women in general. But, though this last consideration is not essential, it is far from being irrelevant. An unprejudiced view of it gives additional strength to the arguments against the disabilities of women, and reinforces them by high considerations of practical utility.

Let us at first make entire abstraction of all psychological considerations tending to show, that any of the mental differences supposed to exist between women and men are but the natural effect of the differences in their education and circumstances, and indicate no radical difference, far less radical inferiority, of nature. Let us consider women only as they already are, or as they are known to have been; and the capacities which they have already practically shown. What they have done, that at least, if nothing else, it is proved that they can do. When we consider how sedulously they are all trained away from, instead of being trained towards, any of the occupations or objects reserved for men, it is evident that I am taking a very humble ground for them, when I rest their case on what they have actually achieved. For, in this case, negative evidence is worth little, while any positive evidence is conclusive. It cannot be inferred to be impossible that a woman should be a Homer, or an Aristotle, or a Michael Angelo, or a Beethoven, because no woman has yet actually produced works comparable to theirs in any of those lines of excellence. This negative fact at most leaves the question uncertain, and open to psychological discussion. But it is quite certain that a woman can be a Queen Elizabeth, or a Deborah, or a Joan of Arc, since this is not inference, but fact. Now it is a curious consideration, that the only things which the existing law excludes women from doing, are the things which they have proved that they are able to do. There is no law to prevent a woman from having written all the plays of Shakspeare, or composed all the operas of Mozart. But Queen Elizabeth or Queen Victoria, had they not inherited the throne, could not have been intrusted with the smallest of the political duties, of which the former showed herself equal to the greatest.

If anything conclusive could be inferred from experience, without psychological analysis, it would be that the things which women are not allowed to do are the very ones for which they are peculiarly qualified; since their vocation for government has made its way, and become conspicuous, through the very few opportunities which have been given; while in the lines of distinction which apparently were freely open to them, they have by no means so eminently distinguished themselves. We know how small a number of reigning queens history presents, in comparison with that of kings. Of this smaller number a far larger proportion have shown talents for rule; though many of them have occupied the throne in difficult periods. It is remarkable, too, that they have, in a great number of instances, been distinguished by merits the most opposite to the imaginary and conventional character of women: they have been as much remarked for the firmness and vigour of their rule, as for its intelligence. When, to queens and empresses, we add regents, and viceroys of provinces, the list of women who have been eminent rulers of mankind swells to a great length.[1] This fact is so undeniable, that some one, long ago, tried to retort the argument, and turned the admitted truth into an additional insult, by saying that queens are better than kings, because under kings women govern, but under queens, men.

It may seem a waste of reasoning to argue against a bad joke; but such things do affect people's minds; and I have heard men quote this saying, with an air as if they thought that there was something in it. At any rate, it will serve as well as anything else for a starting point in discussion. I say, then, that it is not true that under kings, women govern. Such cases are entirely exceptional: and weak kings have quite as often governed ill through the influence of male favourites, as of female. When a king is governed by a woman merely through his amatory propensities, good government is not

1. Especially is this true if we take into consideration Asia as well as Europe. If a Hindoo principality is strongly, vigilantly, and economically governed; if order is preserved without oppression; if cultivation is extending, and the people prosperous, in three cases out of four that principality is under a woman's rule. This fact, to me an entirely unexpected one, I have collected from a long official knowledge of Hindoo governments. There are many such instances: for though, by Hindoo institutions, a woman cannot reign, she is the legal regent of a kingdom during the minority of the heir; and minorities are frequent, the lives of the male rulers being so often prematurely terminated through the effect of inactivity and sensual excesses. When we consider that these princesses have never been seen in public, have never conversed with any man not of their own family except from behind a curtain, that they do not read, and if they did, there is no book in their languages which can give them the smallest instruction on political affairs; the example they afford of the natural capacity of women for government is very striking.

probable, though even then there are exceptions. But French history counts two kings who have voluntarily given the direction of affairs during many years, the one to his mother, the other to his sister: one of them, Charles VIII, was a mere boy, but in doing so he followed the intentions of his father Louis XI, the ablest monarch of his age. The other, Saint Louis, was the best, and one of the most vigorous rulers, since the time of Charlemagne. Both these princesses ruled in a manner hardly equalled by any prince among their contemporaries. The emperor Charles the Fifth, the most politic prince of his time, who had as great a number of able men in his service as a ruler ever had, and was one of the least likely of all sovereigns to sacrifice his interest to personal feelings, made two princesses of his family successively Governors of the Netherlands, and kept one or other of them in that post during his whole life (they were afterwards succeeded by a third). Both ruled very successfully, and one of them, Margaret of Austria, was one of the ablest politicians of the age. So much for one side of the question. Now as to the other. When it is said that under queens men govern, is the same meaning to be understood as when kings are said to be governed by women? Is it meant that queens choose as their instruments of government, the associates of their personal pleasures? The case is rare even with those who are as unscrupulous on the latter point as Catherine II: and it is not in these cases that the good government, alleged to arise from male influence, is to be found. If it be true, then, that the administration is in the hands of better men under a queen than under an average king, it must be that queens have a superior capacity for choosing them; and women must be better qualified than men both for the position of sovereign, and for that of chief minister; for the principal business of a prime minister is not to govern in person, but to find the fittest persons to conduct every department of public affairs. The more rapid insight into character, which is one of the admitted points of superiority in women over men, must certainly make them, with anything like parity of qualifications in other respects, more apt than men in that choice of instruments, which is nearly the most important business of every one who has to do with governing mankind. Even the unprincipled Catherine de' Medici could feel the value of a Chancellor de l'Hôpital. But it is also true that most great queens have been great by their own talents for government, and have been well served precisely for that reason. They retained the supreme direction of affairs in their own hands: and if they listened to good advisers, they gave by that fact the strongest proof that their judgment fitted them for dealing with the great questions of government.

Is it reasonable to think that those who are fit for the greater functions of politics, are incapable of qualifying themselves for the less? Is there any reason in the nature of things, that the wives and sisters of princes should, whenever called on, be found as competent as the princes themselves to *their* business, but that the wives and sisters of statesmen, and administrators, and directors of companies, and managers of public institutions, should be unable to do what is done by their brothers and husbands? The real reason is plain enough; it is that princesses, being more raised above the generality of men by their rank than placed below them by their sex, have never been taught that it was improper for them to concern themselves with politics; but have been allowed to feel the liberal interest natural to any cultivated human being, in the great transactions which took place around them, and in which they might be called on to take a part. The ladies of reigning families are the only women who are allowed the same range of interests and freedom of development as men; and it is precisely in their case that there is not found to be any inferiority. Exactly where and in proportion as women's capacities for government have been tried, in that proportion have they been found adequate.

This fact is in accordance with the best general conclusions which the world's imperfect experience seems as yet to suggest, concerning the peculiar tendencies and aptitudes characteristic of women, as women have hitherto been. I do not say, as they will continue to be; for, as I have already said more than once, I consider it presumption in any one to pretend to decide what women are or are not, can or cannot be, by natural constitution. They have always hitherto been kept, as far as regards spontaneous development, in so unnatural a state, that their nature cannot but have been greatly distorted and disguised; and no one can safely pronounce that if women's nature were left to choose its direction as freely as men's, and if no artificial bent were attempted to be given to it except that required by the conditions of human society, and given to both sexes alike, there would be any material difference, or perhaps any difference at all, in the character and capacities which would unfold themselves. I shall presently show, that even the least contestable of the differences which now exist, are such as may very well have been produced merely by circumstances, without any difference of natural capacity. But, looking at women as they are known in experience, it may be said of them, with more truth than belongs to most other generalizations on the subject, that the general bent of their talents is towards the practical. This statement is conformable to all the public history of women, in the present and the past. It is no less borne out by common and daily experience. Let us consider the special nature of the mental capacities most characteristic of a woman of talent. They are all of a kind which fits them for practice, and makes them tend towards it. What is meant by a woman's capacity of intuitive perception? It means, a rapid and correct insight into present fact. It has nothing to do with general principles. Nobody ever perceived a scientific law of nature by intuition, nor arrived at a general rule of duty or prudence by it. These are results of slow and careful collection and comparison of experience; and neither the men nor the women of intuition usually shine in this department, unless, indeed, the experience necessary is such as they can acquire by themselves. For what is called their intuitive sagacity makes them peculiarly apt in gathering such general truths as can be collected from their individual means of observation. When, consequently, they chance to be as well provided as men are with the results of other people's experience, by reading and education, (I use the word chance advisedly, for, in respect to the knowledge that tends to fit them for the greater concerns of life, the only educated women are the self-educated) they are better furnished than men in general with the essential requisites of skilful and successful practice. Men who have been much taught, are apt to be deficient in the sense of present fact; they do not see, in the facts which they are called upon to deal with, what is really there, but what they have been taught to expect. This is seldom the case with women of any ability. Their capacity of "intuition" preserves them from it. With equality of experience and of general faculties, a woman usually sees much more than a man of what is immediately before her. Now this sensibility to the present, is the main quality on which the capacity for practice, as distinguished from theory, depends. To discover general principles, belongs to the speculative faculty: to discern and discriminate the particular cases in which they are and are not applicable, constitutes practical talent: and for this, women as they now are have a peculiar aptitude. I admit that there can be no good practice without principles, and that the predominant place which quickness of observation holds among a woman's faculties, makes her particularly apt to build over-hasty generalizations upon her own observation; though at the same time no less ready in rectifying those generalizations, as her observation takes a wider range. But the corrective to this defect, is access to the experience of the human race; general knowledge—exactly the thing which education can best supply. A woman's mistakes are specifically those of a clever self-educated man, who often sees what men trained in routine do not see, but falls into errors for want of knowing things which have long been known. Of course he has acquired much of the pre-existing knowledge, or he could not have got on at all; but what he knows of it he has picked up in fragments and at random, as women do.

But this gravitation of women's minds to the present, to the real, to actual fact, while in its exclusiveness it is a source of errors, is also a most useful counteractive of the contrary error. The principal and most characteristic aberration of speculative minds as such, consists precisely in the deficiency of this lively perception and ever-present sense of objective fact. For want of this, they often not only overlook the contradiction which outward facts oppose to their theories, but lose sight of the legitimate purpose of speculation altogether, and let their speculative faculties go astray into regions not peopled with real beings, animate or inanimate, even idealized, but with personified shadows created by the illusions of metaphysics or by the mere entanglement of words, and think these shadows the proper objects of the highest, the most transcendant, philosophy. Hardly anything can be of greater value to a man of theory and speculation who employs himself not in collecting materials of knowledge by observation, but in working them up by processes of thought into comprehensive truths of science and laws of conduct, than to carry on his speculations in the companionship, and under the criticism, of a really superior woman. There is nothing comparable to it for keeping his thoughts within the limits of real things, and the actual facts of nature. A woman seldom runs wild after an abstraction. The habitual direction of her mind to dealing with things as individuals rather than in groups, and (what is closely connected with it) her more lively interest in the present feelings of persons, which makes her consider first of all, in anything which claims to be applied to practice, in what manner persons will be affected by it—these two things make her extremely unlikely to put faith in any speculation which loses sight of individuals, and deals with things as if they existed for the benefit of some imaginary entity, some mere creation of the mind, not resolvable into the feelings of living beings. Women's thoughts are thus as useful in giving reality to those of thinking men, as men's thoughts in giving width and largeness to those of women. In depth, as distinguished from breadth, I greatly doubt if even now, women, compared with men, are at any disadvantage.

If the existing mental characteristics of women are thus valuable even in aid of speculation, they are still more important, when speculation has done its work, for carrying out the results of speculation into practice. For the reasons already given, women are comparatively unlikely to fall into the common error of men, that of sticking to their rules in a case whose specialties either take it out of the class to which the rules are applicable, or require a special adaptation of them. Let us now consider another of the admitted superiorities of clever women, greater quickness of apprehension. Is not this preeminently a quality which fits a person for practice? In action, everything continually depends upon deciding promptly. In speculation, nothing does. A mere thinker can wait, can take time to consider, can collect additional evidence; he is not obliged to complete his philosophy at once, lest the opportunity should go by. The power of drawing the best conclusion possible from insufficient data is not indeed useless in philosophy; the construction of a provisional hypothesis consistent with all known facts is often the needful basis for further inquiry. But this faculty is rather serviceable in philosophy, than the main qualification for it: and, for the auxiliary as well as for the main operation, the philosopher can allow himself any time he pleases. He is in no need of the capacity of doing rapidly what he does; what he rather needs is patience, to work on slowly until imperfect lights have become perfect, and a conjecture has ripened into a theorem. For those, on the contrary, whose business is with the fugitive and perishable—with individual facts, not kinds of facts—rapidity of thought is a qualification next only in importance to the power of thought itself. He who has not his faculties under immediate command, in the contingencies of action, might as well not have them at all. He may be fit to criticize, but he is not fit to act. Now it is in this that women, and the men who are most like women, confessedly excel. The other sort of man, however pre-eminent may be his faculties, arrives slowly at complete command of them: rapidity of judgment and promptitude of judicious action, even in the things he knows best, are the gradual and late result of strenuous effort grown into habit.

It will be said, perhaps, that the greater nervous susceptibility of women is a disqualification for practice, in anything but domestic life, by rendering them mobile, changeable, too vehemently under the influence of the moment, incapable of dogged perseverance, unequal and uncertain in the power of using their faculties. I think that these phrases sum up the greater part of the objections commonly made to the fitness of women for the higher class of serious business. Much of all this is the mere overflow of nervous energy run to waste, and would cease when the energy was directed to a definite end. Much is also the result of conscious or unconscious cultivation; as we see by the almost total disappearance of "hysterics" and fainting fits, since they have gone out of fashion. Moreover, when people are brought up, like many women of the higher classes (though less so in our own country than in any other) a kind of hothouse plants, shielded from the wholesome vicissitudes of air and temperature, and untrained in any of the occupations and exercises which give stimulus and development to the circulatory and muscular system, while their nervous system, especially in its emotional department, is kept in unnaturally active play; it is no wonder if those of them who do not die of consumption, grow up with constitutions liable to derangement from slight causes, both internal and external, and without stamina to support any task, physical or mental, requiring continuity of effort. But women brought up to work for their livelihood show none of these morbid characteristics, unless indeed they are chained to an excess of sedentary work in confined and unhealthy rooms. Women who in their early years have shared in the healthful physical education and bodily freedom of their brothers, and who obtain a sufficiency of pure air and exercise in after-life, very rarely have any excessive susceptibility of nerves which can disqualify them for active pursuits. There is indeed a certain proportion of persons, in both sexes, in whom an unusual degree of nervous sensibility is constitutional, and of so marked a character as to be the feature of their organization which exercises the greatest influence over the whole character of the vital phenomena. This constitution, like other physical conformations, is hereditary, and is transmitted to sons as well as daughters; but it is possible, and probable, that the nervous temperament (as it is called) is inherited by a greater number of women than of men. We will assume this as a fact: and let me then ask, are men of nervous temperament found to be unfit for the duties and pursuits usually followed by men? If not, why should women of the same temperament be unfit for them? The peculiarities of the temperament are, no doubt, within certain limits, an obstacle to success in some employments, though an aid to it in others. But when the occupation is suitable to the temperament, and sometimes even when it is unsuitable, the most brilliant examples of success are continually given by the men of high nervous sensibility. They are distinguished in their practical manifestations chiefly by this, that being susceptible of a higher degree of excitement than those of another physical constitution, their powers when excited differ more than in the case of other people, from those shown in their ordinary state: they are raised, as it were, above themselves, and do things with ease which they are wholly incapable of at other times. But this lofty excitement is not, except in weak bodily constitutions, a mere flash, which passes away immediately, leaving no permanent traces, and incompatible with persistent and steady pursuit of an object. It is the character of the nervous temperament to be capable of *sustained* excitement, holding out through long continued efforts. It is what is meant by *spirit*. It is what makes the high-bred racehorse run without slackening speed till he drops down dead. It is what has enabled so many delicate women to maintain the most sublime constancy not only at the stake, but through a long preliminary succession of mental and bodily tortures. It is evident that people of this temperament are particularly apt for what may be called the executive department of the leadership of mankind. They are the material of great orators, great preachers, impressive diffusers of moral influences. Their constitution might be deemed less favourable to the qualities required from a statesman in the cabinet, or from a judge. It would be so, if the consequence necessarily followed that because people are excitable they must always be in a state of excitement. But this is wholly a question of training. Strong feeling is the instrument and element of strong self-control: but it requires to be cultivated in that direction. When it is, it forms not the heroes of impulse only, but those also of self-conquest. History and experience prove that the most passionate characters are the most fanatically rigid in their feelings of duty, when their passion has been trained to act in that direction. The judge who gives a just decision in a case where his feelings are intensely interested on the other side, derives from that same strength of feeling the determined sense of the obligation of justice, which enables him to achieve this victory over himself. The capability of that lofty enthusiasm which takes the human being out of his every-day character, reacts upon the daily character itself. His aspirations and powers when he is in this exceptional state, become the type with which he compares, and by which he estimates, his sentiments and proceedings at other times: and his habitual purposes assume a character moulded by and assimilated to the moments of lofty excitement, although those, from the physical nature of a human being, can only be transient. Experience of races, as well as of individuals, does not show those of excitable temperament to be less fit, on the average, either for speculation or practice, than the more unexcitable. The French, and the Italians, are undoubtedly by nature more nervously excitable than the Teutonic races, and, compared at least with the English, they have a much greater habitual and daily emotional life: but have they been less great in science, in public business, in legal and judicial eminence, or in war? There is abundant evidence that the Greeks were of old, as their descendants and successors still are, one of the most excitable of the races of mankind. It is superfluous to ask, what among the achievements of men they did not excel in. The Romans, probably, as an equally southern people, had the same original temperament: but the stern character of their national discipline, like that of the Spartans, made them an example of the opposite type of national character; the greater strength of their natural feelings being chiefly apparent in the intensity which the same original temperament made it possible to give to the artificial. If these cases exemplify what a naturally excitable people may be made, the Irish Celts afford one of the aptest examples of what they are when left to themselves; (if those can be said to be left to themselves who have been for centuries under the indirect influence of bad government, and the direct training of a Catholic hierarchy and of a sincere belief in the Catholic religion.) The Irish character must be considered, therefore, as an unfavourable case: yet, whenever the circumstances of the individual have been at all favourable, what people have shown greater capacity for the most varied and multifarious individual eminence? Like the French compared with the English, the Irish with the Swiss, the Greeks or Italians compared with the German races, so women compared with men may be found, on the average, to do the same things with some variety in the particular kind of excellence. But, that they would do them fully as well on the whole, if their education and cultivation were adapted to correcting instead of aggravating the infirmities incident to their temperament, I see not the smallest reason to doubt.

Supposing it, however, to be true that women's minds are by nature more mobile than those of men, less capable of persisting long in the same continuous effort, more fitted for dividing their faculties among many things than for travelling in any one path to the highest point which can be reached by it: this may be true of women as they now are (though not without great and numerous exceptions), and may account for their having remained behind the highest order of men in precisely the things in which this absorption of the whole mind in one set of ideas and occupations may seem to be most requisite. Still, this difference is one which can only affect the kind of excellence, not the excellence itself, or its practical worth: and it remains to be shown whether this exclusive working of a part of the mind, this absorption of the whole thinking faculty in a single subject, and concentration of it on a single work, is the normal and healthful condition of the human faculties, even for speculative uses. I believe that what is gained in special development by this concentration, is lost in the capacity of the mind for the other purposes of life; and even in abstract thought, it is my decided opinion that the mind does more by frequently returning to a difficult problem, than by sticking to it without interruption. For the purposes, at all events, of practice, from its highest to its humblest departments, the capacity of passing promptly from one subject of consideration to another, without letting the active spring of the intellect run down between the two, is a power far more valuable; and this power women pre-eminently possess, by virtue of the very mobility of which they are accused. They perhaps have it from nature, but they certainly have it by training and education; for nearly the whole of the occupations of women consist in the management of small but multitudinous details, on each of which the mind cannot dwell even for a minute, but must pass on to other things, and if anything requires longer thought, must steal time at odd moments for thinking of it. The capacity indeed which women show for doing their thinking in circumstances and at times which almost any man would make an excuse to himself for not attempting it, has often been noticed: and a woman's mind, though it may be occupied only with small things, can hardly ever permit itself to be vacant, as a man's so often is when not engaged in what he chooses to consider the business of his life. The business of a woman's ordinary life is things in general, and can as little cease to go on as the world to go round.

But (it is said) there is anatomical evidence of the superior mental capacity of men compared with women: they have a larger brain. I reply, that in the first place the fact itself is doubtful. It is by no means established that the brain of a woman is smaller than that of a man. If it is inferred merely because a woman's bodily frame generally is of less dimensions than a man's, this criterion would lead to strange consequences. A tall and large-boned man must on this showing be wonderfully superior in intelligence to a small man, and an elephant or a whale must prodigiously excel mankind. The size of the brain in human beings, anatomists say, varies much less than the size of the body, or even of the head, and the one cannot be at all inferred from the other. It is certain that some women have as large a brain as any man. It is within my knowledge that a man who had weighed many human brains, said that the heaviest he knew of, heavier even than Cuvier's (the heaviest previously recorded,) was that of a woman. Next, I must observe that the precise relation which exists between the brain and the intellectual powers is not yet well understood, but is a subject of great dispute. That there is a very close relation we cannot doubt. The brain is certainly the material organ of thought and feeling: and (making abstraction of the great unsettled controversy respecting the appropriation of different parts of the brain to different mental faculties) I admit that it would be an anomaly, and an exception to all we know of the general laws of life and organization, if the size of the organ were wholly indifferent to the function; if no accession of power were derived from the greater magnitude of the instrument. But the exception and the anomaly would be fully as great if the organ exercised influence by its magnitude *only*. In all the more delicate operations of nature—of which those of the animated creation are the most delicate, and those of the nervous system by far the most delicate of these—differences in the effect depend as much on differences of quality in the physical agents, as on their quantity: and if the quality of an instrument is to be tested by the nicety and delicacy of the work it can do, the indications point to a greater average fineness of quality in the brain and nervous system of women than of men. Dismissing abstract difference of quality, a thing difficult to verify, the efficiency of an organ is known to depend not solely on its size but on its activity: and of this we have an approximate measure in the energy with which the blood circulates through it, both the stimulus and the reparative force being mainly dependent on the circulation. It would not be surprising—it is indeed an hypothesis which accords well with the differences actually observed between the mental operations of the two sexes—if men on the average should have the advantage in the size of the brain, and women in activity of cerebral circulation. The results which conjecture, founded on analogy, would lead us to expect from this difference of organization, would correspond to some of those which we most commonly see. In the first place, the mental operations of men might be expected to be slower. They would neither be so prompt as women in thinking, nor so quick to feel. Large bodies take more time to get into full action. On the other hand, when once got thoroughly into play, men's brain would bear more work. It would be more persistent in the line first taken; it would have more difficulty in changing from one mode of action to another, but, in the one thing it was doing, it could go on longer without loss of power or sense of fatigue. And do we not find that the things in which men most excel women are those which require most plodding and long hammering at a single thought, while women do best what must be done rapidly? A woman's brain is sooner fatigued, sooner exhausted; but given the degree of exhaustion, we should expect to find that it would recover itself sooner. I repeat that this speculation is entirely hypothetical; it pretends to no more than to suggest a line of enquiry. I have before repudiated the notion of its being yet certainly known that there is any natural difference at all in the average strength or direction of the mental capacities of the two sexes, much less what that difference is. Nor is it possible that this should be known, so long as the psychological laws of the formation of character have been so little studied, even in a general way, and in the particular case never scientifically applied at all; so long as the most obvious external causes of difference of character are habitually disregarded—left unnoticed by the observer, and looked down upon with a kind of supercilious contempt by the prevalent schools both of natural history and of mental philosophy: who, whether they look for the source of what mainly distinguishes human beings from one another, in the world of matter or in that of spirit, agree in running down those who prefer to explain these differences by the different relations of human beings to society and life.

To so ridiculous an extent are the notions formed of the nature of women, mere empirical generalizations, framed, without philosophy or analysis, upon the first instances which present themselves, that the popular idea of it is different in different countries, according as the opinions and social circumstances of the country have given to the women living in it any specialty of development or non-development. An Oriental thinks that women are by nature peculiarly voluptuous; see the violent abuse of them on this ground in Hindoo writings. An Englishman usually thinks that they are by nature cold. The sayings about women's fickleness are mostly of French origin; from the famous distich of Francis the First, upward and downward. In England it is a common remark, how much more constant women are than men. Inconstancy has been longer reckoned discreditable to a woman, in England than in France; and Englishwomen are besides, in their inmost nature, much more subdued to opinion. It may be remarked by the way, that Englishmen are in peculiarly unfavourable circumstances for attempting to judge what is or is not natural, not merely to women, but to men, or to human beings altogether, at least if they have only English experience to go upon: because there is no place where human nature shows so little of its original lineaments. Both in a good and a bad sense, the English are farther from a state of nature than any other modern people. They are, more than any other people, a product of civilization and discipline. England is the country in which social discipline has most succeeded, not so much in conquering, as in suppressing, whatever is liable to conflict with it. The English, more than any other people, not only act but feel according to rule. In other countries, the taught opinion, or the requirement of society, may be the stronger power, but the promptings of the individual nature are always visible under it, and often resisting it: rule may be stronger than nature, but nature is still there. In England, rule has to a great degree substituted itself for nature. The greater part of life is carried on, not by following inclination under the control of rule, but by having no inclination but that of following a rule. Now this has its good side doubtless, though it has also a wretchedly bad one; but it must render an Englishman peculiarly ill-qualified to pass a judgment on the original tendencies of human nature from his own experience. The errors to which observers elsewhere are liable on the subject, are of a different character. An Englishman is ignorant respecting human nature, a Frenchman is prejudiced. An Englishman's errors are negative, a Frenchman's positive. An Englishman fancies that things do not exist, because he never sees them; a Frenchman thinks they must always and necessarily exist, because he does see them. An Englishman does not know nature, because he has had no opportunity of observing it; a Frenchman generally knows a great deal of it, but often mistakes it, because he has only seen it sophisticated and distorted. For the artificial state superinduced by society disguises the natural tendencies of the thing which is the subject of observation, in two different ways: by extinguishing the nature, or by transforming it. In the one case there is but a starved residuum of nature remaining to be studied; in the other case there is much, but it may have expanded in any direction rather than that in which it would spontaneously grow.

I have said that it cannot now be known how much of the existing mental differences between men and women is natural, and how much artificial; whether there are any natural differences at all; or, supposing all artificial causes of difference to be withdrawn, what natural character would be revealed. I am not about to attempt what I have pronounced impossible: but doubt does not forbid conjecture, and where certainty is unattainable, there may yet be the means of arriving at some degree of probability. The first point, the origin of the differences actually observed, is the one most accessible to speculation; and I shall attempt to approach it, by the only path by which it can be reached; by tracing the mental consequences of external influences. We cannot isolate a human being from the circumstances of his condition, so as to ascertain experimentally what he would have been by nature; but we can consider what he is, and what his circumstances have been, and whether the one would have been capable of producing the other.

Let us take, then, the only marked case which observation affords, of apparent inferiority of women to men, if we except the merely physical one of bodily strength. No production in philosophy, science, or art, entitled to the first rank, has been the work of a woman. Is there any mode of accounting for this, without supposing that women are naturally incapable of producing them?

In the first place, we may fairly question whether experience has afforded sufficient grounds for an induction. It is scarcely three generations since women, saving very rare exceptions, have begun to try their capacity in philosophy, science, or art. It is only in the present generation that their attempts have been at all numerous; and they are even now extremely few, everywhere but in England and France. It is a relevant question, whether a mind possessing the requisites of first-rate eminence in speculation or creative art could have been expected, on the mere calculation of chances, to turn up during that lapse of time, among the women whose tastes and personal position admitted of their devoting themselves to these pursuits. In all things which there has yet been time for—in all but the very highest grades in the scale of excellence, especially in the department in which they have been longest engaged, literature (both prose and poetry)—women have done quite as much, have obtained fully as high prizes as many of them, as could be expected from the length of time and the number of competitors. If we go back to the earlier period when very few women made the attempt, yet some of those few made it with distinguished success. The

Greeks always accounted Sappho among their great poets; and we may well suppose that Myrtis, said to have been the teacher of Pindar, and Corinna, who five times bore away from him the prize of poetry, must at least have had sufficient merit to admit of being compared with that great name. Aspasia did not leave any philosophical writings; but it is an admitted fact that Socrates resorted to her for instruction, and avowed himself to have obtained it.

If we consider the works of women in modern times, and contrast them with those of men, either in the literary or the artistic department, such inferiority as may be observed resolves itself essentially into one thing: but that is a most material one; deficiency of originality. Not total deficiency; for every production of mind which is of any substantive value, has an originality of its own—is a conception of the mind itself, not a copy of something else. Thoughts original, in the sense of being unborrowed—of being derived from the thinker's own observations or intellectual processes—are abundant in the writings of women. But they have not yet produced any of those great and luminous new ideas which form an era in thought, nor those fundamentally new conceptions in art, which open a vista of possible effects not before thought of, and found a new school. Their compositions are mostly grounded on the existing fund of thought, and their creations do not deviate widely from existing types. This is the sort of inferiority which their works manifest: for in point of execution, in the detailed application of thought, and the perfection of style, there is no inferiority. Our best novelists in point of composition, and of the management of detail, have mostly been women; and there is not in all modern literature a more eloquent vehicle of thought than the style of Madame de Stael, nor, as a specimen of purely artistic excellence, anything superior to the prose of Madame Sand, whose style acts upon the nervous system like a symphony of Haydn or Mozart. High originality of conception is, as I have said, what is chiefly wanting. And now to examine if there is any manner in which this deficiency can be accounted for.

Let us remember, then, so far as regards mere thought, that during all that period in the world's existence, and in the progress of cultivation, in which great and fruitful new truths could be arrived at by mere force of genius, with little previous study and accumulation of knowledge—during all that time women did not concern themselves with speculation at all. From the days of Hypatia to those of the Reformation, the illustrious Heloisa is almost the only woman to whom any such achievement might have been possible; and we know not how great a capacity of speculation in her may have been lost to mankind by the misfortunes of her life. Never since any considerable number of women have begun to cultivate serious thought, has originality been possible on easy terms. Nearly all the thoughts which can be reached by mere strength of original faculties, have long since been arrived at; and originality, in any high sense of the word, is now scarcely ever attained but by minds which have undergone elaborate discipline, and are deeply versed in the results of previous thinking. It is Mr. Maurice, I think, who has remarked on the present age, that its most original thinkers are those who have known most thoroughly what had been thought by their predecessors: and this will always henceforth be the case. Every fresh stone in the edifice has now to be placed on the top of so many others, that a long process of climbing, and of carrying up materials, has to be gone through by whoever aspires to take a share in the present stage of the work. How many women are there who have gone through any such process? Mrs. Somerville, alone perhaps of women, knows as much of mathematics as is now needful for making any considerable mathematical discovery: is it any proof of inferiority in women, that she has not happened to be one of the two or three persons who in her lifetime have associated their names with some striking advancement of the science? Two women, since political economy has been made a science, have known enough of it to write usefully on the subject: of how many of the innumerable men who have written on it during the same time, is it possible with truth to say more? If no woman has hitherto been a great historian, what woman has had the necessary erudition? If no woman is a great philologist, what woman has studied Sanscrit and Slavonic, the Gothic of Ulphila and the Persic of the Zendavesta? Even in practical matters we all know what is the value of the originality of untaught geniuses. It means, inventing over again in its rudimentary form something already invented and improved upon by many successive inventors. When women have had the preparation which all men now require to be eminently original, it will be time enough to begin judging by experience of their capacity for originality.

It no doubt often happens that a person, who has not widely and accurately studied the thoughts of others on a subject, has by natural sagacity a happy intuition, which he can suggest, but cannot prove, which yet when matured may be an important addition to knowledge: but even then, no justice can be done to it until some other person, who does possess the previous acquirements, takes it in hand, tests it, gives it a scientific or practical form, and fits it into its place among the existing truths of philosophy or science. Is it supposed that such felicitous thoughts do not occur to women? They occur by hundreds to every woman of intellect. But they are mostly lost, for want of a husband or friend who has the other knowledge which can enable him to estimate them properly and bring them before the world: and even when they are brought before it, they generally appear as his ideas, not their real author's. Who can tell how many of the most original thoughts put forth by male writers, belong to a woman by suggestion, to themselves only by verifying and working out? If I may judge by my own case, a very large proportion indeed.

If we turn from pure speculation to literature in the narrow sense of the term, and the fine arts, there is a very obvious reason why women's literature is, in its general conception and in its main features, an imitation of men's. Why is the Roman literature, as critics proclaim to satiety, not original, but an imitation of the Greek? Simply because the Greeks came

first. If women lived in a different country from men, and
had never read any of their writings, they would have had a
literature of their own. As it is, they have not created one,
because they found a highly advanced literature already created. If there had been no suspension of the knowledge of
antiquity, or if the Renaissance had occurred before the Gothic
cathedrals were built, they never would have been built. We
see that, in France and Italy, imitation of the ancient literature stopped the original development even after it had commenced. All women who write are pupils of the great male
writers. A painter's early pictures, even if he be a Raffaelle,
are undistinguishable in style from those of his master. Even a
Mozart does not display his powerful originality in his earliest
pieces. What years are to a gifted individual, generations are
to a mass. If women's literature is destined to have a different
collective character from that of men, depending on any difference of natural tendencies, much longer time is necessary
than has yet elapsed, before it can emancipate itself from the
influence of accepted models, and guide itself by its own impulses. But if, as I believe, there will not prove to be any
natural tendencies common to women, and distinguishing their
genius from that of men, yet every individual writer among
them has her individual tendencies, which at present are still
subdued by the influence of precedent and example: and it
will require generations more, before their individuality is
sufficiently developed to make head against the influence.

It is in the fine arts, properly so called, that the *primâ facie*
evidence of inferior original powers in women at first sight
appears the strongest: since opinion (it may be said) does
not exclude them from these, but rather encourages them, and
their education, instead of passing over this department, is in
the affluent classes mainly composed of it. Yet in this line of
exertion they have fallen still more short than in many others,
of the highest eminence attained by men. This shortcoming,
however, needs no other explanation than the familiar fact,
more universally true in the fine arts than in anything else;
the vast superiority of professional persons over amateurs.

Women in the educated classes are almost universally taught
more or less of some branch or other of the fine arts, but
not that they may gain their living or their social consequence
by it. Women artists are all amateurs. The exceptions are only
of the kind which confirm the general truth. Women are taught
music, but not for the purpose of composing, only of execut-
ing it: and accordingly it is only as composers, that men, in
music, are superior to women. The only one of the fine arts
which women do follow, to any extent, as a profession, and
an occupation for life, is the histrionic; and in that they are
confessedly equal, if not superior, to men. To make the comparison fair, it should be made between the productions of
women in any branch of art, and those of men not following
it as a profession. In musical composition, for example, women
surely have produced fully as good things as have ever been
produced by male amateurs. There are now a few women,
a very few, who practise painting as a profession, and these
are already beginning to show quite as much talent as could
be expected. Even male painters (*pace* Mr. Ruskin) have not
made any very remarkable figure these last centuries, and it will
be long before they do so. The reason why the old painters were
so greatly superior to the modern, is that a greatly superior class
of men applied themselves to the art. In the fourteenth and fif-
teenth centuries the Italian printers were the most accomplished
men of their age. The greatest of them were men of encyclopædi-
cal acquirements and powers, like the great men of Greece. But
in their times fine art was, to men's feelings and conceptions,
among the grandest things in which a human being could excel;
and by it men were made, what only political or military distinction now makes them, the companions of sovereigns, and
the equals of the highest nobility. In the present age, men
of anything like similar calibre find something more important
to do, for their own fame and the uses of the modern world,
than painting: and it is only now and then that a Reynolds
or a Turner (of whose relative rank among eminent men I
do not pretend to an opinion) applies himself to that art.
Music belongs to a different order of things; it does not re-

quire the same general powers of mind, but seems more de-
pendant on a natural gift: and it may be thought surprising
that no one of the great musical composers has been a woman.
But even this natural gift, to be made available for great
creations, requires study, and professional devotion to the
pursuit. The only countries which have produced first-rate composers, even of the male sex, are Germany and Italy—countries in which, both in point of special and of general cultivation, women have remained far behind France and England,
being generally (it may be said without exaggeration) very
little educated, and having scarcely cultivated at all any of
the higher faculties of mind. And in those countries the men
who are acquainted with the principles of musical composition must be counted by hundreds, or more probably by thousands, the women barely by scores: so that here again, on
the doctrine of averages, we cannot reasonably expect to see
more than one eminent woman to fifty eminent men; and the
last three centuries have not produced fifty eminent male composers either in Germany or in Italy.

There are other reasons, besides those which we have now
given, that help to explain why women remain behind men,
even in the pursuits which are open to both. For one thing,
very few women have time for them. This may seem a paradox; it is an undoubted social fact. The time and thoughts of
every woman have to satisfy great previous demands on them
for things practical. There is, first, the superintendence of the
family and the domestic expenditure, which occupies at least
one woman in every family, generally the one of mature years
and acquired experience; unless the family is so rich as to
admit of delegating that task to hired agency, and submitting
to all the waste and malversation inseparable from that mode
of conducting it. The superintendence of a household, even
when not in other respects laborious, is extremely onerous to
the thoughts; it requires incessant vigilance, an eye which no
detail escapes, and presents questions for consideration and
solution, foreseen and unforeseen, at every hour of the day,
from which the person responsible for them can hardly ever

shake herself free. If a woman is of a rank and circumstances which relieve her in a measure from these cares, she has still devolving on her the management for the whole family of its intercourse with others—of what is called society, and the less the call made on her by the former duty, the greater is always the development of the latter: the dinner parties, concerts, evening parties, morning visits, letter writing, and all that goes with them. All this is over and above the engrossing duty which society imposes exclusively on women, of making themselves charming. A clever woman of the higher ranks finds nearly a sufficient employment of her talents in cultivating the graces of manner and the arts of conversation. To look only at the outward side of the subject: the great and continual exercise of thought which all women who attach any value to dressing well (I do not mean expensively, but with taste, and perception of natural and of artificial *convenance*) must bestow upon their own dress, perhaps also upon that of their daughters, would alone go a great way towards achieving respectable results in art, or science, or literature, and does actually exhaust much of the time and mental power they might have to spare for either.[2] If it were possible that all this number of little practical interests (which are made great to them) should leave them either much leisure, or much energy and freedom of mind, to be devoted to art or speculation, they must have a much greater original supply of active

2. "It appears to be the same right turn of mind which enables a man to acquire the *truth*, or the just idea of what is right, in the ornaments, as in the more stable principles of art. It has still the same centre of perfection, though it is the centre of a smaller circle.— To illustrate this by the fashion of dress, in which there is allowed to be a good or bad taste. The component parts of dress are continually changing from great to little, from short to long; but the general form still remains: it is still the same general dress which is comparatively fixed, though on a very slender foundation; but it is on this which fashion must rest. He who invents with the most success, or dresses in the best taste, would probably, from the same sagacity employed to greater purposes, have discovered equal skill, or have formed the same correct taste, in the highest labours of art."—*Sir Joshua Reynolds' Discourses,* Disc. vii.

faculty than the vast majority of men. But this is not all. Independently of the regular offices of life which devolve upon a woman, she is expected to have her time and faculties always at the disposal of everybody. If a man has not a profession to exempt him from such demands, still, if he has a pursuit, he offends nobody by devoting his time to it; occupation is received as a valid excuse for his not answering to every casual demand which may be made on him. Are a woman's occupations, especially her chosen and voluntary ones, ever regarded as excusing her from any of what are termed the calls of society? Scarcely are her most necessary and recognised duties allowed as an exemption. It requires an illness in the family, or something else out of the common way, to entitle her to give her own business the precedence over other people's amusement. She must always be at the beck and call of somebody, generally of everybody. If she has a study or a pursuit, she must snatch any short interval which accidentally occurs to be employed in it. A celebrated woman, in a work which I hope will some day be published, remarks truly that everything a woman does is done at odd times. Is it wonderful, then, if she does not attain the highest eminence in things which require consecutive attention, and the concentration on them of the chief interest of life? Such is philosophy, and such, above all, is art, in which, besides the devotion of the thoughts and feelings, the hand also must be kept in constant exercise to attain high skill.

There is another consideration to be added to all these. In the various arts and intellectual occupations, there is a degree of proficiency sufficient for living by it, and there is a higher degree on which depend the great productions which immortalize a name. To the attainment of the former, there are adequate motives in the case of all who follow the pursuit professionally: the other is hardly ever attained where there is not, or where there has not been at some period of life, an ardent desire of celebrity. Nothing less is commonly a sufficient stimulus to undergo the long and patient drudgery, which, in the case even of the greatest natural gifts, is absolutely required for great eminence in pursuits in which we already possess so many splendid memorials of the highest genius. Now, whether the cause be natural or artificial, women seldom have this eagerness for fame. Their ambition is generally confined within narrower bounds. The influence they seek is over those who immediately surround them. Their desire is to be liked, loved, or admired, by those whom they see with their eyes: and the proficiency in knowledge, arts, and accomplishments, which is sufficient for that, almost always contents them. This is a trait of character which cannot be left out of the account in judging of women as they are. I do not at all believe that it is inherent in women. It is only the natural result of their circumstances. The love of fame in men is encouraged by education and opinion: to "scorn delights and live laborious days" for its sake, is accounted the part of "noble minds," even if spoken of as their "last infirmity," and is stimulated by the access which fame gives to all objects of ambition, including even the favour of women; while to women themselves all these objects are closed, and the desire of fame itself considered daring and unfeminine. Besides, how could it be that a woman's interests should not be all concentrated upon the impressions made on those who come into her daily life, when society has ordained that all her duties should be to them, and has contrived that all her comforts should depend on them? The natural desire of consideration from our fellow creatures is as strong in a woman as in a man; but society has so ordered things that public consideration is, in all ordinary cases, only attainable by her through the consideration of her husband or of her male relations, while her private consideration is forfeited by making herself individually prominent, or appearing in any other character than that of an appendage to men. Whoever is in the least capable of estimating the influence on the mind of the entire domestic and social position and the whole habit of a life, must easily recognise in that influence a complete explanation of nearly all the apparent differences between women and men, including the whole of those which imply any inferiority.

As for moral differences, considered as distinguished from intellectual, the distinction commonly drawn is to the advantage of women. They are declared to be better than men; an empty compliment, which must provoke a bitter smile from every woman of spirit, since there is no other situation in life in which it is the established order, and considered quite natural and suitable, that the better should obey the worse. If this piece of idle talk is good for anything, it is only as an admission by men, of the corrupting influence of power; for that is certainly the only truth which the fact, if it be a fact, either proves or illustrates. And it *is* true that servitude, except when it actually brutalizes, though corrupting to both, is less so to the slaves than to the slave-masters. It is wholesomer for the moral nature to be restrained, even by arbitrary power, than to be allowed to exercise arbitrary power without restraint. Women, it is said, seldomer fall under the penal law —contribute a much smaller number of offenders to the criminal calendar, than men. I doubt not that the same thing may be said, with the same truth, of negro slaves. Those who are under the control of others cannot often commit crimes, unless at the command and for the purposes of their masters. I do not know a more signal instance of the blindness with which the world, including the herd of studious men, ignore and pass over all the influences of social circumstances, than their silly depreciation of the intellectual, and silly panegyrics on the moral, nature of women.

The complimentary dictum about women's superior moral goodness may be allowed to pair off with the disparaging one respecting their greater liability to moral bias. Women, we are told, are not capable of resisting their personal partialities: their judgment in grave affairs is warped by their sympathies and antipathies. Assuming it to be so, it is still to be proved that women are oftener misled by their personal feelings than men by their personal interests. The chief difference would seem in that case to be, that men are led from the course of duty and the public interest by their regard for themselves, women (not being allowed to have private interests of their own) by their regard for somebody else. It is also to be considered, that all the education which women receive from society inculcates on them the feeling that the individuals connected with them are the only ones to whom they owe any duty—the only ones whose interest they are called upon to care for; while, as far as education is concerned, they are left strangers even to the elementary ideas which are presupposed in any intelligent regard for larger interests or higher moral objects. The complaint against them resolves itself merely into this, that they fulfil only too faithfully the sole duty which they are taught, and almost the only one which they are permitted to practise.

The concessions of the privileged to the unprivileged are so seldom brought about by any better motive than the power of the unprivileged to extort them, that any arguments against the prerogative of sex are likely to be little attended to by the generality, as long as they are able to say to themselves that women do not complain of it. That fact certainly enables men to retain the unjust privilege some time longer; but does not render it less unjust. Exactly the same thing may be said of the women in the harem of an Oriental: they do not complain of not being allowed the freedom of European women. They think our women insufferably bold and unfeminine. How rarely it is that even men complain of the general order of society; and how much rarer still would such complaint be, if they did not know of any different order existing anywhere else. Women do not complain of the general lot of women; or rather they do, for plaintive elegies on it are very common in the writings of women, and were still more so as long as the lamentations could not be suspected of having any practical object. Their complaints are like the complaints which men make of the general unsatisfactoriness of human life; they are not meant to imply blame, or to plead for any change. But though women do not complain of the power of husbands, each complains of her own husband, or of the husbands of her friends. It is the same in all other cases of servitude, at least in the commencement of the emancipatory movement.

The serfs did not at first complain of the power of their lords, but only of their tyranny. The Commons began by claiming a few municipal privileges; they next asked an exemption for themselves from being taxed without their own consent; but they would at that time have thought it a great presumption to claim any share in the king's sovereign authority. The case of women is now the only case in which to rebel against established rules is still looked upon with the same eyes as was formerly a subject's claim to the right of rebelling against his king. A woman who joins in any movement which her husband disapproves, makes herself a martyr, without even being able to be an apostle, for the husband can legally put a stop to her apostleship. Women cannot be expected to devote themselves to the emancipation of women, until men in considerable number are prepared to join with them in the undertaking.

4

There remains a question, not of less importance than those already discussed, and which will be asked the most importunately by those opponents whose conviction is somewhat shaken on the main point. What good are we to expect from the changes proposed in our customs and institutions? Would mankind be at all better off if women were free? If not, why disturb their minds, and attempt to make a social revolution in the name of an abstract right?

It is hardly to be expected that this question will be asked in respect to the change proposed in the condition of women in marriage. The sufferings, immoralities, evils of all sorts, produced in innumerable cases by the subjection of individual women to individual men, are far too terrible to be overlooked. Unthinking or uncandid persons, counting those cases alone which are extreme, or which attain publicity, may say that the evils are exceptional; but no one can be blind to their existence, nor, in many cases, to their intensity. And it is perfectly obvious that the abuse of the power cannot be very much checked while the power remains. It is a power given, or offered, not to good men, or to decently respectable men, but to all men; the most brutal, and the most criminal. There is no check but that of opinion, and such men are in general within the reach of no opinion but that of men like themselves. If such men did not brutally tyrannize over the one human being whom the law compels to bear everything from them, society must already have reached a paradisiacal state. There could be no need any longer to curb men's vicious propensities. Astræa must not only have returned to earth, but the heart of the worst man must have become her temple. The law of servitude in marriage is a monstrous contradiction to all the principles of the modern world, and to all the experience through which those principles have been slowly and painfully worked out. It is the sole case, now that negro slavery has been abolished, in which a human being in the plenitude of every faculty is delivered up to the tender mercies of another human being, in the hope forsooth that this other will use the power solely for the good of the person subjected to it. Marriage is the only actual bondage known to our law. There remain no legal slaves, except the mistress of every house.

It is not, therefore, on this part of the subject, that the question is likely to be asked, *Cui bono?* We may be told that the evil would outweigh the good, but the reality of the good admits of no dispute. In regard, however, to the larger question, the removal of women's disabilities—their recognition as the equals of men in all that belongs to citizenship—the opening to them of all honourable employments, and of the training and education which qualifies for those employments—there are many persons for whom it is not enough that the inequality has no just or legitimate defence; they require to be told what express advantage would be obtained by abolishing it.

To which let me first answer, the advantage of having the most universal and pervading of all human relations regulated by justice instead of injustice. The vast amount of this gain to human nature, it is hardly possible, by any explanation or illustration, to place in a stronger light than it is placed by the bare statement, to any one who attaches a moral meaning to words. All the selfish propensities, the self-worship, the unjust self-preference, which exist among mankind, have their source and root in, and derive their principal nourishment from, the present constitution of the relation between men and women. Think what it is to a boy, to grow up to manhood in the belief that without any merit or any exertion of his own, though he may be the most frivolous and empty or the most ignorant and stolid of mankind, by the mere fact of being born a male he is by right the superior of all and every one of an entire half of the human race: including probably some whose real superiority to himself he has daily or hourly occasion to feel; but even if in his whole conduct he habitually follows a woman's guidance, still, if he is a fool, she thinks that of course she is not, and cannot be, equal in ability and judgment to himself; and if he is not a fool, he does worse— he sees that she is superior to him, and believes that, notwithstanding her superiority, he is entitled to command and she is bound to obey. What must be the effect on his character, of this lesson? And men of the cultivated classes are often not aware how deeply it sinks into the immense majority of male minds. For, among right-feeling and well-bred people, the inequality is kept as much as possible out of sight; above all, out of sight of the children. As much obedience is required from boys to their mother as to their father: they are not permitted to domineer over their sisters, nor are they accustomed to see these postponed to them, but the contrary; the compensations of the chivalrous feeling being made prominent, while the servitude which requires them is kept in the background. Well brought-up youths in the higher classes thus often escape the bad influences of the situation in their early years, and only experience them when, arrived at manhood, they fall under the dominion of facts as they really exist. Such people are little aware, when a boy is differently brought up, how early the notion of his inherent superiority to a girl arises

in his mind; how it grows with his growth and strengthens
with his strength; how it is inoculated by one schoolboy upon
another; how early the youth thinks himself superior to his
mother, owing her perhaps forbearance, but no real respect;
and how sublime and sultan-like a sense of superiority he
feels, above all, over the woman whom he honours by admitting her to a partnership of his life. Is it imagined that all
this does not pervert the whole manner of existence of the
man, both as an individual and as a social being? It is an
exact parallel to the feeling of a hereditary king that he is
excellent above others by being born a king, or a noble by
being born a noble. The relation between husband and wife
is very like that between lord and vassal, except that the wife
is held to more unlimited obedience than the vassal was. However the vassal's character may have been affected, for better
and for worse, by his subordination, who can help seeing that
the lord's was affected greatly for the worse? whether he was
led to believe that his vassals were really superior to himself,
or to feel that he was placed in command over people as good
as himself, for no merits or labours of his own, but merely
for having, as Figaro says, taken the trouble to be born. The
self-worship of the monarch, or of the feudal superior, is
matched by the self-worship of the male. Human beings do
not grow up from childhood in the possession of unearned
distinctions, without pluming themselves upon them. Those
whom privileges not acquired by their merit, and which they
feel to be disproportioned to it, inspire with additional humil-
ity, are always the few, and the best few. The rest are only
inspired with pride, and the worst sort of pride, that which
values itself upon accidental advantages, not of its own achieving. Above all, when the feeling of being raised above the
whole of the other sex is combined with personal authority
over one individual among them; the situation, if a school
of conscientious and affectionate forbearance to those whose
strongest points of character are conscience and affection, is
to men of another quality a regularly constituted Academy or
Gymnasium for training them in arrogance and overbearing-

ness; which vices, if curbed by the certainty of resistance in their intercourse with other men, their equals, break out towards all who are in a position to be obliged to tolerate them, and often revenge themselves upon the unfortunate wife for the involuntary restraint which they are obliged to submit to elsewhere.

The example afforded, and the education given to the sentiments, by laying the foundation of domestic existence upon a relation contradictory to the first principles of social justice, must, from the very nature of man, have a perverting influence of such magnitude, that it is hardly possible with our present experience to raise our imaginations to the conception of so great a change for the better as would be made by its removal. All that education and civilization are doing to efface the influences on character of the law of force, and replace them by those of justice, remains merely on the surface, as long as the citadel of the enemy is not attacked. The principle of the modern movement in morals and politics, is that conduct, and conduct alone, entitles to respect: that not what men are, but what they do, constitutes their claim to deference; that, above all, merit, and not birth, is the only rightful claim to power and authority. If no authority, not in its nature temporary, were allowed to one human being over another, society would not be employed in building up propensities with one hand which it has to curb with the other. The child would really, for the first time in man's existence on earth, be trained in the way he should go, and when he was old there would be a chance that he would not depart from it. But so long as the right of the strong to power over the weak rules in the very heart of society, the attempt to make the equal right of the weak the principle of its outward actions will always be an uphill struggle; for the law of justice, which is also that of Christianity, will never get possession of men's inmost sentiments; they will be working against it, even when bending to it.

The second benefit to be expected from giving to women the free use of their faculties, by leaving them the free choice of their employments, and opening to them the same field of occupation and the same prizes and encouragements as to other human beings, would be that of doubling the mass of mental faculties available for the higher service of humanity. Where there is now one person qualified to benefit mankind and promote the general improvement, as a public teacher, or an administrator of some branch of public or social affairs, there would then be a chance of two. Mental superiority of any kind is at present everywhere so much below the demand; there is such a deficiency of persons competent to do excellently anything which it requires any considerable amount of ability to do; that the loss to the world, by refusing to make use of one-half of the whole quantity of tolent it possesses, is extremely serious. It is true that this amount of mental power is not totally lost. Much of it is employed, and would in any case be employed, in domestic management, and in the few other occupations open to women and from the remainder indirect benefit is in many individual cases obtained, through the personal influence of individual women over individual men. But these benefits are partial; their range is extremely circumscribed; and if they must be admitted, on the one hand, as a deduction from the amount of fresh social power that would be acquired by giving freedom to one-half of the whole sum of human intellect, there must be added, on the other, the benefit of the stimulus that would be given to the intellect of men by the competition; or (to use a more true expression) by the necessity that would be imposed on them of deserving precedency before they could expect to obtain it.

This great accession to the intellectual power of the species, and to the amount of intellect available for the good management of its affairs, would be obtained, partly, through the better and more complete intellectual education of women, which would then improve *pari passu* with that of men. Women in general would be brought up equally capable of understanding business, public affairs, and the higher matters of speculation, with men in the same class of society; and the select few of the one as well as of the other sex, who were qualified not only to comprehend what is done or thought by others, but to think or do something considerable themselves, would meet with the same facilities for improving and training their capacities in the one sex as in the other. In this way, the widening of the sphere of action for women would operate for good, by raising their education to the level of that of men, and making the one participate in all improvements made in the other. But independently of this, the mere breaking down of the barrier would of itself have an educational virtue of the highest worth. The mere getting rid of the idea that all the wider subjects of thought and action, all the things which are of general and not solely of private interest, are men's business, from which women are to be warned off—positively interdicted from most of it, coldly tolerated in the little which is allowed them—the mere consciousness a woman would then have of being a human being like any other, entitled to choose her pursuits, urged or invited by the same inducements as any one else to interest herself in whatever is interesting to human beings, entitled to exert the share of influence on all human concerns which belongs to an individual opinion, whether she attempted actual participation in them or not—this alone would effect an immense expansion of the faculties of women, as well as enlargement of the range of their moral sentiments.

Besides the addition to the amount of individual talent available for the conduct of human affairs, which certainly are not at present so abundantly provided in that respect that they can afford to dispense with one-half of what nature proffers; the opinion of women would then possess a more beneficial, rather than a greater, influence upon the general mass of human belief and sentiment. I say a more beneficial, rather than a greater influence; for the influence of women over the general tone of opinion has always, or at least from the earliest known period, been very considerable. The influence of mothers on the early character of their sons, and the desire of young men to recommend themselves to young women, have in all recorded times been important agencies in the forma-

tion of character, and have determined some of the chief
steps in the progress of civilization. Even in the Homeric age,
αἰδώς towards the Τρωάδας ελκεσίπεπλους is an acknowledged
and powerful motive of action in the great Hector. The moral
influence of women has had two modes of operation. First, it
has been a softening influence. Those who were most liable
to be the victims of violence, have naturally tended as much
as they could towards limiting its sphere and mitigating its
excesses. Those who were not taught to fight, have naturally
inclined in favour of any other mode of settling differences
rather than that of fighting. In general, those who have been
the greatest sufferers by the indulgence of selfish passion, have
been the most earnest supporters of any moral law which
offered a means of bridling passion. Women were powerfully
instrumental in inducing the northern conquerors to adopt the
creed of Christianity, a creed so much more favourable to
women than any that preceded it. The conversion of the
Anglo-Saxons and of the Franks may be said to have been
begun by the wives of Ethelbert and Clovis. The other mode
in which the effect of women's opinion has been conspicuous,
is by giving a powerful stimulus to those qualities in men,
which, not being themselves trained in, it was necessary for
them that they should find in their protectors. Courage, and
the military virtues generally, have at all times been greatly
indebted to the desire which men felt of being admired by
women: and the stimulus reaches for beyond this one class
of eminent qualities, since, by a very natural effect of their
position, the best passport to the admiration and favour of
women has always been to be thought highly of by men. From
the combination of the two kinds of moral influence thus exercised by women, arose the spirit of chivalry: the peculiarity
of which is, to aim at combining the highest standard of the
warlike qualities with the cultivation of a totally different
class of virtues—those of gentleness, generosity, and self-
abnegation, towards the nonmilitary and defenceless classes
generally, and a special submission and worship directed towards women; who were distinguished from the other defence-

less classes by the high rewards which they had it in their power voluntarily to bestow on those who endeavoured to earn their favour, instead of extorting their subjection. Though the practice of chivalry fell even more sadly short of its theoretic standard than practice generally falls below theory, it remains one of the most precious monuments of the moral history of our race; as a remarkable instance of a concerted and organized attempt by a most disorganized and distracted society, to raise up and carry into practice a moral ideal greatly in advance of its social condition and institutions; so much so as to have been completely frustrated in the main object, yet never entirely inefficacious, and which has left a most sensible, and for the most part a highly valuable impress on the ideas and feelings of all subsequent times.

The chivalrous ideal is the acme of the influence of women's sentiments on the moral cultivation of mankind: and if women are to remain in their subordinate situation, it were greatly to be lamented that the chivalrous standard should have passed away, for it is the only one at all capable of mitigating the demoralizing influences of that position. But the changes in the general state of the species rendered inevitable the substitution of a totally different ideal of morality for the chivalrous one. Chivalry was the attempt to infuse moral elements into a state of society in which everything depended for good or evil on individual prowess, under the softening influences of individual delicacy and generosity. In modern societies, all things, even in the military department of affairs, are decided, not by individual effort, but by the combined operations of numbers; while the main occupation of society has changed from fighting to business, from military to industrial life. The exigencies of the new life are no more exclusive of the virtues of generosity than those of the old, but it no longer entirely depends on them. The main foundations of the moral life of modern times must be justice and prudence; the respect of each for the rights of every other, and the ability of each to take care of himself. Chivalry left without legal check all forms of wrong which reigned unpunished throughout society;

it only encouraged a few to do right in preference to wrong, by the direction it gave to the instruments of praise and admiration. But the real dependence of morality must always be upon its penal sanctions—its power to deter from evil. The security of society cannot rest on merely rendering honour to right, a motive so comparatively weak in all but a few, and which on very many does not operate at all. Modern society is able to repress wrong through all departments of life, by a fit exertion of the superior strength which civilization has given it, and thus to render the existence of the weaker members of society (no longer defenceless but protected by law) tolerable to them, without reliance on the chivalrous feelings of those who are in a position to tyrannize. The beauties and graces of the chivalrous character are still what they were, but the rights of the weak, and the general comfort of human life, now rest on a far surer and steadier support; or rather, they do so in every relation of life except the conjugal.

At present the moral influence of women is no less real, but it is no longer of so marked and definite a character: it has more nearly merged in the general influence of public opinion. Both through the contagion of sympathy, and through the desire of men to shine in the eyes of women, their feelings have great effect in keeping alive what remains of the chivalrous ideal—in fostering the sentiments and continuing the traditions of spirit and generosity. In these points of character, their standard is higher than that of men; in the quality of justice, somewhat lower. As regards the relations of private life it may be said generally, that their influence is, on the whole, encouraging to the softer virtues, discouraging to the sterner: though the statement must be taken with all the modifications dependent on individual character. In the chief of the greater trials to which virtue is subject in the concerns of life—the conflict between interest and principle—the tendency of women's influence is of a very mixed character. When the principle involved happens to be one of the very few which the course of their religious or moral education has strongly impressed upon themselves, they are potent auxiliaries to virtue: and their husbands and sons are often prompted by them to acts of abnegation which they never would have been capable of without that stimulus. But, with the present education and position of women, the moral principles which have been impressed on them cover but a comparatively small part of the field of virtue, and are, moreover, principally negative; forbidding particular acts, but having little to do with the general direction of the thoughts and purposes. I am afraid it must be said, that disinterestedness in the general conduct of life—the devotion of the energies to purposes which hold out no promise of private advantages to the family—is very seldom encouraged or supported by women's influence. It is small blame to them that they discourage objects of which they have not learnt to see the advantage, and which withdraw their men from them, and from the interests of the family. But the consequence is that women's influence is often anything but favourable to public virtue.

Women have, however, some share of influence in giving the tone to public moralities since their sphere of action has been a little widened, and since a considerable number of them have occupied themselves practically in the promotion of objects reaching beyond their own family and household. The influence of women counts for a great deal in two of the most marked features of modern European life—its aversion to war, and its addiction to philanthropy. Excellent characteristics both; but unhappily, if the influence of women is valuable in the encouragement it gives to these feelings in general, in the particular applications the direction it gives to them is at least as often mischievous as useful. In the philanthropic department more particularly, the two provinces chiefly cultivated by women are religious proselytism and charity. Religious proselytism at home, is but another word for embittering of religious animosities: abroad, it is usually a blind running at an object, without either knowing or heeding the fatal mischiefs—fatal to the religious object itself as well as to all other desirable objects—which may be produced by the means employed. As for charity, it is a matter in which the immediate effect on the persons directly concerned, and the ultimate consequence to the general good, are apt to be at complete war with one another: while the education given to women—an education of the sentiments rather than of the understanding—and the habit inculcated by their whole life, of looking to immediate effects on persons, and not to remote effects on classes of persons—make them both unable to see, and unwilling to admit, the ultimate evil tendency of any form of charity or philanthropy which commends itself to their sympathetic feelings. The great and continually increasing mass of unenlightened and shortsighted benevolence, which, taking the care of people's lives out of their own hands, and relieving them from the disagreeable consequences of their own acts, saps the very foundations of the self-respect, self-help, and self-control which are the essential conditions both of individual prosperity and of social virtue—this waste of resources and of benevolent feelings in doing harm instead of good, is immensely swelled by women's contributions, and stimulated by their influence. Not that this is a mistake likely to be made by women, where they have actually the practical management of schemes of beneficence. It sometimes happens that women who administer public charities—with that insight into present fact, and especially into the minds and feelings of those with whom they are in immediate contact, in which women generally excel men —recognise in the clearest manner the demoralizing influence of the alms given or the help afforded, and could give lessons on the subject to many a male political economist. But women who only give their money, and are not brought face to face with the effects it produces, how can they be expected to foresee them? A woman born to the present lot of women, and content with it, how should she appreciate the value of self-dependence? She is not self-dependent; she is not taught self-dependence; her destiny is to receive everything from others, and why should what is good enough for her be bad for the poor? Her familiar notions of good are of blessings descending from a superior. She forgets that she is not free, and that the poor are; that if what they need is given to them unearned, they cannot be compelled to earn it: that everybody cannot be taken care of by everybody, but there must be some motive to induce people to take care of themselves; and that to be helped to help themselves, if they are physically capable of it, is the only charity which proves to be charity in the end.

These considerations shew how usefully the part which women take in the formation of general opinion, would be modified for the better by that more enlarged instruction, and practical conversancy with the things which their opinions influence, that would necessarily arise from their social and political emancipation. But the improvement it would work through the influence they exercise, each in her own family, would be still more remarkable.

It is often said that in the classes most exposed to temptation, a man's wife and children tend to keep him honest and respectable, both by the wife's direct influence, and by the concern he feels for their future welfare. This may be so, and no doubt often is so, with those who are more weak than wicked; and this beneficial influence would be preserved and strengthened under equal laws; it does not depend on the woman's servitude, but is, on the contrary, diminished by the disrespect which the inferior class of men always at heart feel towards those who are subject to their power. But when we ascend higher in the scale, we come among a totally different set of moving forces. The wife's influence tends, as far as it goes, to prevent the husband from falling below the common standard of approbation of the country. It tends quite as strongly to hinder him from rising above it. The wife is the auxiliary of the common public opinion. A man who is married to a woman his inferior in intelligence, finds her a perpetual dead weight, or, worse than a dead weight, a drag, upon every aspiration of his to be better than public opinion requires him to be. It is hardly possible for one who is in these bonds, to attain exalted virtue. If he differs in his opinion from the mass—if he sees truths which have not yet dawned upon them, or if, feeling in his heart truths which they nominally recognise, he would like to act up to those truths more conscientiously than the generality of mankind— to all such thoughts and desires, marriage is the heaviest of drawbacks, unless he be so fortunate as to have a wife as much above the common level as he himself is.

For, in the first place, there is always some sacrifice of personal interest required; either of social consequence, or of pecuniary means; perhaps the risk of even the means of subsistence. These sacrifices and risks he may be willing to encounter for himself; but he will pause before he imposes them on his family. And his family in this case means his wife and daughters; for he always hopes that his sons will feel as he feels himself, and that what he can do without, they will do without, willingly, in the same cause. But his daughters—their marriage may depend upon it: and his wife, who is unable to enter into or understand the objects for which these sacrifices are made—who, if she thought them worth any sacrifice, would think so on trust, and solely for his sake—who can participate in none of the enthusiasm or the self-approbation he himself may feel, while the things which he is disposed to sacrifice are all in all to her; will not the best and most unselfish man hesitate the longest before bringing on her this consequence? If it be not the comforts of life, but only social consideration, that is at stake, the burthen upon his conscience and feelings is still very severe. Whoever has a wife and children has given hostages to Mrs. Grundy. The approbation of that potentate may be a matter of indifference to him, but it is of great importance to his wife. The man himself may be above opinion, or may find sufficient compensation in the opinion of those of his own way of thinking. But to the women connected with him, he can offer no compensation. The almost invariable tendency of the wife to place her influence in the same scale with social consideration, is sometimes made a reproach to women, and represented as a peculiar trait of feebleness and childishness of character in them: surely with great injustice. Society makes the whole life of a woman, in the easy classes, a continued self-sacrifice; it exacts from her an unremitting restraint of the whole of her natural inclinations, and the sole return it makes to her for what often deserves the name of a martyrdom, is consideration. Her consideration is inseparably connected with that of her husband, and after paying the full price for it, she finds that she is to lose it, for no reason of which she can feel the cogency. She has sacrificed her whole life to it, and her husband will not sacrifice to it a whim, a freak, an eccentricity; something not recognised or allowed for by the world, and which the world will agree with her in thinking a folly, if it thinks no worse! The dilemma is hardest upon that very meritorious class of men, who, without possessing talents which qualify them to make a figure among those with whom they agree in opinion, hold their opinion from conviction, and feel bound in honour and conscience to serve it, by making profession of their belief, and giving their time, labour, and means, to anything undertaken in its behalf. The worst case of all is when such men happen to be of a rank and position which of itself neither gives them, nor excludes them from, what is considered the best society; when their admission to it depends mainly on what is thought of them personally—and however unexceptionable their breeding and habits, their being identified with opinions and public conduct unacceptable to those who give the tone to society would operate as an effectual exclusion. Many a woman flatters herself (nine times out of ten quite erroneously) that nothing prevents her and her husband from moving in the highest society of her neighbourhood—society in which others well known to her, and in the same class of life, mix freely—except that her husband is unfortunately a Dissenter, or has the reputation of mingling in low radical politics. That it is, she thinks, which hinders George from getting a commission or a place, Caroline from making an advantageous match, and prevents her and her husband from obtaining invitations, perhaps honours, which, for aught she sees, they are as well entitled to as some folks. With such an influence in every

house, either exerted actively, or operating all the more powerfully for not being asserted, is it any wonder that people in
general are kept down in that mediocrity of respectability
which is becoming a marked characteristic of modern times?

There is another very injurious aspect in which the effect,
not of women's disabilities directly, but of the broad line of
difference which those disabilities create between the education and character of a woman and that of a man, requires to
be considered. Nothing can be more unfavourable to that
union of thoughts and inclinations which is the ideal of married life. Intimate society between people radically dissimilar
to one another, is an idle dream. Unlikeness may attract, but
it is likeness which retains; and in proportion to the likeness
is the suitability of the individuals to give each other a happy
life. While women are so unlike men, it is not wonderful that
selfish men should feel the need of arbitrary power in their
own hands, to arrest *in limine* the life-long conflict of inclinations, by deciding every question on the side of their own
preference. When people are extremely unlike, there can be
no real identity of interest. Very often there is conscientious
difference of opinion between married people, on the highest
points of duty. Is there any reality in the marriage union
where this takes place? Yet it is not uncommon anywhere,
when the woman has any earnestness of character; and it is
a very general case indeed in Catholic countries, when she
is supported in her dissent by the only other authority to which
she is taught to bow, the priest. With the usual barefacedness
of power not accustomed to find itself disputed, the influence
of priests over women is attacked by Protestant and Liberal
writers, less for being bad in itself, than because it is a rival
authority to the husband, and raises up a revolt against his
infallibility. In England, similar differences occasionally exist
when an Evangelical wife has allied herself with a husband
of a different quality; but in general this source at least of
dissension is got rid of, by reducing the minds of women to
such a nullity, that they have no opinions but those of Mrs.
Grundy, or those which the husband tells them to have. When

there is no difference of opinion, differences merely of taste may be sufficient to detract greatly from the happiness of married life. And though it may stimulate the amatory propensities of men, it does not conduce to married happiness, to exaggerate by differences of education whatever may be the native differences of the sexes. If the married pair are well-bred and well-behaved people, they tolerate each other's tastes; but is mutual toleration what people look forward to, when they enter into marriage? These differences of inclination will naturally make their wishes different, if not restrained by affection or duty, as to almost all domestic questions which arise. What a difference there must be in the society which the two persons will wish to frequent, or be frequented by! Each will desire associates who share their own tastes: the persons agreeable to one, will be indifferent or positively disagreeable to the other; yet there can be none who are not common to both, for married people do not now live in different parts of the house and have totally different visiting lists, as in the reign of Louis XV. They cannot help having different wishes as to the bringing up of the children: each will wish to see reproduced in them their own tastes and sentiments: and there is either a compromise, and only a half-satisfaction to either, or the wife has to yield—often with bitter suffering; and, with or without intention, her occult influence continues to counterwork the husband's purposes.

It would of course be extreme folly to suppose that these differences of feeling and inclination only exist because women are brought up differently from men, and that there would not be differences of taste under any imaginable circumstances. But there is nothing beyond the mark in saying that the distinction in bringing-up immensely aggravates those differences, and renders them wholly inevitable. While women are brought up as they are, a man and a woman will but rarely find in one another real agreement of tastes and wishes as to daily life. They will generally have to give it up as hopeless, and renounce the attempt to have, in the intimate associate of their daily life, that *idem velle, idem nolle,* which is the recognised bond of any society that is really such: or if the man succeeds in obtaining it, he does so by choosing a woman who is so complete a nullity that she has no *velle* or *nolle* at all, and is as ready to comply with one thing as another if anybody tells her to do so. Even this calculation is apt to fail; dulness and want of spirit are not always a guarantee of the submission which is so confidently expected from them. But if they were, is this the ideal of marriage? What, in this case, does the man obtain by it, except an upper servant, a nurse, or a mistress? On the contrary, when each of two persons, instead of being a nothing, is a something; when they are attached to one another, and are not too much unlike to begin with; the constant partaking in the same things, assisted by their sympathy, draws out the latent capacities of each for being interested in the things which were at first interesting only to the other; and works a gradual assimilation of the' tastes and characters to one another, partly by the insensible modification of each, but more by a real enriching of the two natures, each acquiring the tastes and capacities of the other in addition to its own. This often happens between two friends of the same sex, who are much associated in their daily life: and it would be a common, if not the commonest, case in marriage, did not the totally different bringing-up of the two sexes make it next to an impossibility to form a really well-assorted union. Were this remedied, whatever differences there might still be in individual tastes, there would at least be, as a general rule, complete unity and unanimity as to the great objects of life. When the two persons both care for great objects, and are a help and encouragement to each other in whatever regards these, the minor matters on which their tastes may differ are not all-important to them; and there is a foundation for solid friendship, of an enduring character, more likely than anything else to make it, through the whole of life, a greater pleasure to each to give pleasure to the other, than to receive it.

I have considered, thus far, the effects on the pleasures and benefits of the marriage union which depend on the mere unlikeness between the wife and the husband: but the evil tendency is prodigiously aggravated when the unlikeness is inferiority. Mere unlikeness, when it only means difference of good qualities, may be more a benefit in the way of mutual improvement, than a drawback from comfort. When each emulates, and desires and endeavours to acquire, the other's peculiar qualities, the difference does not produce diversity of interest, but increased identity of it, and makes each still more valuable to the other. But when one is much the inferior of the two in mental ability and cultivation, and is not actively attempting by the other's aid to rise to the other's level, the whole influence of the connexion upon the development of the superior of the two is deteriorating: and still more so in a tolerably happy marriage than in an unhappy one. It is not with impunity that the superior in intellect shuts himself up with an inferior, and elects that inferior for his chosen, and sole completely intimate, associate. Any society which is not improving, is deteriorating: and the more so, the closer and more familiar it is. Even a really superior man almost always begins to deteriorate when he is habitually (as the phrase is) king of his company: and in his most habitual company the husband who has a wife inferior to him is always so. While his self-satisfaction is incessantly ministered to on the one hand, on the other he insensibly imbibes the modes of feeling, and of looking at things, which belong to a more vulgar or a more limited mind than his own. This evil differs from many of those which have hitherto been dwelt on, by being an increasing one. The association of men with women in daily life is much closer and more complete than it ever was before. Men's life is more domestic. Formerly, their pleasures and chosen occupations were among men, and in men's company: their wives had but a fragment of their lives. At the present time, the progress of civilization, and the turn of opinion against the rough amusements and convivial excesses which formerly occupied most men in their hours of relaxation—together with (it must be said) the improved tone of modern feeling as to the reciprocity of duty which binds the husband towards the wife—have thrown the man very much more upon home and its inmates, for his personal and social pleasures: while the kind and degree of improvement which has been made in women's education, has made them in some degree capable of being his companions in ideas and mental tastes, while leaving them, in most cases, still hopelessly inferior to him. His desire of mental communion is thus in general satisfied by a communion from which he learns nothing. An unimproving and unstimulating companionship is substituted for (what he might otherwise have been obliged to seek) the society of his equals in powers and his fellows in the higher pursuits. We see, accordingly, that young men of the greatest promise generally cease to improve as soon as they marry, and, not improving, inevitably degenerate. If the wife does not push the husband forward, she always holds him back. He ceases to care for what she does not care for; he no longer desires, and ends by disliking and shunning, society congenial to his former aspirations, and which would now shame his falling-off from them; his higher faculties both of mind and heart cease to be called into activity. And this change coinciding with the new and selfish interests which are created by the family, after a few years he differs in no material respect from those who have never had wishes for anything but the common vanities and the common pecuniary objects.

What marriage may be in the case of two persons of cultivated faculties, identical in opinions and purposes, between whom there exists that best kind of equality, similarity of powers and capacities with reciprocal superiority in them— so that each can enjoy the luxury of looking up to the other, and can have alternately the pleasure of leading and of being led in the path of development—I will not attempt to describe. To those who can conceive it, there is no need; to those who cannot, it would appear the dream of an enthusiast. But I maintain, with the profoundest conviction, that this, and this only, is the ideal of marriage; and that all opinions, customs, and institutions which favour any other notion of it, or turn the conceptions and aspirations connected with it into any other direction, by whatever pretences they may be coloured, are relics of primitive barbarism. The moral regeneration of mankind will only really commence, when the most fundamental of the social relations is placed under the rule of equal justice, and when human beings learn to cultivate their strongest sympathy with an equal in rights and in cultivation.

Thus far, the benefits which it has appeared that the world would gain by ceasing to make sex a disqualification for privileges and a badge of subjection, are social rather than individual; consisting in an increase of the general fund of thinking and acting power, and an improvement in the general conditions of the association of men with women. But it would be a grievous understatement of the case to omit the most direct benefit of all, the unspeakable gain in private happiness to the liberated half of the species; the difference to them between a life of subjection to the will of others, and a life of rational freedom. After the primary necessities of food and raiment, freedom is the first and strongest want of human nature. While mankind are lawless, their desire is for lawless freedom. When they have learnt to understand the meaning of duty and the value of reason, they incline more and more to be guided and restrained by these in the exercise of their freedom; but they do not therefore desire freedom less; they do not become disposed to accept the will of other people as the representative and interpreter of those guiding principles. On the contrary, the communities in which the reason has been most cultivated, and in which the idea of social duty has been most powerful, are those which have most strongly asserted the freedom of action of the individual—the liberty of each to govern his conduct by his own feelings of duty, and by such laws and social restraints as his own conscience can subscribe to.

He who would rightly appreciate the worth of personal independence as an element of happiness, should consider the value he himself puts upon it as an ingredient of his own. There is no subject on which there is a greater habitual difference of judgment between a man judging for himself, and the same man judging for other people. When he hears others complaining that they are not allowed freedom of action—that their own will has not sufficient influence in the regulation of their affairs—his inclination is, to ask, what are their grievances? what positive damage they sustain? and in what respect they consider their affairs to be mismanaged? and if they fail to make out, in answer to these questions, what appears to him a sufficient case, he turns a deaf ear, and regards their complaint as the fanciful querulousness of people whom nothing reasonable will satisfy. But he has a quite different standard of judgment when he is deciding for himself. Then, the most unexceptionable administration of his interests by a tutor set over him, does not satisfy his feelings: his personal exclusion from the deciding authority appears itself the greatest grievance of all, rendering it superfluous even to enter into the question of mismanagement. It is the same with nations. What citizen of a free country would listen to any offers of good and skilful administration, in return for the abdication of freedom? Even if he could believe that good and skilful administration can exist among a people ruled by a will not their own, would not the consciousness of working out their own destiny under their own moral responsibility be a compensation to his feelings for great rudeness and imperfection in the details of public affairs? Let him rest assured that whatever he feels on this point, women feel in a fully equal degree. Whatever has been said or written, from the time of Herodotus to the present, of the ennobling influence of free government—the nerve and spring which it gives to all the faculties, the larger and higher objects which it presents to the intellect and feelings, the more unselfish public spirit, and calmer and broader views of duty, that it engenders, and the generally loftier platform on which it elevates the individual as a moral, spiritual, and social being—is every particle as true of women as of men. Are these things no important part of individual happiness? Let any man call to mind what he himself felt on emerging from boyhood—from the tutelage and control of even loved and affectionate elders—and entering upon the responsibilities of manhood. Was it not like the physical effect of taking off a heavy weight, or releasing him from obstructive, even if not otherwise painful, bonds? Did he not feel twice as much alive, twice as much a human being, as before? And does he imagine that women have none of these feelings? But it is a striking fact, that the satisfactions and mortifications of personal pride, though all in all to most men when the case is their own, have less allowance made for them in the case of other people, and are less listened to as a ground or a justification of conduct, than any other natural human feelings; perhaps because men compliment them in their own case with the names of so many other qualities, that they are seldom conscious how mighty an influence these feelings exercise in their own lives. No less large and powerful is their part, we may assure ourselves, in the lives and feelings of women. Women are schooled into suppressing them in their most natural and most healthy direction, but the internal principle remains, in a different outward form. An active and energetic mind, if denied liberty, will seek for power: refused the command of itself, it will assert its personality by attempting to control others. To allow to any human beings no existence of their own but what depends on others, is giving far too high a premium on bending others to their purposes. Where liberty cannot be hoped for, and power can, power becomes the grand object of human desire; those to whom others will not leave the undisturbed management of their own affairs, will compensate themselves, if they can, by meddling for their own purposes with the affairs of others. Hence also women's passion for personal beauty, and dress and display; and all the evils that flow from it, in the way of mischievous luxury and social immorality. The love of power and the love of liberty are in eternal antagonism. Where there is least liberty, the passion for power is the most ardent and unscrupulous. The desire of power over others can only cease to be a depraving agency among mankind, when each of them individually is able to do without it: which can only be where respect for liberty in the personal concerns of each is an established principle.

But it is not only through the sentiment of personal dignity, that the free direction and disposal of their own faculties is a source of individual happiness, and to be fettered and restricted in it, a source of unhappiness, to human beings, and not least to women. There is nothing, after disease, indigence, and guilt, so fatal to the pleasurable enjoyment of life as the want of a worthy outlet for the active faculties. Women who have the cares of a family, and while they have the cares of a family, have this outlet, and it generally suffices for them: but what of the greatly increasing number of women, who have had no opportunity of exercising the vocation which they are mocked by telling them is their proper one? What of the women whose children have been lost to them by death or distance, or have grown up, married, and formed homes of their own? There are abundant examples of men who, after a life engrossed by business, retire with a competency to the enjoyment, as they hope, of rest, but to whom, as they are unable to acquire new interests and excitements that can replace the old, the change to a life of inactivity brings ennui, melancholy, and premature death. Yet no one thinks of the parallel case of so many worthy and devoted women, who, having paid what they are told is their debt to society— having brought up a family blamelessly to manhood and womanhood—having kept a house as long as they had a house needing to be kept—are deserted by the sole occupation for which they have fitted themselves; and remain with undiminished activity but with no employment for it, unless perhaps a daughter or daughter-in-law is willing to abdicate in their favour the discharge of the same functions in her younger household. Surely a hard lot for the old age of those who have worthily discharged, as long as it was given to them to discharge, what the world accounts their only social duty. Of such women, and of those others to whom this duty has not been committed at all—many of whom pine through life with the consciousness of thwarted vocations, and activities which

are not suffered to expand—the only resources, speaking generally, are religion and charity. But their religion, though it
may be one of feeling, and of ceremonial observance, cannot
be a religion of action, unless in the form of charity. For
charity many of them are by nature admirably fitted; but to
practise it usefully, or even without doing mischief, requires
the education, the manifold preparation, the knowledge and
the thinking powers, of a skilful administrator. There are few
of the administrative functions of government for which a
person would not be fit, who is fit to bestow charity usefully.
In this as in other cases (pre-eminently in that of the education of children), the duties permitted to women cannot be
performed properly, without their being trained for duties
which, to the great loss of society, are not permitted to them.
And here let me notice the singular way in which the question of women's disabilities is frequently presented to view, by
those who find it easier to draw a ludicrous picture of what
they do not like, than to answer the arguments for it. When
it is suggested that women's executive capacities and prudent
counsels might sometimes be found valuable in affairs of state,
these lovers of fun hold up to the ridicule of the world, as
sitting in parliament or in the cabinet, girls in their teens, or
young wives of two or three and twenty, transported bodily,
exactly as they are, from the drawing-room to the House of
Commons. They forget that males are not usually selected at
this early age for a seat in Parliament, or for responsible
political functions. Common sense would tell them that if
such trusts were confided to women, it would be to such as
having no special vocation for married life, or preferring another employment of their faculties (as many women even
now prefer to marriage some of the few honourable occupations within their reach), have spent the best years of their
youth in attempting to qualify themselves for the pursuits in
which they desire to engage; or still more frequently perhaps,
widows or wives of forty or fifty, by whom the knowledge of
life and faculty of government which they have acquired in
their families, could by the aid of appropriate studies be made

available on a less contracted scale. There is no country of Europe in which the ablest men have not frequently experienced, and keenly appreciated, the value of the advice and help of clever and experienced women of the world, in the attainment both of private and of public objects; and there are important matters of public administration to which few men are equally competent with such women; among others, the detailed control of expenditure. But what we are now discussing is not the need which society has of the services of women in public business, but the dull and hopeless life to which it so often condemns them, by forbidding them to exercise the practical abilities which many of them are conscious of, in any wider field than one which to some of them never was, and to others is no longer, open. If there is anything vitally important to the happiness of human beings, it is that they should relish their habitual pursuit. This requisite of an enjoyable life is very imperfectly granted, or altogether denied, to a large part of mankind; and by its absence many a life is a failure, which is provided, in appearance, with every requisite of success. But if circumstances which society is not yet skilful enough to overcome, render such failures often for the present inevitable, society need not itself inflict them. The injudiciousness of parents, a youth's own inexperience, or the absence of external opportunities for the congenial vocation, and their presence for an uncongenial, condemn numbers of men to pass their lives in doing one thing reluctantly and ill, when there are other things which they could have done well and happily. But on women this sentence is imposed by actual law, and by customs equivalent to law. What, in unenlightened societies, colour, race, religion, or in the case of a conquered country, nationality, are to some men, sex is to all women; a peremptory exclusion from almost all honourable occupations, but either such as cannot be fulfilled by others, or such as those others do not think worthy of their acceptance. Sufferings arising from causes of this nature usually meet with so little sympathy, that few persons are aware of the great amount of unhappiness even now produced by the feeling of a wasted life. The case will be even more frequent, as increased cultivation creates a greater and greater disproportion between the ideas and faculties of women, and the scope which society allows to their activity.

When we consider the positive evil caused to the disqualified half of the human race by their disqualification—first in the loss of the most inspiriting and elevating kind of personal enjoyment, and next in the weariness, disappointment, and profound dissatisfaction with life, which are so often the substitute for it; one feels that among all the lessons which men require for carrying on the struggle against the inevitable imperfections of their lot on earth, there is no lesson which they more need, than not to add to the evils which nature inflicts, by their jealous and prejudiced restrictions on one another. Their vain fears only substitute other and worse evils for those which they are idly apprehensive of: while every restraint on the freedom of conduct of any of their human fellow creatures, (otherwise than by making them responsible for any evil actually caused by it), dries up *pro tanto* the principal fountain of human happiness, and leaves the species less rich, to an inappreciable degree, in all that makes life valuable to the individual human being.

DATE DUE